for
edexcel

Leisure Studies AS

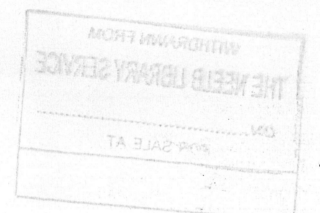

for
edexcel

Leisure Studies

AS

Lindsey Taylor   Ray Barker

Collins

Contents

Unit 3 The Leisure Customer 116–169

About this book

Welcome to AS Leisure Studies. This textbook is written specifically for students taking the Edexcel Leisure Studies award and provides you with the underpinning knowledge to be successful in both the coursework set by your school or college (internal assessment) and the one-and-a-half hour test set by Edexcel (external assessment).

Collins *Leisure Studies AS for Edexcel* is divided into three units. Each unit in the book corresponds to a unit of the Edexcel AS-level Leisure Studies specification.

Unit	Title	How is this unit assessed?
1	The Leisure Industry	Internal assessment
2	Working Practices in Leisure	External test
3	The Leisure Customer	Internal assessment

The units in this book have been divided into topics and each topic provides a manageable chunk of learning covering the subject content of an Edexcel unit. The contents list at the beginning of this book and at the start of each unit will show you how the topics correspond to the Edexcel Leisure Studies AS-level specification.

About this book

● **Explanatory introduction** to the topic explains what you will need to learn about each topic.

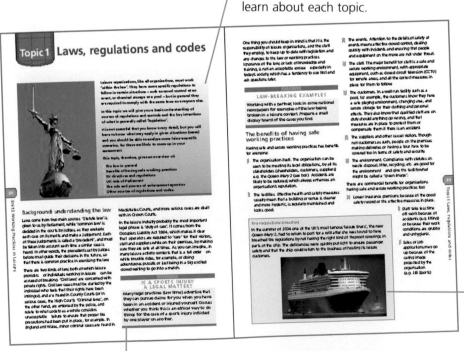

● **Case studies** of real organisations support your learning and set it in context.

● **Activities** provide you with an opportunity to develop your understanding about specific aspects of a topic and practise your skills. Most activities are designed so that you can do them on your own, with a partner or in a small group.

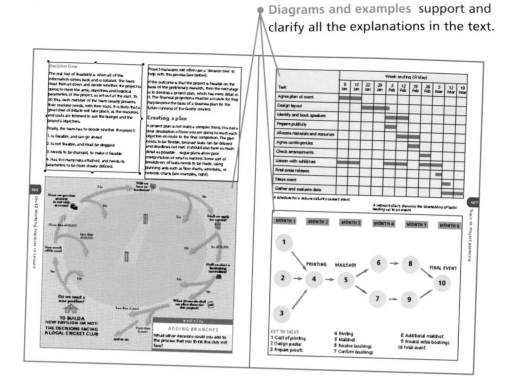

This book has been produced with considerable input from current practitioners in the leisure industry. Each unit contains an **Industry Focus** interview:

Unit 1 The Leisure Industry features Martin Steer, Education and Development Manager at the Institute of Sport and Recreation Management (ISRM)

Unit 2 Working Practices in Leisure features Michael Beadle, Sales Coordinator, Xscape, Castleford, Yorkshire

Unit 3 The Leisure Customer features Katherine Duckworth, Sales and Marketing Manager, Alton Towers Hotels

A wide range of leisure organisations has been included and the table on pages 8–9 will help you to locate them in this book. When you are building your understanding of the industry and completing assessments you will find the internet an invaluable source of information. To help you in your research, details of useful websites are given on page 170.

Good luck with your GCE AS-level studies. This book provides you with interesting, supportive and motivating learning materials that we hope will help you to succeed in your leisure studies course.

7

About this book

Table of organisations used as examples

Unit1   Unit2   **Unit3**

Table of organisations used as examples

Health & Safety Executive	enforcing the law	60
HF Holidays	IIP award winner	89
ILAM	source of expert advice	148
Int. Org. of Standardisation (ISO)	originator of standards	90
ISRM	prof. body serving all sports sectors	35
Keynote Market Research	source of leisure industry data	18
Leis. Ind. Res. Centre (LIRC)	leisure industry statistics	25
McDonald's	staff skills	132
McDonald's	mystery customer	139
McDonald's	public relations	154
Mikrofax Company	stock-control system	97
Mintel Market Research	data/stats on the leisure ind.	17
Nat. Mus. of Photog./Film/TV	customer charter	128
N. Yorks. Moors Nat. Park	customers with specific needs	135
Paralympics	overcoming barriers	44
PMP Consultancy	managers of the Quest award	81
Queen Mary 2	breaching regulations	59
Rank	commercial leisure operator	37
Romsey Golf Club	system user	112
Scot. Nat. Rock Climbing Centre	liquidity problems	105
Sea Life Centre	marketing research	146
Shrewsbury Netball Club	Clubmark award winner	93
Silver Screen	passive leisure example	18
Sony	electronic media provider	25
Sport England	active leisure statistics	22
Sport England	oversees Clubmark awards	92
Stephen Joseph Theatre	customers with specific needs	157
Sutton & Epsom RFC	Clubmark award winner	93
Tameside Council	disability policy	126
Thackray Museum	dealing with groups	123
UCI Cinemas	automatic ticketing systems	113
UK Parliament	source of safety acts	58
UK Sports Councils	quality drives	79
Vue Cinemas	customers with specific needs	127
Warwick Castle	customer service training	133
Welcome Host	customer service training	134
Winchester Council	collaborative project	44
Youth Hostel Association	mission statement	128

This unit will introduce you to what is a very dynamic and diverse industry – an industry which makes a big contribution to our pleasures in life. For workers in the industry it provides employment and income in many different types of organisations and jobs, and the vast size of the industry means that it contributes a lot to our national economy as well as to our lifestyles.

Leisure activities represent many things for different people. A walk in the park can be a simple escape from work or chores – and is free to most people, while someone else may choose to spend hundreds of pounds going heli-skiing in the Rockies, as they chase the ultimate challenge.

Leisure time can be a rare commodity for some people – those who work long hours or who have responsibilities that limit their spare time. Most people have access to leisure facilities such as swimming pools, gyms, sports halls, golf courses and parks, but that is not the case for everyone, and we shall explore why in this unit.

Some people prefer home-based leisure pursuits, with a few friends, while others need team games and competition. You can be sure, however, that the leisure industry will always be inventing new ways to enjoy ourselves, whatever our preference.

Much of the information about leisure products and services comes to our knowledge through the media – in one form or another – so we will also try to show how influential the media can be.

In this unit you will investigate the diversity of the leisure industry to gain a knowledge of its many facets. Much of the knowledge and understanding gained will be helpful for studying the other units in the qualification. Many of the topics which only have a brief mention in this unit will be more developed in the other units: 'Working Practices in Leisure' and 'The Leisure Customer'.

During your studies for this unit we hope that you will be able to make visits to a number of locations and get the opportunity to speak to a range of people working in the industry. Make sure you maximise this experience to build up your own knowledge and understanding. You can also use magazines and the internet to broaden your knowledge of how the media try to influence us to buy products, take trips and spend our leisure pound.

Unit 1

The Leisure Industry

Topic 1 | Types of leisure

Before we can examine leisure types in any detail, we first need to agree on some sort of definition of what leisure is, for it can be interpreted in terms of time, activity, place or motivation. It is also useful to consider what leisure is not – for example, it does not involve the activities we perform at work or our day-to-day chores, even if we derive pleasure from them. The commonly accepted definition of leisure is:

'the time spent outside of work and essential domestic activity'.

In this topic we investigate how we spend our leisure time. This will help to show the diversity of the leisure industry and provide us with a system with which to classify various activities. Leisure activities can be:

- active
- passive
- home-based.

Active leisure

Active leisure pursuits can be low or high impact. Low-impact activities would include things like walking or yoga, which do not expend high levels of energy, usually have little contact or competition, and do not require much equipment. At the other end of the scale are high-impact activities such as kick boxing and rugby, which are high-energy, competitive sports that require quite a lot of equipment.

Motivations and benefits are also important for people with regard to their choice of leisure activities.

Motivations

Motivation can be intrinsic or extrinsic. Intrinsic motivation comes from within and can inspire people in different ways; it may drive some to be the world's fastest athlete or best footballer, whilst others may simply want to do something for personal satisfaction alone.

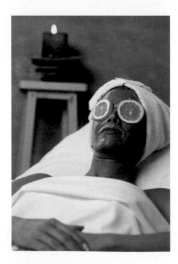

Extrinsic motivation comes from external sources such as parents, role models or friends, who may inspire us to excel at something. Equally though, they can put pressure on us not to participate in something, which usually results in de-motivation and a reduced sense of enjoyment and achievement.

activity

SATISFYING MOTIVATIONS

Consider the following motivations and list some leisure activities you think would satisfy them. Then discuss what gender differences there might be and why.

- relaxation and improvement of health and well-being

- thrills and excitement

- competition

- challenge

- improvement of skills

- fun with friends

- exploration.

Benefits

Taking part in an active leisure pursuit, whether it be high or low impact, has psychological, physical and social benefits:

- It makes or keeps us fit (physical and psychological)

- It improves our general health (physical and psychological)

- It gives us the opportunity to meet new friends (psychological and social)

- It can allow us to travel (psychological)

- Team sports can teach us cooperation (psychological and social)

- It increases our self-esteem (psychological)

- It can enable us to live longer (physical).

TYPES OF ACTIVE PURSUITS

The range of active leisure pursuits is very diverse. Look at the examples in the left-hand column of this table and try to complete the middle column with a range of intrinsic or extrinsic sources. Then go on to add the benefits you think participants might get from their chosen activity. Compare your responses with others in your class. One example is given to get you started.

ACTIVITY	SOURCE OF MOTIVATION	BENEFIT
Sky diving		
Rambling		
Swimming	Extrinsic – friends go	Some physical and social
Playing hockey		
Going to a theme park		
Boxing		

All active leisure pursuits can be seen to have certain common characteristics: they are dynamic; require high levels of motivation and some degree of skill; and are usually practised outside the home, with other people.

However old we are, and whatever time, motivation or skills we have, there is an active leisure pursuit to suit our needs. Active pursuits can be done indoors or out, in a team or individually, in the countryside or in urban areas. Examples of different types of active sports include:

- indoor – badminton, basketball, bowling

- outdoor – jogging, football, canoeing

- team – volleyball, hockey

- individual – horse riding, paragliding

- countryside – hiking, sailing

- urban – keep-fit classes, yoga.

Passive leisure

Passive leisure activities are just as diverse as active ones and, although they do not have the same benefits in terms of health, they share many similar motivations and skills. As with active pursuits, passive activities tend to reflect our age and lifestyle interests, as well as our spending power.

■ **Cinema** – Going to the cinema is not an age-related activity, but with the recent releases of *Shrek 2, Thunderbirds, Harry Potter* and *Spiderman 2*, it is becoming more and more popular with children and young people.

■ **Shopping** – Shopping has become much more popular since the introduction of shopping malls to the UK. Most cities also have pedestrianised shopping zones. Some people are even more adventurous, venturing across the Channel to do their shopping.

■ **Spectator sports** – With a greater range of indoor arenas staging sports events and new stadiums being built, spectator levels have increased. European competitions like the Champions League mean that many fans are also travelling further afield to support their teams.

■ **Shows and concerts** – The numbers attending concerts have increased as larger venues provide a regular circuit for the big performers.

■ **Theatre, opera and jazz concerts** remain popular amongst the older age groups, as well as attracting younger audiences. Many theatres and concert halls have also been the subject of renovation schemes.

■ **Night-time entertainment** – Eating out and 'pubbing and clubbing' are popular amongst teenagers, twentysomethings and couples.

■ **Holidays** – Holidays and short breaks might constitute active leisure, but are often centred around sightseeing and eating out.

■ **Gambling** – Gambling received a boost from the introduction of the National Lottery. Internet gambling has taken off recently, and bingo is also experiencing a revival due to the success of new advertising campaigns.

■ **Events and exhibitions** – There is now a wide variety of events and exhibitions, covering interests from gardening to classic cars. Trade fairs for hobbyists are also becoming more common.

■ **Visitor attractions** – Museums, botanical gardens and stately homes are attracting more and more visitors.

■ **Visiting** – Visiting family and friends may lead to active leisure pursuits, but usually involves passive activities such as socialising and entertaining.

Exhibitions, fairs, shows and concerts all need specialist skills to set up and run. As a result, there are many event companies that make a living from organising passive leisure events, which can be lucrative as they often fill quiet times, tend to bring in people with good spending power, and help raise a venue's profile.

activity

SURVEY OF PASSIVE PURSUITS

Prepare a survey to carry out in class to investigate:

• the range of passive pursuits (not home-based)

• who people pursue their activities with

• what the average weekly leisure spend is

• what motivates people to do their preferred activity.

Analyse your findings to assess whether any trends emerge.

Home-based leisure

According to the Leisure Industries Research Centre (LIRC), home-based leisure activities fall into one of four categories – reading, home entertainment, house and garden, hobbies and pastimes.

Reading

Although book sales have been boosted by the internet, the discounts offered by online book shops have led to a gradual decline in high-street sales. Book superstores with café areas and internet access are likely to supersede traditional book shops. Even with new online versions now available, the magazine sector remains strong.

Home entertainment

We have seen the arrival of the digital revolution with cable, digital and satellite TV, DVDs and CD-Roms flooding the home entertainment market. However, the biggest increase in the home entertainment market has been in the use of computers and computer games.

House and garden

More and more people are buying and developing property for profit. There has also been an increase in the number of people buying second homes abroad. The DIY market has also experienced growth (8–10%), due in part to the number of DIY-related TV programmes and magazines.

Gardening, an activity traditionally popular amongst older age groups, has benefited from the current demographic conditions – that is we have an ageing population. Gardening programmes and magazines have also contributed to the growth in this market.

Hobbies and pastimes

There has been a recent trend to fuse traditional and modern concepts. Electronic toys are particularly popular, and keeping a pet as a hobby is ever popular despite increasing pet-care costs.

Current developments in leisure

Over the last generation, leisure – whether it be active, passive or home-based – has become a consumable item. We are now willing to pay for more of our leisure activities than ever before. Leisure has become a commodity; leisure goods and services are there to be bought and sold.

Over the last five years leisure spending has increased, even though leisure is considered 'non-essential'. This is in line with other spending, which tends to be higher when consumer confidence and the economy are growing. In trying to accommodate our ever-greater demands, the leisure industry has become rather fragmented, with both large and small providers competing for our custom.

Annual consumer expenditure on sport

	Expenditure (£million)	% of total (rounded)
SPORT GOODS		
Clothing & footwear	3,086	20
Equipment	969	7
Boats	768	5
Publications	639	4
Goods total	*5,462*	*36*
SPORT SERVICES		
Health & fitness	1,243	8
Participant sports	1,681	11
Spectator sports	813	5
Gambling	3,111	20
TV/video	1,542	10
Travel	987	7
Other	398	3
Services total	*9,775*	*64*
TOTAL	**15,237**	**100**

Source: Chris Gratton, *Leisure Management*, 2002. Figures are for 2000.

To summarise the current situation:

• Leisure makes a significant contribution to society and to the economy.

• New technology has had a big impact, as have new consumer values.

• We all participate in and enjoy leisure in one way or another.

So why are so many people still 'money rich and leisure-time poor'?

Topic 2 The value of the leisure industry

In this topic we explore the range, scale and importance of the leisure industry, both in the UK and in the whole of Europe.

If you consider the impact that Euro 2004 had on Portugal's economy and image, and how much the Olympic Games contributed to development in Athens, you can see the scale, importance and value of the leisure industry. Consider also how many people in Greece may have been encouraged to play football after the Greek team's win at Euro 2004, and how many people pick up a tennis racket during the annual Wimbledon tournament. Clearly, sport and leisure also have an influence on our social lives. Big sporting events like these, along with the diverse other leisure activities on offer, give the leisure industry global importance.

This topic covers:

- the value of the leisure industry in general
- the economic value of the interactive media market, theme parks and multi-leisure sites
- the social value of health and well-being, fun, trends and developments.

The various values of leisure

First we must decide what we mean by 'value', as the perceived value of leisure can differ between individuals, just as motivations do.

Active sports participants may find value in the skills they learn, the money they make or the camaraderie of being part of a team. Passive participants, on the other hand, may find value in the excitement of watching or gambling on a sport, or in simply being able to relax and unwind.

The value of home-based leisure activities often stems from the sense of satisfaction and achievement that comes from acquiring or developing new skills.

Leisure activities that take place outside the home, whether active or passive, usually give value through the potential for travel, discovery and social interchange.

The difference in the value placed on leisure activities has given rise to a debate as to whether leisure time should be spent productively or simply in play and personal development. Whilst some people take the view that we should spend our leisure time doing something useful or worthwhile like charity work, others feel that our leisure time should be spent in self expression – through art or dance, for example.

Economic value

'Economic value' considers the quantitative side of leisure: the growth in sales; the amount of consumer spending; the numbers of people employed in leisure-related jobs and so on, which in economic terms gives value to the 'gross domestic product' – what we produce in the UK. Understanding these types of figures and trends is important when planning developments, creating new products and investing in venues, as the information gathered can guide companies, local authorities and voluntary clubs in their plans for the future.

The leisure industry has profited from the recent economic climate, as leisure organisations can make more accurate predictions and are more confident of investments and expansion in periods of financial stability. The UK has also experienced a steady decline in unemployment over the last decade. This has led to a greater sense of job security and generated a 'feel-good factor', which in turn benefits the leisure market.

We now consider, in greater detail, the value of some of the markets that have been a key part of the leisure industry growth.

The interactive media market

At the end of the 1990s, Mintel reported strong growth in the home-based electronic leisure market. The strong future for e-commerce, also predicted by Mintel, has now been realised, as we shop extensively online for both essential purchases and leisure products. On account of our new shopping habits, staffing levels have risen dramatically amongst call-centre staff and internet workers.

There has also been an upward trend in spending on multimedia and interactive services. The Leisure Industries Research Centre (LIRC) has predicted further growth in this market, especially with the cessation of analogue TV in 2013 and the introduction of new digital, satellite and pay per view (PPV) channels, which offer greater choice.

Theme parks

Spending was buoyant at the start of the century, as parks improved their rides and new technology was introduced. The market leader was Pearson plc, who own Chessington World of Adventures and Alton Towers.

Seasonality is the big problem for theme parks, and operators are working hard to augment income streams by offering corporate days, accommodation, parties and functions, and educational visits. Income from increased admissions and in-park spending have nevertheless kept the theme park sector quite profitable.

Multi-leisure sites

This market is typified by all the facilities being 'under one roof' or highly clustered, thereby overcoming the weather problems from which the outdoor parks suffer. A typical multi-leisure site would combine some or all of the following types of facilities:

- Warner Village
- McDonald's
- Ask
- Frankie & Benny's
- Wendy's
- Hollywood Bowl
- Leisure / health and fitness centres

Some top multi-leisure performers have been: Allied Leisure, First Leisure, Granada, and Rank.

This is an emergent sector that generates value in terms of jobs and income, and often creates a 'development multiplier effect' (see diagram), as other businesses group around.

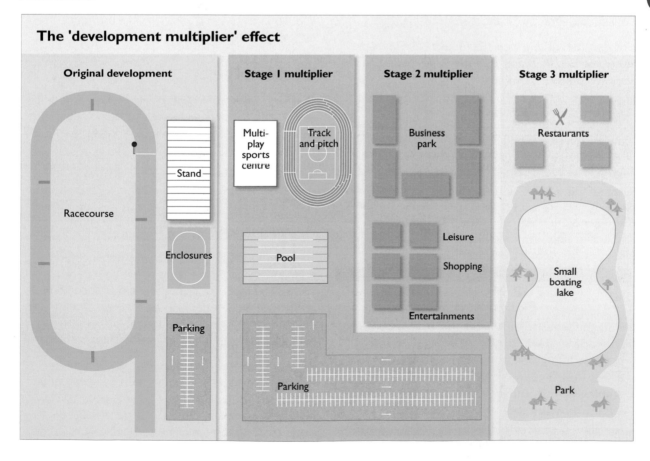

The 'development multiplier' effect

Original development — Racecourse, Stand, Enclosures, Parking

Stage I multiplier — Multi-play sports centre, Track and pitch, Pool, Parking

Stage 2 multiplier — Business park, Leisure, Shopping, Entertainments

Stage 3 multiplier — Restaurants, Small boating lake, Park

Growth in the rest of Europe

Similar levels of growth are also found in the rest of Europe, especially in the developing economies of Eastern Europe. Some examples include:

- Europa Park in Germany has around 3.5 million visitors a year and has recently expanded to include a new Roman-style hotel with themed rooms, a children's area, a health and fitness area with pools, an open-air stage, and a new major ride. You can visit www.europa.de for further details. How will this benefit the local economy?

- Silver Screen is opening a new cinema site in Warsaw designed by a UK-based company. It also has a multi-level café and bar, and is in a retail development complex.

- Le Meridian Villion has built a new opera hall in the Lithuanian capital, Vilnius, with a convention centre, a library, a business centre and a restaurant to complement its existing health and spa facilities.

- The fashionable Swiss resort of Interlaken has seen a new hotel built, which boasts extensive spa services, holistic therapies and massage. Visit www.victoria-jungfrau.ch for further details.

- DiR, the Spanish health-club operator now has twelve clubs based entirely in Barcelona. DiR appoint and train all their own staff on site.

You can further investigate European developments every week in the *Leisure Opportunities* magazine at www.worldleisurenews.com.

Current value updates

Estimates of the current value of the leisure industry from Keynote Market Research group give:
- growth at five to six per cent until 2002. This was not uniform growth, however. Although the cinema and games software sectors were booming, others including the health and fitness sector, were showing signs of slowing down.

---

activity
THE TOP MULTI-LEISURE PERFORMERS

Visit the website of Allied Leisure, First Leisure, Granada or Rank (or any other multi-leisure provider) and look at the company reports to assess the company's diversity, value, employment, turnover and profits. Compare its results with those of other companies.

- spending in 2002 at £120 billion (8% of all consumer spending).
- numbers employed at just over 522,000.

Clearly the leisure industry is vast both in scale and in importance to the UK, Europe and beyond.

Future growth

The government has announced that it wants to achieve 70 per cent participation in sport and physical activity by 2020. This will have massive implications for the economy and for investment in resources. The Sport Industry Research Centre in Sheffield estimates that to do this:

- Consumer spending on leisure activities would have to double

- Value added to the economy by sports would double.

- Employment in the industry would need to double.

- Savings on health might be as much as £2.4 billion.

- Additional tax income for the government would be over £8 billion.

This projects an image of a real 'win-win' situation. Considering that current rates of participation are at about 30 per cent, do you think the government's targets are achievable?

Social value

To help us understand the social value of sport and leisure, and their impact on our spending habits and choice of leisure activities, we shall briefly explore three areas:

- health and well-being
- fun
- trends and developments.

Health and well-being

The health and fitness industry has experienced a huge boost in recent times as we have become more aware about and more willing to spend time on our health. Sales of exercise clothing and fitness equipment have increased, and people are joining spas, gyms and sports clubs in ever-greater numbers.

Many people see sport, recreation and leisure activities as a means of staying healthy, getting fit, or relieving stress, and are willing to spend time and money on them. Both the commercial and non-commercial sectors welcome such individuals as they tend to be very committed to their particular activities and keep themselves fitter and healthier, thereby reducing illness, days off work, and visits to their doctors – something which the government is trying to encourage. Organised activities give social as well as fitness value, as they enable us to meet and make new friends.

Fun

Leisure activities usually involve an element of fun for participants; if we did not enjoy a certain activity we would not continue with it. Fun activities make us feel happy; the body releases endorphins (chemicals) in the brain which make us feel good and therefore want more!

Trends and developments

We gain some value from our leisure pursuits through changes in society and technology. The government is keen to extend equality of access and opportunity to leisure premises through disability and equality legislation (Disability Act 2000). There has been growth in female versions of sports such as soccer and rugby, as well as increased opportunities for disabled people to participate in sport at all levels. Greater mobility allows us to travel further to pursue our hobbies, sports or activities, and greater disposable income means that we are also able to spend more on our favourite pastimes and products.

From technology we have gained the ability to play more effectively: high-tech golf clubs enable you to hit the ball further, and easy-to-use DIY materials allow the enthusiast to undertake projects without expert help.

activity

IDENTIFY SOME TRENDS

Try to identify two or three further social trends or technological developments that have contributed to the social value of leisure. One example is given to get you started.

TYPE OF DEVELOPMENT OR TREND	SOCIAL / FUN OR HEALTH BENEFITS
Use of Lottery funding for sport or arts facilities	*Groups can visit and play/learn together*

Leisure activities have great social value as they:

- make us 'feel good'
- give us enjoyable purposes away from work or study
- allow us to make friends.

Personal benefits that also add to their value are that:

- skills and abilities can be improved
- status can be created
- motivations and well-being can be increased.

We cannot quantify these benefits or estimate their real value, but they are inherent in all our leisure activities.

Topic 3 Participation rates

Participation rates give a strong indication of the popularity of activities, as well as a clear idea of their geographic scale and importance. The nature of the population means that some activities are naturally more popular than others. Statistics on participation rates are useful for facility planners, product developers and health providers. For the commercial sector, information about the numbers of people participating in particular activities is a key factor in producing their business strategies. Participation data is valuable to many organisations and individuals in the leisure industry. This section illustrates some common sources of information on participation rates, as well as examining participation rates and trends for leisure activities and variations in participation.

Participation contributes as much to the leisure industry as do economic and social value. For many people, being able to take part in an activity is what they value about the leisure industry. Not everyone is able to participate in leisure, however, and we will look at issues surrounding non-participation in a later section.

This topic covers:

■ participation in leisure activities
■ variations in participation
■ regional differences.

Participation in leisure activities

Our source of data on participation rates is the General Household Survey.

The General Household Survey (GHS) is a 'multi-purpose continuous survey' carried out by the Social Survey Division of the Office for National Statistics (ONS), which collects information on a range of topics from people living in private households in Great Britain. The survey began in 1971 and has been carried out every year since.

The GHS has documented the major changes in households, families and lifestyle that have occurred over the last 30 years, including changes in participation in sport and leisure.

Sport participation

The 2002 survey first established how many people took part in some form of sport, game or physical activity. 75% of adults had taken part in the twelve months prior to the interview. (Excluding people whose only activity was walking, the rate was 66%.) In the four weeks before interview, 59% of adults had taken part (43% excluding the walkers).

The five most popular sports, games or physical activities among adults were:

■ walking (46%)

■ swimming (35%)

■ keep fit/yoga (22%)

■ cycling (19%)

■ cue sports (17%).

As in previous years, men were more likely than women to participate in sporting activities. In 1996, 54% of men and 38% of women had participated in at least one activity (excluding walking) in the four weeks before interview. By 2002 participation had fallen to 51% of men, and 36% of women.

In general, participation rates decreased with age. Excluding walking, 72% of 16 to 19 year olds participated. This fell to 54% of adults aged 30 to 44, and fell again to 14% of adults aged 70 and over.

Adults living in Scotland were slightly more likely than those living in England or Wales to have participated in at least one activity, mainly due to the greater proportion of people who had been walking.

Leisure participation

Leisure participation

The 2002 General Household Survey collected data about adult participation in a range of passive and home-based leisure activities.

The most popular of the selected activities was watching television (99%), followed by listening to the radio (88%). These participation rates have been constant since 1996. The proportion of adults who said they listened to records or tapes has increased steadily from 62% in 1977 to 83% in 2002. The proportion of adults who read books was the same in 2002 as in 1996 (65%).

In terms of adult participation in the arts, it was reported that:

- 11% had sung or played a musical instrument
- 11% had danced
- 9% had painted, drawn or done printmaking or sculpture
- 4% had written stories, plays or poetry
- 3% had voluntarily helped with the running of an arts/cultural event or organisation
- 2% had performed in a play, drama or rehearsed for a performance.

There were differences in participation rates in the arts by age and gender. Men and women in the youngest age group (16 to 19) were the most likely to have performed in a play, painted, or written stories, plays or poetry. Participation rates for performing in plays and painting decreased with age. Women were almost twice as likely as men to have been dancing (14% compared with 8%). The peak ages for dancing were 16 to 19 for women (33%) and 20 to 24 for men (15%). Women were more than twice as likely as men to have attended a leisure or recreational class (10% of women compared with 4% of men).

Future surveys will inevitably have to cover electronic media as well as, or instead of, the more traditional activities.

You can visit the site at www.statistics.gov.uk.

Variations in participation

More detailed examples of trends and statistics can be found on the Sport England website, which presents case studies that highlight regional variation throughout England. Sport England's research has found that the eastern region of England has the highest participation rates for sport, with over 37% of adults taking part in sport at least four times a week. The national average is closer to 32%.

Participation rates are highest among the ABC1 categories (professionals and managers) in the 16 to 35 age group, and over 10% of adults are members of sports clubs. (This is a long way below the European average, however, and does not meet the government's targets for participation.) There are lower rates among older age groups, ethnic minorities and women.

Active England

In order to achieve higher participation rates, more funding and resources are clearly required, and there needs to be a change in the way people think about participation. The Active England programme (see below) is one of the projects designed to increase participation.

Active England Programme

Active England is a £108 million community sport investment programme run jointly by the New Opportunities Fund and Sport England. The programme aims to encourage creative approaches to raising physical activity levels and sports participation rates in England. The government's strategy for delivering its sport and physical activity objectives, 'Game Plan', set a target for 70 per cent of the population in England to be reasonably active by 2020. The Active England programme aims, by 2005, to create and support sustainable innovative multi-activity environments in areas of social, sport and health deprivation in England. It also seeks to increase participation in sport and physical activity among all sections of society, but particularly amongst those which are typically under-represented in sport and physical activity participation. The programme is supporting a number of innovative projects that have demonstrated their ability to work towards this vision. Sport England will manage the delivery of the programme and the grant application process through its nine regional offices in England. The Regional Sports Boards will have a fixed amount of funding allocated to manage the programme, and projects will be assessed against local priorities and the overall programme objectives.

activity

SPORT ENGLAND AND PARTICIPATION

Visit the Sports England website at www.sportengland.org and assess its findings on participation rates amongst your age group. Compare activities to those quoted in the GHS and evaluate how they plan to encourage us to adopt more active lifestyles.

Regional differences

There is great variation in the regional popularity of particular sports. Such regional differences may be caused by a number of factors:

- type of terrain/climate
- population profile/demographics
- local traditions
- provision, facilities and location
- seasonal variations.

Type of terrain and climate

Mountainous regions offer good terrain for adventure activities such as biking, climbing, canoeing and skiing, whilst coastal areas offer less strenuous outdoor pursuits – boating, rambling and fossil-hunting, for example.

Population profile/demographics

The population profile of an area can affect the availability and popularity of activities. For example, within retirement towns around the UK, activities like bowls, walking and gardening are popular, whereas in towns with younger populations there are higher participation rates for electronic- or entertainment-based leisure activities. Leisure providers need to be aware of the local population profile in order to offer the types of activity that are likely to be popular.

The UK now has a higher proportion of elderly people than ever before, as people are healthier and are living longer. Statistics from Mintel show that in the period 1999–2003, there was an 11 per cent drop in the number of 25–34 year olds, but an increase of 12 per cent in the 55–64 age range. Such population changes have to be taken into account by leisure providers.

Local traditions

Traditions are a great guide as to what activities might be popular in a particular area. Rugby union and rugby league have great traditional heartlands. Rugby league is well established in the north of England, whilst rugby union is more common in Scotland, Wales and the south of England.

There is a great theatre tradition in London, with its famous West End boasting more than forty theatres that are open all year round.

Many towns host their own traditional leisure events or fairs to reflect local history and regional differences. Examples of this include the Highland Games in Scotland, folk singing in old fishing ports, and agricultural shows in rural areas. Similar examples from elsewhere in Europe are German beer festivals, the running of the bulls in Pamplona in the Basque country, French Celtic festivals in Brittany, and Spanish religious fiestas.

Provision, facilities and location

The commercial sector evaluates which locations are likely to attract the most customers; cities are favoured for their density and diversity of potential customers and, therefore, tend to have the bigger and better venues. Cities with good stadiums and pools can bid for large (sporting) events and host international championships such as the Olympics. It is important that purpose-built facilities are used by the public after such events to justify the initial expense. Rural areas tend to have fewer facilities and, therefore, people who live in the countryside may have to travel some distance to indoor sports and entertainment venues.

Seasonal variations

Participation rates also vary according to the seasons. Sports particularly affected by seasonal variations include tennis and cricket, which, as they require good weather, have to be played in summer unless there is good indoor provision. In this way, seasonal variations can affect an activity's popularity. Similarly, apart from skiing, fewer people participate in outdoor activities in the winter when the weather conditions are more challenging. Tourist activities increase in the summer as holidays have a knock-on effect on our participation rates.

activity

OTHER REGIONAL DIFFERENCES

Try to identify some other regional differences by comparing your region with another in the UK or elsewhere in Europe. Use the factors listed above to guide your research.

Topic 4 The commercial sector

The commercial sector of the leisure industry is made up of organisations that are purely profit-oriented, such as the UK-based companies Whitbread, Rank and Allied, and international companies like Nike, McDonald's and Disney. It is important to understand how these private, limited, or multinational companies function and how they compare to non-commercial organisations. To do this we need to examine:

- the scope and diversity of the commercial sector
- the nature of commercial providers
- the range of products and services they provide
- updates on areas such as health and fitness, tourism and entertainment.

The commercial leisure sector has undergone a rapid period of growth (around 7% per year on average, according to Mintel). Factors that have contributed to this growth are population changes, steady employment rates and a stable economy. However, in recent years there has been a slowing in some sectors, and some commentators feel that saturation point may have been reached.

With the diversity of products and services on offer, competition between leisure providers is fierce. Such competition is another defining characteristic of the commercial sector.

The scope and diversity of the commercial sector

The commercial sector comprises a wide range of leisure providers including:

- food outlets
- entertainment venues
- health and fitness chains
- hotels
- retail operators.

These have been augmented by 'out of town' multi-leisure complexes, which are often sited on green belt or derelict industrial land when space is at a premium in city centres. In this type of development, many types of leisure organisation are housed under one roof, or on one site. Recently the government has tried to encourage more city-centre development with facilities catering for night-time leisure needs and the regeneration of poorer downtown areas.

The commercial sector, which is always chasing increased profits and market share, frequently finds itself in a state of flux as take-overs, mergers, and 'buy outs' occur. Popular brands usually remain the same, but the owners may not. In fact you may only be aware of the brand name – Tussaud's, Centre Parcs or Alton Towers – but these are often different to the commercial owners.

activity

WHO OWNS WHAT?

Working in small teams, look at different business or corporate websites, and try to find out who owns what amongst the following public limited companies: First Leisure, Hilton group, Pearsons, Granada. Prepare a display board showing your findings.

Food outlets

Food and drink establishments have increased in popularity, with more than three-quarters of adults regularly visiting pubs, and two-thirds eating out. Other popular outlets are fast food restaurants and takeaways.

Entertainment venues

Entertainment venues are attracting more and more visitors. Cinemas are the most popular, followed by theatres, arenas, arcades and bowling alleys. Multiplex cinemas are now more modern and comfortable; and regular showings of the latest Hollywood blockbusters mean that young people are going in ever-increasing numbers.

Discos, nightclubs and gambling venues have also profited through targeting young people who, with higher disposable incomes, have developed a tendency to party at weekends.

Health and fitness chains

Over the last decade we have seen a huge increase in the number of health and fitness venues throughout the UK and in the rest of Europe. Some names which spring to mind are Esporta, Cannon's, Next Generation, David Lloyd, Fitness First and Virgin Active. The intense competition for market share amongst the major operators has led to greater choice and higher standards for customers. Hotels have also entered the market by opening their own pool and gym facilities to non-residents, and through partnership arrangements. Much of this expansion has been fuelled by our concern for health; the problem of obesity; stress at work; and, of course, our desire to look and feel good!

The growth of multiple operations looks set to continue, but operators will need to keep an eye on demographic changes. The number of 15–24 year-olds is set to rise, along with the over 55s, but there is also likely to be a fall in the numbers of those aged 25 to 34.

Retail operators

On the publishing side of the sector, book and magazine sales have been hard hit by the impact of the internet. However, LIRC reports that there is still a profitable future ahead for magazine vendors, and new lifestyle magazines are doing particularly well.

The electronic sector of the leisure industry has also seen a period of growth, with digital technology leading the way. LIRC suggests that DVDs, CD-Roms, minidiscs, digital TVs and cameras, computers, and audio systems can now be found in as many as 80 per cent of homes. This is good news for stores like Comet and Dixons and manufacturers such as Sony and Philips.

Finally, the markets for DIY, gardening, photography, toys and pets are all in a healthy trading position due to social trends and buying habits. LIRC estimate the market value of this area at the end of 2003 to have been £8.5 billion. Gardening for leisure has also become more popular, and multi-facility garden centres have become visitor attractions with cafés, play areas and shops as well as plants and gardening equipment, to increase customer enjoyment and spending.

The nature of commercial providers

It is important to understand how commercial sector organisations operate in comparison to non-commercial organisations. Most commercial businesses have a board of directors that makes strategic decisions about what the company will do. These directors have to answer to the shareholders, who can be anyone from members of the general public to other large organisations that may have nothing to do with leisure but can see the chance of gaining good dividends from the company's profitability. The next level down is the management level, made up of managers who implement the company's policies and make the decisions for the general running of the company. Depending on the nature of the organisation, these managers may be in charge of a division, region, department or team of staff. In these departments, sections and divisions are the staff who are responsible for dealing with the company's equipment, services or customers.

At the lower levels of a commercial organisation, the managerial and operational structure is very similar to that of non-commercial leisure organisations.

We can represent this type of structure in an organisational chart:

SHAREHOLDERS IN THE COMPANY

▲

BOARD OF DIRECTORS

▼

DIVISION / REGION / FACILITY / DEPARTMENTAL MANAGERS

▼

OPERATIONS STAFF: TECHNICIANS / RECEPTIONISTS / INSTRUCTORS / GUIDES / ASSISTANTS

The executive board members will pass down their instructions for profit-making to the managers. Companies also need to ensure that other aspects of their business are in good order such as:

- retaining customers
- maintaining quality standards
- ensuring safety measures are adequate
- keeping staff motivated
- developing products and new services.

The leisure industry does not just include large firms and multi-nationals. In fact, much of the industry is made up of small and medium-sized organisations (SMEs). There are also sole traders, partnerships, small limited companies or family-run businesses that only employ a few people.

Although SMEs do not have as much in the way of resources, marketing or finance at their disposal, they are still profit-motivated and, despite having far fewer employees than the larger organisations, SMEs nevertheless offer a huge range of leisure activities.

Range of products and services

To ensure customer satisfaction, commercial leisure operators should provide appropriate services to complement the products they offer.

- A holiday is a leisure product (travel and accommodation) requiring additional services such as currency conversion, travel insurance, tourist excursions, and so on. Travel operators must make provision for these additional requirements – or work in partnership with other commercial organisations – to ensure their availability.

- A visit – to a castle or a theme park – is a leisure experience that could be classed as a product. The services you might also expect during your visit could include: toilet facilities, guides, a café, polite staff, and so on.

The café is an important part of the visit.

- Eating out is a leisure experience, as you buy a product – the meal. The service attached to such a purchase would include efficient service and a clean table, crockery and cutlery.

- Sports rackets, football boots and golf clubs are all leisure products, but we usually expect a range of services to go with them: guidance on maintaining them; the ability to return the purchase if unsuitable; and a well-informed sales person.

Commercial companies are always aiming for repeat business – that is, to give us such a good product or service that we book with them again or revisit their premises, and maybe even make recommendations to friends. In an effort to please existing customers or attract new ones, leisure operators are always keen to launch new and exciting services and products.

In Unit 3 you will find out the importance of customer service, but some key ideas might be summed up in these familiar phrases:

> *'give value for money'*
> *'get it right first time – every time'*
> *'make sure products are fit for purpose'*
> *'keep the customer satisfied'*

Commercial leisure organisations evaluate how well they are doing in terms of sales and customer satisfaction by using a number of means, including:

- performance targets, e.g. retention rates, tickets sold

- customer-satisfaction surveys

- numbers of complaints or returns.

Companies judge the quality of their services as well as the quantities of their products sold by making comparisons with their competitors and with their previous years' performances, to ensure they are staying competitive, working efficiently, and maintaining a good public image.

The importance of excellent customer service cannot be over-emphasised, for the commercial leisure sector is 'people based'. Satisfied customers tend to remain loyal, and customer loyalty means repeat business.

Selling leisure products and services needs teamwork, training and time. Leisure operators need to have a good business plan in place to convince investors that their scheme will work, give them a return on their investments and make profits for shareholders. Any business plan will not only have to give detailed profit and loss forecasts, but also include details of the marketing strategy, to ensure a steady stream of customers to keep the business viable. (You can read more of marketing and business plans in Topic 6.)

It is also worth considering the potential problems and issues faced by commercial operators:

- Accidents can ruin reputations and close operations.

- Seasonal variations can mean income dries up and staff have to be paid off.

- Income can become too low to keep the business viable.

- Business rates and taxes can go up and legislation can change.

- Staff may strike for more pay.

Updates on some sectors

- The Health and Fitness industry – At the beginning of 2004 an assessment by Plimsoll Porfolio analysts reported that, of the top 500 companies in the sector, half were making less than a 2% profit (12% is more usual). Of these, only 62 were returning even 10%, while over 50 operators were showing losses for the second year running. This is not good news for this sector – has saturation point been reached?

- Tourism and accommodation – VisitBritain, the UK tourist organisation, reports that numbers were up by 2% . In order to exceed the 2002 earnings total of £12 billion, the UK tourist industry must achieve a target of 25 million visitors.

- Entertainment – Legislation on gambling has been relaxed, but pub 'happy hours' have been curtailed in an effort to clamp down on binge-drinking. Cinemas have benefited from a stream of blockbusters. Multi-faceted entertainment is the current theme of developments – we can now eat, drink, play, shop and be entertained under one roof.

Topic 4 The commercial sector

| activity |

A LOCAL EXAMPLE

With a partner, investigate one commercial leisure operator (venue or facility) in your town, in terms of its:
- current product range
- supporting services
- methods of evaluating success and satisfaction
- operating difficulties.

Identify three issues that might affect it, and set out some recommendations for what it could do to overcome these problems.

The non-commercial sector

Although the commercial sector of the leisure industry has the biggest profile, there are two other sectors that support our leisure needs. These are the public sector (local authorities) and the 'not for profit' sector (amateur and voluntary clubs and bodies) which support and provide for the 'grass roots' of UK sport and leisure, offering free or low-cost resources and activities to the community.

Both of these sectors are finding that, in order to survive alongside commercial operations, they are having to adopt increasingly business-like ways of meeting targets; coping with shrinking budgets; and making cost savings, without reducing value for money.

Our investigation of these two sectors will be carried out in a similar way to that used in our examination of commercial operators. For both local authorities and for voluntary organisations we look at:

- the scope of provision
- the nature of their operations
- their range of products and services.

The scope of provision

The public sector

The principal remit of local authorities is to cater for markets that commercial operators are not interested in: non-profitable areas or groups of participants who cannot afford commercial prices. In any borough, district, metropolitan or county council you could expect to find the following facilities as part of the local leisure provision:

- swimming pools
- leisure centres
- sports halls
- pitches
- parks
- libraries
- museums
- children's play areas.

Some coastal local authorities may also have marinas, caravan parks, beaches and lakes in their portfolio of resources; city authorities may have to manage major international venues; and rural authorities might have extensive national parks or moorland to manage. Some local authorities have part-share or control in leisure venues since they own the land, but may franchise or let out the premises to a commercial operator to generate additional revenue. Most local authorities will share the responsibility for leisure provision between educational, leisure and community services; these work together to avoid duplication of resources and funding.

No two local authorities have exactly the same types of resources or manage their resources in exactly the same way. It is not compulsory for local authorities to provide leisure and sports facilities and, therefore, each is unique in what it does and how it does it. As a result, there is a great diversity of leisure provision across the UK.

In a climate of declining leisure budgets, many local authorities are finding it difficult to afford the costs of both maintaining old and providing new leisure facilities. Many facilities are old and need extensive refurbishment or even demolition, and local authorities are not able to meet the capital requirements for new-build unless partnership schemes can be created.

Some old facilities, like this Lido, have been successfully refurbished.

activity

YOUR LOCAL AUTHORITY FACILITIES

Make a list of your own local authority facilities. Try to assess how many are old and how many are new and, with some further research, what plans there are for expansion or closure.

The voluntary sector

The voluntary sector is made up of specialist organisations that cater for a specific leisure activity or hobby, or for groups of people who 'club' together for their own benefit.

The voluntary sector is fragmented. Every city, town and village has an array of clubs, societies, teams, groups, bodies and associations, which, in effect, cover the whole range of active, passive and home-based leisure.

Here are just a few examples:

- tennis clubs
- pub football teams
- chess clubs
- photography societies
- swimming associations
- book clubs
- hockey leagues
- chatrooms
- amateur dramatic groups
- choirs or bands.
- after-school clubs
- keep-fit groups
- parents and toddlers groups
- tea dance groups.

The scope of the voluntary sector is vast, with specialities to suit local needs or conditions and population preferences. Coastal towns are likely to have sailing and maybe surfing clubs; cities will have the greatest diversity due to population density; clubs and groups in rural areas are likely to have lower member numbers due to the lower population density and lack of provision.

The voluntary sector provides all types of leisure pursuit for all types of people as long as there are sufficient members to keep it alive. The previous examples underline the importance of the social aspect of leisure, whilst the following examples of clubs emphasise the importance of competition:

- golf and tennis tournaments
- swimming galas
- equestrian events
- five-a-side football competitions.

The following types of group activity are associated with learning and developing new skills:

- coaching courses
- night-school classes
- amateur-dramatic or operatic clubs
- art groups
- computer clubs.

activity

YOUR VOLUNTARY PROVISION

From your own knowledge and from looking at newspapers, internet sites, or visiting sports centres or tourist information centres, compile a display board to show the range of examples of voluntary provision in your area.

Many clubs are associated with national bodies that cover the whole of the UK – for example the Youth Hostels Association, the Women's Institute and the Arts Council. Other groups, like the Scout and Guide Associations and the Young Men's Christian Association (YMCA) are global. At the last count there were over 200 national organisations in the UK, with more than eight million members. Sports, arts, young people's, religious, environmental, charitable and community groups have the highest representation.

The YHA hostel at Bogle Hole, Yorkshire

The Central Council for Physical Recreation (CCPR).

As the independent voice of UK Sport, the CCPR:

- Is the umbrella organisation for the national governing and representative bodies of sport and recreation in the UK.
- Is at the forefront of sports politics.
- Is completely independent of any form of Government control.
- Has no responsibility for allocating funds.
- Is strictly non-party and will support or oppose proposed measures only on the basis of their perceived value to sport and recreation.

Who do we represent?

It is estimated that 29 million people regularly take part in sport or some form of physical recreation. From rugby to country dancing, from motor racing to rambling, the range of sporting and physical endeavours available to the public is enormous.

All these activities are administered and promoted by a governing or representative body. It is these bodies that make up the membership of the CCPR. We work on behalf of:

- 270 national governing and representative bodies.
- 150,000 voluntary clubs.
- Millions of individuals who participate.

Scope and independence

The objectives of our members are immensely wide ranging – from encouraging people to volunteer on wet Sunday mornings to help at an under-10's football match, right up to developing medal-winning, international squads.

Our membership includes well known organisations such as the Football Association and the Lawn Tennis Association, as well as much smaller, less well known bodies such as the Medau Society and the British Ultimate Federation. We also represent many organisations that have a supporting role in the area such as teaching unions, youth groups, and HM Armed Services.

Our independence from Government is a vital component of our impartiality. It enables the members to assess the interests of sport and recreation with a completely objective viewpoint and then to make representations to the Government, Sports Councils and other agencies whose view and decisions impact on sport and recreation.

Source: www.ccpr.org

The Central Council for Physical Recreation (see box above) is a unique national body as it represents all sports governing bodies, is seen as a voluntary sector organisation, (though it has professionals working there) and is also independent of government. In fact, it existed even before the sports councils did, so has a strong history of representing grassroots and amateur sports in the UK.

The nature of operations

The public sector

Like commercial providers, local authorities also need someone to be responsible for making decisions and guiding strategies. This is usually done by a group of elected councillors, who each take responsibility for managing an area of the community. They do this in conjunction with professionals who are trained or qualified in leisure management.

Nowadays, local authorities have to be as well managed as commercial providers in order to make effective and efficient use of resources for the benefit of the local community. A management system called 'Best Value' – later superseded by Competitive Performance Assessment (CPA) – was introduced to ensure local authorities meet certain performance targets; consult their customers; and compare themselves to other similar bodies, to monitor their progress. Such monitoring is not always well received but, as local authorities are responsible for taxpayers' money, they need to be held accountable for spending it wisely.

Each year the professional officers prepare a budget for their plans and submit it to the council for approval. On the basis of the budget, new capital works can be undertaken and levels of income (revenue) and subsidy can be set. The income from profitable areas is often used to subsidise other non-profitable services.

The voluntary sector

Like local authorities, voluntary organisations usually have a committee that oversees their activities. However, unlike those in commercial and local authorities, voluntary committee members are usually unpaid, except in the larger national associations such as sports clubs, hostels, charities and youth groups.

Most voluntary organisations function on minimal budgets, often surviving solely through sponsorship from the commercial sector. They are unlikely to own their own premises and usually rent or hire them from the local authority. This type of arrangement is called 'synergy'.

LOCAL AUTHORITIES PROVIDE PREMISES OR GROUNDS

COMMUNITY PROVIDES PEOPLE

COMMERCIAL SECTOR PROVIDES SPONSORSHIP

activity

A LOCAL EXAMPLE OF SYNERGY

Working in a small team and using the diagram above, identify a local example of this type of arrangement. Sum up the key points at each stage.

Voluntary clubs often have a constitution (some basic rules and structure) by which they run themselves. Volunteers who run the clubs are usually very motivated, and their contribution to leisure in their local community should not be underestimated. Voluntary clubs and Trusts have some advantages over commercial operators; because of their nature, the government grants voluntary organisations certain financial allowances such as rates relief, no VAT charges, and no tax on profit.

Range of products and services

We have now looked at a range of examples of organisations and services that are found in the non-commercial sector. The following tables present some examples, which may give you ideas for further research and could be used for your assessment.

TYPES OF LOCAL AUTHORITIES	LEISURE SERVICES
County councils	Museums, parks and libraries
District councils	Local tennis courts and pitches
Community and parish councils	Bowling greens and pathways
Borough councils	Pools and leisure centres
Metropolitan councils	Stadiums and athletic tracks

NON-COMMERCIAL NATIONAL ORGANISATIONS	LEISURE SERVICES
The National Trust	Coastal paths
The Forestry Commission	Forest trails and picnic sites
English Heritage	Stately homes and gardens
The Environment Agency	Waterways and lakes
Sport England	Sports advice, schemes and funding
Youth Hostels Association	Accommodation and courses
Arts Council	Advice, guidance and funding

Aims, objectives, funding and marketing

In this section we look in more detail at the purposes, aims and objectives of leisure providers, and how these are managed and evaluated, with a focus on funding, working partnerships and marketing. Topics are covered under the following headings:

- **The purposes of leisure organisations**
- **The nature of aims and objectives**
- **Managing people and resources**
- **Funding sources, revenue streams and partnerships**
- **Marketing strategies.**

The purposes of leisure organisations

Commercial organisations

In the process of trying to make a profit and provide a financial return for investors, commercial organisations also try to influence our lifestyle choices in terms of our:

- buying habits
- interests
- fashions, fads and fancies.

Commercial support, through the production of goods or promotion of services, or through sponsorship, inventions and innovations has, in many cases, created or kept a sport or hobby alive. Examples of this include:

- TV coverage of snooker
- the creation of new recreational toys
- sponsorships of sports tournaments and leagues.

So although commercial organisations are driven by profit, their actions can also be seen to have both direct and indirect benefits for sport and leisure; the increase in the number of commercial leisure clubs has helped to generate new approaches to health and fitness, while also creating new jobs.

In recent years, commercial providers have become aware of the value of appearing to act altruistically, giving more to their local communities in the form of sponsorship, donations, free use of premises and goods. By raising their public image in this way, organisations hope to attract more customers and, therefore, make more money.

activity

ASSESS A COMMERCIAL PROVIDER

Identify a commercial leisure provider and, using company reports, assess :
- their main purpose and products/services
- the profits they make
- the support or sponsorship they give back to the community.

The voluntary sector

Voluntary organisations are far more socially oriented. Their purpose is to help people achieve their leisure needs. Socialisation is also a purpose for voluntary groups, as they often bring together people with common interests, backgrounds or experiences.

Membership of a club can also create:

- a collective voice on certain issues (political pressure)

- a sense of identity (wearing a uniform)

- opportunities that an individual might not have (safety in numbers or meeting the opposite sex)

- new roles and responsibilities (secretary, treasurer)

- status or image (leader, captain, chairperson).

The public sector

The primary purpose of local authorities is to serve the needs of their communities, and most will have a strategic plan that includes leisure and recreation. Local authorities try to provide for areas that the commercial sector does not, and that the voluntary sector can not, such as:

- providing and maintaining pitches, playing areas and courts.

- ensuring everyone has access to facilities for health and fitness purposes.

- managing parks and gardens, which have been created or given to the authority.

- supporting library, gallery and museum provision.

- providing entertainment in the form of theatres, cinemas and arts centres.

---

activity

YOUR LOCAL SITUATION

In groups, evaluate your own local authority or a local voluntary leisure organisation and try to assess their purpose and the leisure users and groups they cater for. How could they go about monitoring their success? Discuss what you would like to see them concentrate on.

Local authorities can provide support for voluntary groups and private developers in the form of land, grants, advice, use of halls and so on, so they have a collaborative purpose too. They also have a regulatory function, preventing unsightly buildings, unsafe practices or unhealthy situations developing. In essence, local authorities have three main purposes: service, support and control.

National bodies

National organisations such as the Football Association, the National Trust and the Guide movement, have all been set up to manage areas that commercial operators are not interested in, that local authorities cannot cater for and that voluntary clubs are too dispersed to cover.

Their general purposes are similar to those of local authorities: to develop, promote and support their members and any activities they do. Such bodies also tend to exert some sort of control over their members – to prevent drug taking in sport or bad conduct, for example.

Libraries, such as this one in York, are provided by local authorities.

The nature of aims and objectives

Once strategic plans and purposes have been established, the next step for an organisation is to set out one or two aims and a set of objectives. Before we go any further, it is important to first understand the difference between an aim and an objective, as they are often confused.

An aim is a vision of what an organisation would like to happen. For example, the North Yorkshire coastline is currently undergoing a period of regeneration, and the local councils have a joint vision of: 'achieving the renaissance of the North Yorkshire Coast by 2020'. Commercial operators also have vision statements. The Trafford Centre in Manchester, for example, promotes the aim of: 'being a centre of excellence for both the retailers that trade in it and the people who visit it'.

An objective, on the other hand, is a measurable target that is set in order to help achieve an aim or vision. Objectives are usually set at various stages so that progress can be measured. Examples might include:

- selling 1000 tickets for every concert as part of an aim to make £1million.

- completing every assignment on time as part of getting a qualification.

- making a 10 per cent profit on every product sold as part of a business plan.

These types of objectives are all measurable. An objective needs to be a quantity of some sort that can be evaluated at the end of a set period of time. The most common way to remember how to set objectives is to use the mnemonic 'SMART'. All objectives should be:

Specific – to the tasks set

Measurable – by quantities of some sort

Achievable – within the scope of the team

Realistic – appropriate for the organisation

Timed – set to a given time.

Using objectives enables you to set targets or goals at the outset of a project or financial year, for example, which can then be compared to the eventual outcomes. It is a case of checking expectations against reality, forecasts against actual performance.

This type of evaluation process is now being carried out by non-commercial as well as commercial organisations. Both types of organisation produce plans, and both are judged on performance.

Managing people and resources

Organisations and services need careful planning, as they all involve the management of people (staff and customers) and resources.

Managing staff

Managing staff means ensuring that they can do their jobs effectively so that customers are satisfied with the service they receive. Some key aims are:

■ teamwork

■ clear objectives

■ effective leadership

■ excellent communications

■ comprehensive training.

Managing customers

Managing customers involves:

■ meeting and satisfying needs

■ presenting a professional image

■ adjusting and being flexible to demands

■ being polite and knowledgeable

■ communicating clearly.

activity

AIMS, OBJECTIVES, EVALUATION

Working in a small group, imagine you are working for a leisure company that has been asked to stage an event (you can decide the nature of this). Decide on the following:
• the aim of the event, and invent a vision statement for it.
• three different types of objectives by which you could judge its success.
• an evaluation system to capture team, event and customer feedback.

Managing resources

Managing resources means:

■ looking after equipment

■ maintaining the building or premises

■ providing support services for clients

■ stocking up with supplies.

All of this is usually monitored and checked by supervisors and managers.

activity

HOW DO THEY MANAGE?

Working in groups, investigate how an organisation of your choice manages its staff, customers or resources and how they evaluate their progress.

The Institute of Sport and Recreation Management

The Institute of Sport and Recreation Management (ISRM) is a national organisation set up to support professionals from any of the three industry sectors (commercial, local authority or voluntary). The ISRM is one of the leading sport and recreation associations serving leisure professionals (membership is also open to students).

The mission statement of the ISRM makes its role very clear:

'to lead, develop and promote professionalism in the management of sport and recreation'.

To achieve this aim the ISRM offer a range of products and services to members including:

- courses and seminars, to improve qualifications and operational knowledge
- facility management and development resources, such as videos and manuals
- publications, such as research reports and safety posters
- access to consultants in a range of leisure management aspects, such as risk assessment, contracts and use of new technology
- technical support and advisory services for legal affairs.

Information on all these and other services is available on the ISRM's website, www.isrm.co.uk, and is also sent out to members through a regular mailshot and a professional journal.

Martin Steer is the Education and Development Manager at the ISRM. Martin feels that his primary role is to raise management standards, making his aims fit with the overall ISRM strategy. 'I work hard to try and ensure that examples of "best practice" are spread to members across the country and everyone in the association gets an opportunity for "continuous professional development" (CPD).

In recent years we have created a range of courses and qualifications from first Level 2, right up to Master's Level 5 in sport and recreation operations and management.'

The ISRM works with many partners in the leisure industry:

- The British Standards Institution (BSI)
- The Child Protection in Sport Unit
- The Department for Culture, Media and Sport (DCMS)
- The Central Council of Physical Recreation (CCPR)
- All UK sports councils and UK Sport
- The World Health Organisation (WHO)

You can learn more by visiting the website or contacting the ISRM at info@isrm.co.uk. Student memberships are currently only £25 per year.

Funding sources, revenue streams and partnerships

It is important to understand the difference between funding sources and revenue streams. In a sense they are the 'before' and 'after' of finance. Funding is the capital needed to build or create something; revenue is the income you make from it after it has been built.

Funding sources

Commercial companies have the broadest range of funding sources (capital). They can:

- plough back some of their profits
- offer shares on the stock market
- approach a bank for a loan
- find investors who have capital of their own who might invest in the company.

One source that commercial companies cannot apply to is the National Lottery.

For non-commercial organisations like local authorities, the process of fund-raising is much more difficult. Although they receive government funding, this has to be spent on *all* services, not solely leisure, so there may not be much to spare. If one of their facilities makes a profit, some of this may then have to be ploughed into capital developments. Another strategy would be to increase council taxes for local residents, but this would not be a popular political move. Local authorities sometimes sell off land to developers and use the proceeds to build new leisure or sports facilities; however, suitable sites are not always available. To overcome the problem of raising capital, local authorities may go into partnership with the commercial sector or apply for funding from other sources including:

- The National Lottery
- Urban renewal, rural development or regeneration schemes
- Sport Action Zones
- European social development funds.

For voluntary organisations, raising capital is a huge task. Many will have to take on long-term savings/fund-raising schemes to achieve any improvements. Fund-raising events could include car boot sales, sponsored runs, walks and swims or discos and fairs. Non-commercial clubs and organisations can also apply for grants to local authorities, national organisations or the National Lottery.

Revenue streams

Revenue streams are vital to the sustainability or viability of a new facility. Revenue is needed to pay for staff wages and maintenance of the premises.

Revenue streams are created from fees, entry charges and ticket sales (primary spend) and the sale of goods and services on the premises such as kit, souvenirs and food (secondary spend).

Revenue might be added to by donations from former members, sponsorship by local businesses, the hiring out of facilities, or franchising.

In order to overcome the problem of not being able to function like a company, some local authorities set

Raising capital for even quite small projects can be a huge task.

a c t i v i t y
WHERE DID THE MONEY COME FROM?
Identify three new schemes in your area that represent examples of the scenarios presented above. What sources of funding have helped them raise the capital? There may well be several sources for any one scheme.

up what is called a 'trust' which can operate autonomously from the council to benefit leisure facility users. This allows local authorities to make and recycle profits and also has certain tax advantages.

Partnerships

Partnership schemes have become quite popular (see below). Local authorities simply approach private sector developers (or vice versa) to build the facilities, which are then leased back to them. In this way, both organisations create a revenue stream.

Private–Public Partnerships

The capital that local authorities require to achieve their leisure expansion plans has been estimated by Business in Sport and Leisure (BISL) to be over £3 billion. As we saw earlier, there are many constraints on how local authorities can access or raise capital. Partnership solutions to this problem are often called PPPs: Private–Public Partnerships. The government approves PPPs, and the funding processes and contracts are overseen by the Department of the Environment, Transport and the Regions. Some schemes cover all four aspects of capital and revenue – Design, Build, Finance, Operate (DBFO schemes). New facilities that have been created through partnership working include leisure centres, swimming complexes, golf courses and theatres. Can you identify any near you?

Major building projects often need PPP funding.

Unit 1 The Leisure Industry

Partnership arrangements are common throughout Europe, with companies offering their recreation grounds for community use. In Belgium, as in the UK, joint provision is common, with schools using facilities during the week and other community groups and clubs utilising them in the evening or at weekends. In Sweden, private firms, local authorities and the government all collaborate to support recreation and hold tournaments and events with neighbouring countries (Norway and Finland) through commercial connections. In many other European countries (Switzerland, Holland and Austria), companies fund recreation schemes for employees to help them recover their strength and fitness following illness or surgery. They are a bit like GP-referral schemes in the UK, whereby patients are recommended to follow specially designed programmes at approved local gyms as part of their recovery. Statistics show that exercise regimes for employees also help improve productivity.

Marketing strategies

Marketing has become a powerful tool. Considerable market research goes into identifying consumer needs and wants, enabling organisations to target specific groups or sections of the community. This is called 'market segmentation': we are all categorised into leisure types and targeted by marketing in the form of mailshots, internet ads, TV advertising and in-store offers to encourage us to spend more.

Marketing strategies are one of the key tools used by commercial providers. They try to offer the right product to us at the right price, selling it at the right place through effective promotion. These four Ps make up the 'marketing mix'.

Strategies for commercial providers tend to target certain segments of the population, with product brands they hope are right for them such as:

■ Leisure clothing aimed at teenagers

■ Sports drinks for active sportsmen and women

■ Holiday products such as cruises for the over-50s.

All strategies seek to attract customers and keep them loyal, hence the large range of loyalty schemes that reward you for shopping with certain suppliers.

Non-commercial providers have a much harder task as they usually have much smaller marketing budgets. Because they have to serve everyone, local authorities need a generic strategy. Voluntary clubs and associations will have some age-groups in mind, but do tend to focus on 'junior' members, in the hope that they will remain loyal as they grow older. Every

organisation should have a customer-focused strategy and a flexible approach to applying it.

Most marketing strategies are based on good market intelligence, which is gained through research and should be ongoing and help steer the implementation of the strategies.

A successful marketing strategy: trainers for teenagers

The Rank Organisation, one of the world's biggest leisure-oriented companies, identifies four activities around which they design all their products and services, and which inform their strategies throughout Europe:

- Eating and drinking
- Boy meets girl
- Gambling
- Family holidays.

These have become 'stable mass-market business areas'.

Eurocamp's strategy has been to repeat its UK success in the rest of Europe, and create revenue streams from German, French, Austrian and Swiss clients, whilst continually diversifying to suit the different holiday needs of people from each country.

Whitbread and First Leisure both try to manage diversified portfolios of products and services such as bingo, fitness clubs, seaside attractions and theatres. Repeat business is the mainstay of their success.

activity

COMPARING COMPANY STRATEGIES

Working in groups, identify the strategic approaches that Stakis, Allied, and Ladbrokes have taken recently (using their company reports or website information) and compare them in terms of success and failure. Present your findings to the rest of the class.

Topic 7 Factors affecting consumer demand

Customer needs and wants can change frequently in the leisure industry; what was fashionable and popular ten years ago can often be considered outdated today. A number of factors have contributed to changes in consumer demand, including:

- leisure time
- disposable income
- demographic changes
- social trends and life-stages
- car and home ownership
- health awareness.

Leisure time

Our leisure time has undoubtedly increased as our economy has undergone a gradual change from one based on manufacturing and manual labour to one based on service. The majority of workplaces today are clean and comfortable environments, in stark contrast to the dusty, smelly, noisy factories of early last century. But how does all of this affect leisure time?

In the early twentieth century, the works outing to the seaside was the leisure event of the year for many working people.

In Victorian and Edwardian times, only the wealthy had enough time or resources to spend on leisure pursuits; working-class people worked on the land or in factories, some for up to six or even seven days a week. Leisure time was a rare commodity and was usually limited to special events two or three times a year. Shifts were long and pay was poor.

In comparison, we now have a five-day week and guaranteed paid holidays around which to organise our leisure time. This has helped generate an increase in consumer demand for leisure goods and services.

One trend that has developed in the UK is that of people working longer hours to achieve more in terms of pay and status; UK workers tend to work far longer hours than other European workers. This has created what is termed the 'money rich, time poor' scenario, which has resulted in intensive spending on leisure to compensate for lack of time. Leisure has become a commodity; we now pay for most of our leisure activities, indulging ourselves at weekends to counteract stressful working weeks. Obviously this is not the case for everyone; some people have welcomed the increase in leisure time, particularly those who retire early or take a gap year between school and university.

SURVEYING THE WORKERS

Working with a partner, design a questionnaire that you could use for a survey on the leisure-time allocation of working people. It should cover:

- how long each weekday they spend on leisure in comparison to weekends.
- how often they carry out their hobby/activity/sport and for how long.
- how much more time would they like for leisure in a week.
- how they divide their leisure time between activities and holidays.

Disposable income

The money left over after bills and other dues are paid is called 'disposable income' and, as real incomes have grown (at about 2% per year for the last decade) disposable income has grown too. In recent years the UK has enjoyed high levels of employment and a general wage increase, which gives us confidence and security. Add to that the low level of interest rates and we have been quite happy to run up 'consumer debt' on our credit cards, much of which is spent on leisure goods and services like:

- home entertainment
- the home and garden
- eating, drinking and clubbing
- gambling
- sightseeing, day trips and short breaks
- holidays and holiday homes.

In 2002 it was estimated that we spent nearly £120 billion on leisure and recreation, which amounted to 18 per cent of all consumer spending.

Not everyone is able to spend so much, however. It is easy to identify the division between the 'haves' and 'have nots' in our society today, as the unemployed and the low-paid fall lower in the social stratification and leisure stakes.

Demographic changes

Demographic change means alterations to the population profile. In the UK some current demographic trends are having a discernable effect on consumer demand and product supply.

The first is that we have an ageing population; at the turn of the last century, around half of the population were over 50. Commercial organisations, including leisure providers, are increasingly looking to attract older consumers as they tend to either have good earning power if they are in work, or good disposable income if they are retired. As a result, many more goods and services, activities and events, and programmes and facilities are now provided for this 'grey market'.

A second demographic change is the reduction in numbers in the 24–35 age bracket. This has reduced the market for suppliers and made it highly competitive.

Another demographic change is the increase in the number of single parents; there are now more extended families and children being brought up by single parents than ever before. Single-parent families usually have lower disposable income, less leisure time and restricted access to leisure services. In order to attract this group, leisure organisations have to tailor their products to suit their specific needs.

Leisure providers are looking to attract the 'grey market'.

WHAT DO THEY WANT?

Can you identify what the following suppliers might provide to help attract the over-50s or single-parent families?

LEISURE OPERATOR	OVER-50s	SINGLE-PARENT FAMILIES
Local sports and leisure centre		
Swimming pool		
Pub		
Theatre or cinema		
Holiday company		

Social trends and life stages

A number of notable social trends that have affected leisure demands are:

- Marrying later – many women are continuing with their careers for longer and, as a result, are marrying later. Many couples tend to cohabit for a number of years before getting married.

- Smaller families – people are having fewer children and later too, in order to maintain their careers and the level of their disposable income.

- Work/life balance – many working people struggle to find a balance between domestic duties and work commitments. We seem to have developed a rather unhealthy attitude to work, putting in long hours to achieve promotion or bonuses.

- Flexible working practices – more employers are offering staff the opportunity to work 'flexi-time' to suit their busy lifestyles or parenting needs.

- Health awareness in the older population – older people are living longer, are becoming increasingly aware of the benefits of healthy eating and exercise.

- Obesity problems for the young – young people are eating too much junk food and have poor exercise regimes.

- Holiday homes – due to low interest rates and a strong pound, many families are buying second homes abroad.

- Short breaks – with European travel now cheaper and quicker, short breaks are becoming increasingly popular.

- Theme parks have become our new playgrounds for thrills.

- Electronic leisure products, for example Playstations, mobile phones and games consoles, are especially popular amongst young people.

activity

PREDICTING FUTURE DEMANDS

Working in small groups, analyse the life trends listed above and, through the eyes of a leisure company, decide how you would meet the predicted change in demands. Prepare a display of your suggestions to show the rest of the class.

Our leisure trends tend to change as we grow older – and become less active. Leisure providers are aware of this and try to target our leisure habits accordingly, with products and services to match. In partnership with the government, Sport England is actively encouraging us to have a lifelong attitude to activity, so that as we lose the agility, ability and strength to do more energetic sports, we keep active by opting for less demanding, passive activities instead.

Car and home ownership

Car ownership has been a major factor in the growth and direction of leisure trends and consumer demand. Ownership of a car facilitates many aspects of leisure such as visiting family and friends, going on a day or shopping trip, or going on a driving holiday.

As cars have become cheaper and more reliable, most families now have access to a car for their work and leisure needs. Cars have truly liberated the modern family. Car manufacturers have responded by fitting cars with a combination of safety, comfort and leisure features. However, we should not forget the cost to the environment and the potential clashes with other people's leisure habits. Cars cause noise and air pollution, congestion, need huge parking spaces and require disposal. The government has to try and combat these negative factors and, ultimately, we all pay for cars, through higher taxes and a poorer environment.

Nearly two-thirds of people in the UK now own their own homes and, consequently, buy more home-based goods and materials. The range of products for use in and around the home has boomed, whilst ownership of second homes has also added new dimensions to holiday habits, leisure times and spending. Home ownership is less common in other parts of Europe, where renting occurs more, e.g. Spain.

Health awareness

Another factor that has led to a change in our leisure demands is greater health awareness, brought about by:

- advertising campaigns
- government documents (for schools and health)
- better education
- research by sports scientists
- events run by big charities such as the Heart Foundation.

The commercial sector has responded by creating new venues for us to pursue our health and fitness ideals; the public sector has responded by providing more facilities and schemes; the government has produced plans such as 'Lifelong Learning', which try to encourage us to start early and keep going into old age. Magazines and television are both major promoters of health products and services. The National Lottery has also had a big impact on health, by funding the creation of facilities for local health and fitness schemes.

Healthy Competition

In an article published in *Sports Management* (Vol. 1, Issue 1, 2003), Tom McNab, a well-known sports writer, argues that we should be using competition to help health and fitness. He makes a number of points:

- There has been an increase in the range of sports undertaken (to the detriment of some mainstream ones) which means people have more choice and can find an activity that they enjoy, which they can do at their own level for a number of years.

- Big gains have been made by health club memberships, better education and lifestyle magazines supporting healthy lifestyle.

- The main problem is our increasingly sedentary lifestyles, which mean that we all burn fewer calories.

- Research has shown that regular exercise can prolong life spans.

- A couple of hours of Physical Education per week in schools is not going to have any real effect on the level of children's health and fitness, as PE activities are too 'games' orientated.

- Flexible ways of playing have become important – artificial turf, mixed sessions, timings and junior levels are important too.

- The government should use legislation and taxation to tackle the problems of health and fitness.

activity

YOUR 'GET FIT' CAMPAIGN

Discuss some of the ideas in the 'Healthy Competition' article, and produce your own 'get fit' campaign ideas for schools. Design a poster to promote your scheme and ask your PE teacher or sports tutor to judge which is the best from the point of view of a) design, and b) content and ideas.

Topic 8 Barriers to participation

It is important to be aware of the inequality of access to leisure provision, and the barriers that prevent some people or groups from participating as freely as others. Although many organisations in the leisure industry actively campaign to overcome these barriers, problems of participation still persist around the country.

Barriers to participation can be related to:

- economic factors
- choice
- lifestyle and aspirations
- disability access and provision
- issues of equity and diversity.

It is also important to consider what measures have been put in place and what future solutions are planned to ensure equality of access to leisure provision.

Economic factors

Economic factors are those that affect our personal financial circumstances:

- People on a low wage do not have enough disposable income to spend on leisure activities. This is particularly true for students and those just starting out but also, at the other end of the age spectrum, people surviving on a state pension.

- People who are unemployed because they live in an area with few jobs or one which has been hit by factory closures tend to concentrate on the basic essentials like food, shelter and clothing. Leisure activities or goods are not a priority.

- People can suffer from poverty through a combination of factors: poor education, poor skills, living in an impoverished area, and bad influences. These are not all due to economic factors, but often stem from them. Poorer people may have free time, but no inclination or means to use it for recreational purposes.

- People saving for something (for example, a deposit on a house, a car or a wedding) will often cut back on their leisure spending until they achieve their target. This is not enforced hardship, but an economic path taken by choice.

- For lone parents or large extended families, the domestic budget can be very tight, leaving little to spend on leisure activities.

- New and young borrowers are often fully stretched paying mortgages and other household bills, which limits their disposable income.

- Other economic factors may affect leisure provision. Organisations may struggle to pay for facilities, equipment, transport, staff and so on.

Choice

Choice-related factors that prevent participation have a number of sources:

- Poor or no local provision – this can be an issue for both urban and rural populations, where no facilities exist, commercial operators do not find them viable or what is there is not well managed or is vandalised.

- Poor or no public transport provision – this is certainly a problem for rural people, but surprisingly it can be the same for urban dwellers. In many areas bus routes do not always follow the most convenient path or don't run late at night.

- Lack of awareness of what facilities are available – those seeking to increase their leisure activity may not know where to obtain information or even know what goes on at their local leisure centre. Good publicity is the answer here.
- Lack of choice in leisure provision can also be a constraint – activities may be limited by old facilities (church halls, low-roof buildings) or by a lack of suitably qualified coaches or instructors. Sponsorship might be a way to boost choice, or someone in the club could go on a coaching course to improve skills in the club.

Old community buildings are not always suitable for leisure provision.

Many sports colleges have received government funding in order to further develop their facilities. In addition, many academies and centres of excellence have been set up around the country, increasing access and opportunities for young and talented people. Local councils have been able to provide more leisure facilities by working in partnership with commercial developers.

activity
SOLVING CHOICE-RELATED PROBLEMS

Some solutions have been made for each of the choice-related problems mentioned above. Devise others and insert them into the following table. One example is given to get you started.

CONSTRAINT	SOLUTION
Lack of knowledge of how to play or do something	*Invite a coach/instructor for a taster session*
Poor provision	
Poor transport	
Lack of awareness	
Lack of choice	

Lifestyle and aspirations

In a leisure context, 'lifestyle' means our leisure choices and habits; 'aspirations' are what we hope to achieve through our leisure pursuits.

Lifestyles differ greatly from person to person. Factors like wealth, free time and transport will facilitate participation, whilst a lack of them will inhibit participation. Where there is some degree of choice about how we live, we create our own lifestyle – deciding the type of clothes to wear, the food to eat, the friends to have, the work to do and the leisure activities to undertake.

So for many people, leisure activities have to fit in with their perceived or preferred lifestyle. For members of the upper middle classes (socio-economic groups A and B), lifestyles might be typified by: driving top-of-the-range cars; taking several foreign holidays a year; being a member of a exclusive leisure club; and holding dinner parties or dining out at top restaurants.

The average middle-class family will probably shop at department stores; have a four-wheel-drive vehicle or people carrier; attend a local leisure centre; and holiday in Spain.

Our leisure pursuits are part of the image of ourselves that we wish to project to others. Inequalities in access to leisure activities can create a division between the 'haves' and the 'have nots', and this can cause those who fall into the latter category to develop a poor self-image and have low self-esteem.

This leads us into a discussion of 'aspirations' – targets we set for ourselves. In leisure terms we can aspire to:

- improve our skills
- be able to free-fall parachute
- take a trip in a hot-air balloon
- own a top-of-the-range stereo system
- speak a foreign language
- visit the Grand Canyon.

You will no doubt have some aspirations of your own. Aspirations provide us with the intrinsic motivation to apply ourselves to achieve our targets or realise our dreams. Aspirations need reinforcement – a little success or encouragement goes a long way. Extrinsic motivation is also important; poor role models can prove detrimental and cause us to become apathetic or disillusioned.

Disability access and provision

We have now discussed some of the barriers that able-bodied people face in terms of participation, but access for disabled people is even more problematic. The factors that affect able-bodied people can apply to disabled people too, however, many of the traditional problems are much more practical in nature. The issue of disabled access and provision has only really been tackled in the last 10 years, spurred on by the Disability Discrimination Act 2000.

In many ways, sport has led the way in terms of improving access to leisure activities, and involving disabled people (see example of a successful collaborative project below). Much more publicity and exposure is now being given to disabled athletes and competitions such as the Commonwealth Games, the London Marathon and the Paralympics. You can check out recent developments on the English Federation for Disability Sport website, at http://www.efds.co.uk.

Disability need not stop people enjoying leisure pursuits. Some disabled athletes compete at the highest level.

Successful collaborative project

In January 2004, a collaborative project between Winchester Council, the NHS, and a group of adults with learning difficulties, proved quite a success. An initial 10-week programme saw a range of people with learning difficulties working with a local fitness instructor. Screening and selection for the scheme was made on the basis of advice from local GPs. Baseline fitness measurements were made at the start. The exercise regime encouraged participants to take a range of suitable activities for 35-40 minutes once a week for 10 weeks. Assistants and dieticians supported the group and the participants responded well. The final evaluation stated that:

- the clients clearly enjoyed themselves; some lost weight; most became more competent at the activities.

- levels of self-confidence rose and anxiety levels fell.

- all participants wanted to come back for more.

Clearly this programme was a major success, setting an example for others to follow suit.

activity
HELPING DISABLED PEOPLE PARTICIPATE

Working with a partner, try to complete the following chart with examples of the improvements that have been made to help disabled people participate in leisure activities. One example is given to get you started.

LEISURE ACTIVITY	HOW ACCESS HAS BEEN IMPROVED
Sailing	Specially adapted boats and trained instructors
Skiing	
Home-based electronic leisure	
Abseiling	
	Parking
	Signage
	Prosthetics

Legislation has forced organisations to adapt their facilities to improve disabled access to leisure activities and opportunities, by providing:

- ramps into museums
- lifts for libraries
- low-level counters for receptions
- special fittings and toilets
- training for staff
- extra space in planes and cinemas
- inclusiveness in the school curriculum.

Issues of equity and diversity

These issues can be very sensitive and emotive for some people. In this context equity means 'equality of access' and diversity means 'choice'.

Equity really means fairness in leisure contexts – a fair allocation of resources; a fair distribution of finance; a fair share of access to provision. Plans that can be put in place to ensure greater equity include:

- giving equal funding to all groups wanting to participate
- creating equality of leisure opportunities throughout the UK
- setting the same criteria for resources for everybody
- making provision for all levels of participant, and for all ages
- offering opportunities for all types of interaction: recreational, competitive, social, cultural, educational
- making leisure activities more affordable
- ensuring leaders and coaches are trained to apply equitable and ethical practices.

Such parameters need to be applied to all kinds of leisure activities as they provide good guidelines for achieving equality and equity. Diversity of opportunity means also providing appropriate choices to cater for different cultures, which is particularly important in the multicultural society we live in today.

Diversity of provision can start at school level, with a range of leisure pursuits being offered through after-school clubs. Provision should also be made in the community to celebrate cultural diversity.

There's no reason why women shouldn't play football.

Access and opportunity can be denied because of:

- Gender – Many sports are traditionally male-dominated or inaccessible to women.
- Ethnicity – Racist attitudes may prevent someone joining a club. Wider issues include things like some Asian women not being able to participate in mixed gender activities.
- Social class – Based on income, type of housing and levels of mobility.
- Economic status – Derived from employment type, disposable income and level of education.
- Cultural values – For certain cultures it is not acceptable to play sport or gamble, for example.

45

---

activity

DISCUSS THE BARRIERS

Working as a small group, discuss the barriers to participation listed below and give three examples of leisure activities they might apply to. Create your own chart to illustrate the material.
- medical conditions
- limited resources
- lack of skill
- time.

Sports

The sports sector has probably received the greatest boost in terms of innovation and new technology through National Lottery and private–public partnership (PPP) funding. New stadiums and leisure centres have been built, and sports academies have been set up. Sports venues often lead the way for further regeneration projects. Such facilities incorporate a huge range of innovative features and new technological ideas:

■ CCTV for scanning crowds

■ new running track materials

■ underground heating systems

■ swipe-card access and electronically controlled access and exit routes

■ lighting controls to diffuse bright light above playing surfaces

■ sliding roofs.

On indoor courts, tennis can be played all the year round.

activity

SPORTS: WHAT'S NEW?

Working with a partner, identify one innovative feature or use of new technology at each of the sports venues listed below.

VENUE	INNOVATIVE FEATURE OR USE OF NEW TECHNOLOGY
A stadium	
A pool	
A leisure centre	
A water-based venue	
Indoor climbing location	
A retail outlet	

The following examples (from *Sports Management*, Vol. 7, issue 3, 2003) will give you a more detailed insight:

> **Lawn Tennis Association's Tennis Academy, Loughborough**
> Four indoor acrylic hard courts, three outdoor courts, plus three American clay courts. The site was chosen because of its proximity to Sports Science lecturers and coaching experts at Loughborough University. The lighting and surfaces were designed and installed by Halmo Sports, one of the leaders in innovative design. Facilities are said to be 'cutting edge'.
>
> **National Aquatic Centre, Dublin**
> The brief was to combine a top-class competition pool with a leisure pool to generate income. An innovative approach was required to achieve the right balance between leisure and competitive swimming, including changing rooms to suit both athletes and the general public. The result is a main tank with two submersible booms that can be moved to create a competitive short course pool. The diving pool also has a moveable boom and floor. Support facilities give space for the media, judges and marshals, and for drugs testing to be carried out. The leisure pool is flooded with natural light, and has water slides, a wave machine, and a kids' pool and play area. A café, gym and fitness studios, and sauna, spa, and steam rooms complement the main facilities.

Every major sports and leisure organisation has its own website. Here are a few examples to check out:

http://www.clublasanta.com/
A health and fitness resort on Lanzarote

http://www.leisureopportunities.co.uk
Leisure jobs and developments

http://www.earthcentre.org.uk
Centre for environmental awareness

http://www.strategicleisure.co.uk   Leisure consultants

http://www.sta.co.uk Association of swimming teachers

Further improvements in communications are likely with the introduction of new technology including fibre optics, satellite transmissions and the use of new materials like Kevlar, Milor and carbon fibre, which are used in the making of racing sails for yachts.

Innovative approaches to some traditional sports include kitesurfing, skyboarding and other extreme sports like base jumping and cave diving, which have pushed the boundaries of adventure sports to their limits.

Holiday activities

Holiday activities have also benefited from advances in technology, with the introduction of:

- better short- and long-haul flights

- innovative approaches to ticketing

- budget airlines and new destinations

- modern cruise liners that are literally floating leisure complexes

All this – and planes, too

Changi Airport, Singapore offers a number of leisure facilities and activities. Passengers can:

- access the internet at any of the transit lounges
- watch a blockbuster movie at the cinema
- sit in a themed TV lounge
- freshen up, shower, take a nap or have a work out at the Fitness and Lifestyle Centre
- eat or drink at any one of a number of cafés
- do some shopping in the various boutiques
- have a swim, get a tan or have a haircut
- visit the range of gardens around the terminal
- choose between several city tours of Singapore
- take part in a game show (see below).

- virtual tours of resorts and accommodation

- computer-controlled take-off and landing

- new types of holidays, for example short city breaks and adventure weekends

- high-speed trains

- a greater choice of budget hotels

- airports with every facility for the passengers (see box, below, left).

In addition, much more travel booking is now done on the internet, and space tourism has even become reality for one American millionaire!

It is clear from all the examples given that the leisure industry is one of the leading industries in terms of innovation and the use of new technology. The pace of change is rapid, and our hunger for new ideas, activities and leisure products quite insatiable.

The future will see this level of creativity grow as corporations chase profits on a global basis and new market economies emerge. It is also worth remembering that for every new idea that hits the leisure market, hundreds have failed. The lifespan of new products can be limited as there is a constant demand for something newer, better and cheaper.

For smaller companies operating in niche markets survival can be tough, due to the domination of global corporations and changes in customer expectations.

One emerging trend is the development of multiple venues – properties are being built to house cinemas, shops, bars and nightclubs, tenpin bowling alleys, bingo halls, casinos and arcades. Family-oriented entertainment looks likely to be another growth area.

activity

EFFECTS AND IMPLICATIONS

In class, discuss the following:
1. New technology encourages us to stay home and 'play' with electronic games. What wider effects does this have?
2. Leisure activities and products are now commodities. What implications does this have?
3. How can small companies compete with large multinational companies or corporations?

In studying the leisure industry, it is important to understand both the power and various dimensions of the media. In this topic, therefore, we analyse the influence of the media on our lifestyles and our leisure habits and choices. We also examine the positive and negative aspects of each common medium as well as exploring media-related issues.

In such a competitive industry, effective use of the media can be crucial to an organisation's success; if a leisure organisation fails to communicate successfully it is unlikely to achieve its objectives or satisfy its customers, who can take their custom elsewhere very quickly.

Television

With digital and satellite television in addition to terrestrial channels, we can now receive coverage of sporting events from anywhere in the world. New channels dedicated to sport and leisure mean that you can turn on your television at almost any time to watch a sporting event or purchase leisure goods.

The advertising slots during and between programmes are aimed at the type of audience likely to be watching. In this way, children's programmes are interspersed with adverts for toys and games; big football matches with male-oriented adverts (e.g. cars); and romantic films with female-oriented adverts, all of which try to influence the buying habits of the particular target audience.

Television is a powerful medium and, as analogue is replaced by digital, there is likely to be an increase in the number of channels dedicated to leisure activities such as DIY, gardening and cookery. The Leisure Industry Research Centre (LIRC) estimates that by 2010 we will have over 400 channels to choose from; in 2003 over 50 per cent of homes already had satellite television.

Sport has led the way in establishing 'pay as you go', cable and subscription channels, which in 2003 were estimated to attract around 11 million viewers.

Perhaps the issue for discussion here is the value of the ever-expanding range of television programmes.

With more and more soap operas, reality TV shows and repeats on our screens, would you agree that maybe quality has been replaced by quantity?

Radio

The UK has a wide range of radio stations. Each station has a similar function in terms of reporting and presenting programmes, but they have slightly different purposes:

- commercial local radio is motivated by the profit brought in by advertising (e.g. Capital, Heart).

- public service national radio is non-profit making and, as its name suggests, aims to provide the public with a free information and entertainment service (e.g. BBC Radio 1, 2, 3, 4 and 5).

■ In-house voluntary radio is usually amateur in nature and produces simple formats of discussion and music – hospital radio, for example.

Radio is not as powerful a medium as television but nevertheless, during the day, it can reach huge local and national audiences and thus influence opinions, choices and views. The advent of digital radio will bring more specialist channels to a wider audience.

BBC Radio 5 Live is a particularly well respected sport and news channel. Some local stations will invite phone-ins so there is a chance for listeners to participate and put their views on air. Radio 2 is very popular and follows a live leisure magazine format. Radio 1 has always been popular for up-and-coming DJs, who are particularly influential in terms of music and fashion, two key leisure spending areas. Radios 3 and 4 are more news and opinion-focused, with classical music, current affairs and drama programmes and are principally targeted at older listeners.

The press

By the press we mean national and local newspapers such as:

■ The 'heavies': *The Independent, The Times, Guardian*

■ The 'tabloids': *Mirror, Sun, Daily Star*

■ The locals: *Evening Standard*, daily press and weekly Gazettes

According to LIRC, newspapers account for about 40 per cent of what we read. They have a powerful influence on the information we receive and thus the opinions we form and, of course, also carry adverts for leisure products and services.

Newspaper sales have declined in recent years due to competition from television and the internet; indeed some newspapers have gone out of business. It is likely that every newspaper will eventually have to have an online equivalent, in addition to adopting a smaller format.

LIRC reports that sales of local newspapers have actually remained stable as they have developed into information sources for local news, events, leisure activities, television listings and classified advertising.

Magazines and books

Like the other media products, magazines are targeted at different age groups, lifestyle types and genders. Branding is a key concept in establishing and retaining a customer-base of people pursuing a particular leisure activity or those with a specific interest or hobby. Consumers have increasingly sophisticated tastes, so further segmentation and branding are likely, which might mean shorter lifespans for magazines as readers switch allegiance.

There are now hundreds of different magazines.

According to LIRC, books currently account for around a quarter of sales of reading material.

Choice of reading matter can vary enormously from person to person. Some examples might be:

- gardening or DIY manuals
- sports skills handbooks
- romantic novels
- travel guides
- biographies

People's motivations for reading are as diverse as the books they read. Readers may seek escapism or self-improvement, or require instruction or information.

In order to compete against increasing competition from online booksellers like Amazon, bookshops have to diversify. In the USA, bookshops have developed into 'culture stores' and 'lifestyle superstores'.

Electronic media

The electronic media have had as great an influence on the leisure habits of the under-20s as television had on older generations. Examples include:

- Video – The video market is still a billion-dollar industry although videos are being superseded by DVDs, and may eventually be replaced by downloadable movies. Videos have a strong influence on young people; fantasy films, thrillers and films containing violence are claimed to have a negative effect. Videos often carry trailers advertising similar films, which helps generate repeat business. Nowadays producers try to get their videos out as quickly as possible after the film is released, or else 'pirate' versions can flood the market, regardless of copyright protection.

- Audio equipment – Most people who own a television also have a music system, and car owners are also likely to have a radio or cassette/CD player in their vehicle. The music industry caters for all tastes. Music is a very influential medium, especially for young people; it has an effect on the clothes they wear, the image they project and the issues they consider to be relevant. Walkmans and mini disc players are used by joggers, students and walkers, as they combine one leisure activity with another.

- Computers – The computer market is a £2 billion industry, according to LIRC. Computers are not solely used for leisure purposes of course, but they do have many leisure uses, including games, internet access and digital photography uploads.

Computers are likely to surpass all other mediums in terms of influence on twenty-first century leisure.

- Mobile phones – Mobile phones can make calls, take pictures and short films, play music and connect to the internet. They are a must-have item and a very important communication tool for young people – a true leisure toy.

Benefits, problems and issues with the media

In this section we highlight some of the problems created by the media. Using the charts provided, add your own examples to those given:

Television

POSITIVE INFLUENCES	NEGATIVE ASPECTS
Can inform about nature, the planet and other leisure activities	Can have negative influences on children if it is their only leisure 'toy'

Radio

POSITIVE INFLUENCES	NEGATIVE ASPECTS
Callers can give their opinions on air	Allows a lot of bias to creep in

The press

POSITIVE INFLUENCES	NEGATIVE ASPECTS
Provides up-to-date information about leisure activities	Journalists sometimes fabricate or embellish

Exercising and listening to music at the same time.

Magazines and books

POSITIVE INFLUENCES	NEGATIVE ASPECTS
Source of information or entertainment	*Limited to those who can read well*

Electronic media

POSITIVE INFLUENCES	NEGATIVE ASPECTS
Fast, global, high capacity	*Can be expensive to purchase*

Both commercial and non-commercial organisations use the media as a marketing tool to influence customers' spending, participation and lifestyles.

The media is a leisure sector in its own right, transmitting opinions and information around the globe. Clever wording, illustrations and graphics can influence us if we allow them to. It is important, therefore, not to take the accuracy of media reports for granted, as events are sometimes staged for the camera and stories can be sensationalised.

Television

Sporting events have become commodities that are bought and sold by the media. The rights to broadcast major events often sell for millions, and this source of revenue is very important for the sports industry as it helps sustain sports leagues and competitions. To increase viewing figures, many sports events are now shown at peak viewing times, and some games have even been adapted to make them more suitable for television – for example the colour of squash balls has been changed. On the negative side, television playbacks can sometimes undermine a refereeing decision or the spectators' attitude to a player or official.

Radio

Radio is a much less influential medium, but a more affordable one for smaller leisure organisations in terms of advertising. The real benefit of radio is that it can reach both local and national audiences.

The press

Some reporters will go to any lengths to get a story (often with no real substance) just to try and sell more papers. Such sensationalist stories can be harmful to the subjects, and the intrusion of paparazzi journalists and photographers is despised by sports stars. The poor quality of some tabloid reporting gives the press a bad name and, despite there being a press code, it is often flagrantly ignored. However, as an advertising medium, the press is still very widely used by leisure providers.

The enthusiasm of the press can make life difficult for sports stars.

activity

HOW GOOD IS NEWSPAPER REPORTING?

Compare two or three tabloid newspapers with the 'heavies' and evaluate the quality of reporting on sport and leisure stories.

Magazines and books

As leisure purchases, apart from instructional books and classics, books tend to have a relatively short shelf-life, which limits their influence. Nevertheless, magazines can be quite influential in terms of fashion, lifestyle, and choice of leisure activities.

Electronic media

Two of the major issues surrounding the electronic media industry are 'pirate' versions of CDs and DVDs flooding the market and the speed that technology advances – making products quickly outdated or redundant, and putting pressure on consumers to buy the very latest equipment.

activity

THE MEDIA: YOUR VERDICT

Debate whether, on balance, the media has a good or a bad influence on our leisure lifestyles. Which media do you think have the most influence? Why?

How UNIT 1 is assessed

Unit 1 is assessed by coursework. The evidence should be in four parts, which we suggest you present as four sections within a portfolio.

The following guidance outlines how you can achieve the assessment requirements for each of the four parts. The final sections give you advice on the presentation of your evidence and on improving your grades.

1. The diversity of the leisure industry (an understanding of the range, scale and importance of the leisure industry to the UK and Europe)

1.0 Introduction
Give a brief overview of what leisure might mean to different people, and define what is meant by leisure and give an overview of its diversity.

1.1 Active leisure activities
Describe a range of active pursuits you can take part in as leisure activities and say why they are described as 'active'.

1.2 Passive leisure activities
Describe a range of passive pursuits you can take part in as leisure activities and say why they are described as 'passive'.

1.3 Home-based leisure pursuits
Describe a range of home-based pursuits you can take part in as leisure activities and say why they are described as 'home-based'.

1.4 Regional variations
Where there are differences in activities or locations in the UK and other parts of Europe, highlight a range of these.

1.5 Summary
Draw together a range of ideas to show the diversity of the industry in the UK and other parts of Europe.

1.6 Scale of the industry
This is measured in values which show employment levels and spending on leisure in the UK and other parts of Europe. You need to present accurate information which illustrates these, and give reasons why there are differences.

1.7 Importance of the industry
This can be shown by presenting accurate participation rates and trends, for regions of the UK and for various other European countries, giving reasons why there are differences.

2. The nature of the sectors in the industry (the differences between the commercial and non-commercial sectors within the leisure industry)

2.0 Introduction
Give an overview of why leisure organisations need to be 'business-like' to help them achieve their aims and objectives.

2.1 The commercial sector
Provide some examples of commercial-sector providers, and their facilities and activities.

2.2 The commercial sector
Explain the main characteristics, aims and objectives of commercial leisure providers.

2.3 The non-commercial sector
Provide some examples of non-commercial-sector providers, voluntary and public, and their facilities and activities, using examples from real providers.

2.4 The non-commercial sector
Explain the main characteristics, aims and objectives of non-commercial leisure providers, both voluntary and public, using examples from real providers.

2.5 The commercial sector and non-commercial sector differences
Provide a summary of the main differences between the two sectors.

2.6 Commercial funding sources
Explain the different funding sources and revenue streams that the commercial sector employs, using examples from real providers.

2.7 Non-commercial funding sources
Explain the different funding sources and revenue streams that the non-commercial sector employs, using examples from real providers.

2.8 Marketing strategies
Explain the marketing strategies that each sector uses, using examples from real providers.

2.9 Partnership initiatives
Summarise examples of partnership initiatives, and give examples.

3. Current developments in the industry (research into current developments in the leisure industry)

3.0 Introduction
Give an overview of the changing nature of the leisure industry, giving examples of products and services that are losing or gaining appeal and popularity.

3.1 Recent innovations
Provide evidence of recent change in areas which have seen new innovations and activities, such as extreme sports and home-based leisure.

3.2 Technology
Illustrate understanding, and give examples, of the use of new technology in leisure contexts, such as with home-based leisure.

3.3 Influence of the media
Explain the role the media has in influencing change, appeal and popularity of leisure activities. Describe how many leisure organisations 'target' their local community sections and groups with appropriate products and services. Your evidence can be drawn from local providers.

Improving your grades

Generally, you will get better grades by giving more comprehensive explanations, including better examples and showing a deeper understanding of each topic. Your school or college should be able to advise you in more detail, or you could visit the Edexcel website: edexcel.org.uk for more guidance.

4. Reasons for participation and non-participation (conclusions drawn regarding reasons for participation and non-participation in leisure activities, and suggestions of ways to overcome barriers to participation)

4.0 Introduction
Explain how demand is created by people who want to participate, and supply is given by providers. Give examples.

4.1 Factors creating demand and participation
Explain the increases in leisure time, car ownership, health awareness, income, employment, and population changes, which have contributed to increased participation over the last decade or so.

4.2 Factors working against demand and participation
Explain the range and nature of factors such as economic ones (poverty, unemployment) poor choice, transport, provision, lifestyles, aspirations and inequality – taken from local and national studies.

4.3 Barriers to participation
Explain some examples of disability and access factors, and cultural and equity issues such as gender, ethnicity and location. Explain clearly where your evidence has come from, e.g. research statistics and reports.

General guidelines on presentation of assignments

Whilst the way in which you present your assessment evidence will not directly affect your grade, it is important that you strive to present it in a professional and well-structured way. The following are a few tips on achieving good presentation.

1. All assignments should be word processed, using a suitable font, such as Ariel. Try to avoid 'casual' fonts, such as Comic Sans.

2. You can use a different font for titles if you wish, but do not use more than two fonts in your work.

3. Be consistent in your font size. Generally, 14 or 16 is suitable for titles, and 12 for the main text.

4. Only use bold for titles – not the whole report.

5. Use italics and 'quotation marks' to show when you have copied text from another source, and indicate the source in brackets after the quote.

6. If you choose to use more than one colour in your work, limit this to two, e.g. blue for titles and black for the main text.

7. Avoid using 'Wordart' for titles!

8. Use 1.5 line spacing throughout your work.

9. Do not cut and paste cartoon-style clipart into your work.

10. If you use photographs in your work, label each image underneath.

11. Insert page numbers into your finished work.

The leisure industry, like any other, has to have systems to work with and practices for staff to follow, whatever the facility or venue. Good working practices and systems cover a whole range of operational situations, but for the purposes of this unit we will be focusing on three main areas, each of which has an important role to play – for both staff and customers:

• Safe working practices, including all the relevant legislation
• Quality systems – Quest, IIP, ISO 9001, Charter Mark and Clubmark
• Business systems, including accounting, project planning, and membership and ticketing systems.

By studying the first four topics you should be able to gain an insight into the essential factors in assuring health and safety, and appreciate the key intentions of legislation designed to protect us at work and play. You should also be able to get a good idea how people currently working in the industry apply the rules, regulations and guidelines laid down for them. This unit's assessment will also expect you to know how to do likewise – and the consequences of not following health and safety guidelines properly.

Many of the 'quality awards' in the industry are based on organisations having good systems and practices in place, and in the next three topics you will be made aware of some awards in operation at the moment. Quality systems in the leisure industry cover staff and facility operations and you need to know the essential aims and objective of these, along with just how they are implemented.

The final topics of the unit deal with financial accounting systems, which provide the basis of planning, monitoring and controlling the financial progress of an organisation. Some practice exercises are provided for you, so that you are well prepared for the unit's assessment. These final topics also take you through some principles of project planning and the importance of running a membership and ticketing scheme for an organisation, with an emphasis on electronic solutions.

The unit ends with some guidance on how it will be assessed. As this unit is externally tested, the topics throughout will feature some case studies in line with the assessment style. You should also make some site visits to ensure that you see and hear how systems are implemented and operated first-hand.

Unit 2

Working Practices in Leisure

- Inspections, such as health and hygiene, safety or environmental, are passed easily.

- Healthy, safe and secure environments help put up productivity amongst staff, because they are more confident and have good resources to work with.

activity

BENEFITS, DANGERS, PROBLEMS

1 What benefits might there be for a leisure organisation which installed closed-circuit television cameras around its premises?
2 What dangers could you anticipate a swimming pool might present to the public and staff?
3 How can customer service benefit from good working practices?
4 What problems might need covering for a large event held at a leisure centre, e.g. a concert or county sports tournament?

EU directives and regulations

The EU health and safety regulations, which originally came into effect in 1992, are commonly called the 'six-pack' and cover a range of working practices:

- Health and safety at work

- Workplace regulations

- Manual handling operations

- Provision and use of work equipment

- Personal protective equipment

- Display screen equipment.

These will be updated and covered in more detail with a leisure bias later in the unit. It is important to remember, however, that these EU regulations take precedence over UK-based law, for EU courts can overturn UK verdicts if they do not comply with EU law. This has often been the case where human rights have been breached – unfair dismissal of staff in leisure centres, for example, or discrimination on the grounds of age or sex.

The basis for most of the EU regulations is that individuals or organisations must carry out 'risk assessments' and take measures to prevent unsafe working practices from causing accidents. We will cover risk assessment later in more detail too.

UK Acts of Parliament

Examples of UK Acts of Parliament which are likely to apply to leisure contexts are:

- The Health and Safety at Work Act 1974 – 'HASAWA' for short

- The Control of Substances Hazardous to Health 1994 – 'COSHH' for short

- The Reporting of Injuries, Diseases, and Dangerous Occurrences Regulations – 'RIDDOR' for short.

The role and powers of enforcement agencies

We have already mentioned the power of the police to bring a 'criminal' action against anyone who breaks the law. We have also mentioned that 'civil' actions can be brought by individuals.

However there are other organisations that have a role in regulating, controlling and enforcing legislation. The two with the greatest relevance to leisure contexts are:

- The Health and Safety Executive (HSE) – a national government organisation

- Local authorities.

HSE
Health & Safety Executive

HSE inspectors are usually experts in particular aspects of safety, such as fire or crowd control, and provide consultation and advisory services for organisers of big events or companies planning new attractions. They are always involved when an accident has happened and the cause needs to be investigated, such as when a theme park ride has broken.

Local authorities have enforcement powers too, usually exercised by their officers from environmental health, who can inspect all types of leisure premises – souvenir shops, kitchens, pools, sports halls and gyms, for example – to assess how healthily and safely they are being run.

The role of the enforcement agencies is to carry out assessments of venues, facilities and buildings. To do this they have quite a few powers – they are allowed to make their inspections at almost any time, for example, and take evidence such as samples or photographs. Based on their findings, they may decide upon one of four courses of action:

1. (the most desirable) Allow operations to continue, because safety measures are adequate or good.
2. Issue an 'improvement notice' requiring action to remedy a problem (e.g. have faulty plumbing fixed) within a set number of days, but allow operations to continue.
3. Stop operations by issuing a 'prohibition notice', because measures or systems are inadequate – faulty wiring, for example, or no safety guards on machinery.
4. (the least desirable) Begin a prosecution for ignoring a statutory safety requirement, i.e. a requirement laid down by the law. This might result in a fine or imprisonment.

activity

THE POWER OF THE HSE

Visit the HSE website at http:///www.hse.gov.uk to find:
• what other powers they have
• what areas of leisure they can inspect
• examples of what happens when non-compliance takes place.

Other sources of regulations and codes

Besides those we have already mentioned, there are a number of lesser organisations who have enforcement powers of some sort – mostly national associations or governing bodies such as the Football Association. These bodies often issue codes of conduct which players or members have to comply with, and failure to do so can lead to bans or being struck off the membership list.

Many leisure-oriented organisations, such as RoSPA, the Environment Agency, ASA and Outdoor Adventure, issue their own guidance, giving codes of behaviour for specific leisure activities (see skiing example, below). There are no automatic sanctions for not following these guidelines, but if something goes wrong and someone ends up in court, not having followed a recognised code would greatly increase their chances of being found negligent.

Many awarding bodies in sport have 'standards' which their coaches have to apply while working with young people. These include the FA, who require police checks for all coaches as well as first aid training.

activity

FIND YOUR OWN EXAMPLE

Try to identify a governing body's 'standard' or an association's code of practice for a leisure activity. Assess how easy it is to follow and what the most important features are, for participants and coaches.

The Skiway Code

The English Ski Council issues the Skiway Code – a code of practice adapted from the International Ski Federation rules for skiers. It has 10 safety points, including:

• Make sure your equipment is safe.
• Adapt your speed to suit the terrain, snow and weather conditions.
• Act responsibly and allow other skiers freedom of movement.
• When stopping or joining a piste look up and down the slope and keep to the side.
• Observe all the warning and guide signs.
• Offer your assistance if there is an accident.

Safe working practices

General 'safe working practices' legislation applies to all leisure organisations and premises, whether it be a gym, hotel, arena or pool. Much of the legislation is based on the 'old' Health and Safety at Work Act 1974 (HASAWA), which will be our starting point for this topic.

In 1992 a number of general European regulations (the six-pack) came into force covering the workplace, which to a great extent superseded HASAWA, but also brought in legislation to reflect new working practices, e.g. with display screens, new equipment and the wearing of protective clothing – aspects very relevant to leisure locations. These, therefore, will provide the second area of focus for this topic.

We will also cover three other general Acts concerned with health and safety:

- ■ COSHH 1994 – implemented to 'control substances hazardous to health'
- ■ RIDDOR 1995 – designed to cover 'the reporting of injuries, diseases and dangerous occurrences'
- ■ DDA – Disability Discrimination Acts 1994 and 2000 [Note: Knowledge of the DDA Acts is not required for your assessment of this unit.]

Health and Safety at Work Act 1974 (HASAWA)

HASAWA established some general principles, which governed working practices in the UK for nearly 20 years. The main intention of the Act was to make everyone aware and responsible for safety at work, not just the owners or supervisors, but managers and operatives too (see main points, right).

Staff responsibilities

Under HASAWA, leisure staff would have to ensure that:

- Customers are safe at all times when changing, swimming or playing
- Materials and equipment are stored correctly and out of the way in proper store rooms
- Notices, signs and information about safety procedures are clearly displayed
- Any maintenance processes are carried out as per the required schedule, e.g. gym equipment, lifts and escalators
- Locations around the facility and practices that the staff are supposed to carry out are checked regularly.

Employers' responsibilities

Under HASAWA, employers in the leisure industry would have to ensure that:

- Staff take care of their own and colleagues' health and safety, and know how to do so
- Action is taken on any faults or repairs reported or logged
- Staff are trained to use equipment safely, and follow the manufacturers' recommendations
- Training and awareness of staff is kept up to date.

HASAWA was reviewed and amended in 1999. Amending legislation is necessary from time to time to help it keep up with changes in the workplace brought about by new technology, research or ideas – or sometimes following an accident.

The 1999 update of HASAWA, brought in some important changes:

1. 'Risk assessment' became the basis of all safety checks. This means identifying hazards, assessing how dangerous they are and what action is needed to make them safe. (Risk assessment will be examined in more depth on page 72.)

2. Special measures for the protection of young people and pregnant workers were introduced – police checks on anyone working with young people, and regular health checks for pregnant workers.

3. It became compulsory for an organisation or facility to have a written safety plan.

4. It became compulsory for an organisation or building to appoint a safety officer.

5. Emergency procedures now have to be agreed and practised – for fire and bomb threats, and for evacuation of large numbers quickly.

The European regulations of 1992 (the six-pack)

Many of the 1999 additions to HASAWA were based on knowledge gained from recent incidents and from improvements suggested since the European regulations were introduced in 1992. These regulations themselves will no doubt be reviewed soon, but let us take a look at their essential points.

The Management of Health and Safety at Work 1992

This regulation brought in the idea of risk assessments being required and the need for employers and employees to take action where a hazard is identified. This means that staff cannot see it as the management's responsibility to report a faulty electrical socket, for example – it is everyone's responsibility. Everyone in the staff team becomes a risk assessor, and the employer must take action once a problem is reported.

The Workplace Regulations 1992

These regulations provided some minimum standards for the working environment relating to the health, safety and welfare of staff and customers. The following requirements give you an idea of how the regulations work in the leisure context:

1. In administrative areas – staff must have adequate space to work and any workstations must be set up correctly for height, light and seating. Smoking has become almost totally banned from these areas.

2. In playing and changing areas – heating, lighting and ventilation must be maintained at recognised levels for comfort, e.g. around 21° C, with a free flow of air and low glare bulbs. In leisure areas such as ice rinks, ski slopes, or indoor spas, suitable clothing must be provided for staff.

activity

SLOPPY ABOUT SAFETY

Working with a partner, evaluate this scenario and decide what you think is the best action – for the manager, and for the staff – to keep everyone comfortable, but also safer:

The administration staff in the main office of a busy corporate events company have become very sloppy in their storage of marketing literature and their use of office equipment.

Boxes of leaflets are piled five high around some walls, and staff leave cables and flexes for their computers, faxes and telephones, in untidy bundles around their desks. Some staff are fed up with this as they can see the dangers, but others appear not to care. The manager operates from another room and rarely goes into the main office, but someone has sent him an email complaining.

3. Doors, windows and any escalators or lifts must meet fire-retardant standards, be unobstructed, and of a safe material (e.g. shatter-proof glass) and have emergency stop buttons or crash bars for escape.

4. Water, washing, toilets and cleanliness are all covered, and standards are set for freshness of water, adequacy of supply, good waste control and adequate male and female provision. Staff should also have an adequate restroom for breaks.

5. Maintenance of indoor and outdoor areas is necessary to ensure that dust, rust, litter and spillages are cleaned up. This also requires proper storage for cleaning fluids and chemicals such as bleach, lubricating oil and pool-purifying materials.

activity
WRITE YOUR OWN WORKPLACE REGULATIONS

Imagine that you are a consultant and you have been called in to a leisure centre (with indoor and outdoor areas and wet- and dry-side provision) to provide guidance on what should be done to meet young children's needs. Working with one or two others, see what ideas you can come up with for points 1–5 above.

Manual Handling Operations Regulations 1992

These are very relevant regulations for leisure workers because they are often asked to carry, lift and move equipment, boxes, mats and other types of sports kit. The regulations set out how to manage loads better by suggesting that before you begin the task, you:

1. Think about redesigning the task – by breaking it into smaller 'chunks' or using some lifting or carrying gear.

2. Carry out a risk assessment to identify the things that could go wrong and decide if you can still manage the task safely in those circumstances.

3. Ask to be trained in shifting the load, ask for better lighting if that will help or ask for the load to be repositioned to shorten the lift.

Provision and Use of Work Equipment Regulations 1991

These regulations, which are sometimes called 'PUWER' for short, are meant to ensure the provision of safe working equipment and its proper use. Some leisure industry examples will help:

activity
MOVING AND LIFTING SAFELY – ON ICE

Consider yourself the floor supervisor at a major arena, which stages concerts, shows, fairs and diverse events such as indoor motorbike trials and monster truck demonstrations. The next show due in is an ice show with twenty-five cartoon-themed acts to present. What issues do you think your staff will have to face in moving sets, sound equipment and large floats on the ice, sometimes in dimmed lighting? Work with a partner who can take the role of the show manager, expressing all their needs, to decide what manual handling and machine-based lifting might be involved.

- Poolside, there might be a lifting hoist for disabled people, which needs correct use so as not to drop them into the pool, and maintenance as it is in a humid atmosphere and parts may rust.

- Theme parks with a range of rides are particularly susceptible to mechanical failure if proper maintenance and safety checks are not carried out.

- Museums may well have large displays that need cleaning with electric machines.

- Staff in botanical gardens have to carefully consider how the tall hothouse plants or trees are reached, e.g. by using climbing equipment.

Michael Beadle, Sales Coordinator, Xscape, Castleford (Yorkshire)

Michael has to have a range of skills for his job. He has to sell the various aspects of Xscape to prospective customers. As part of his job, he attends exhibitions at a variety of locations, manning the Xscape stand. He also looks after tours of the building, and every three weeks he takes his turn as duty manager.

Safety on the slopes

Xscape consider that the health and safety of their clients is of primary importance while they are 'at play'. If we take the 'climbing zone' for example, all instructors are qualified to a very high standard. On the 'snow slope', skiers have to have a minimum standard of 'linked turns', be able to control speed and use 'button tows' well. While Xscape supply all equipment (skis, sticks, boots, and helmets where necessary) visitors can hire clothing and are advised to bring gloves too. Advice and guidance is available at the time of booking, and around the slopes, which are supervised.

Formula for success

Xscape in Castleford is an example of one leisure development following another (the development multiplier effect). Here, as with Milton Keynes' Xscape, the business strategy has been to build next to large shopping malls where there is already a regular set of customers of the type that might also use the facility. Both locations also have good motorway access and nearly 8 million people within a 1-hour drive time. This formula is being repeated at Braehead (Glasgow) too, and a further three Xscapes are planned for the UK. The 'synergy' of real snow slopes, climbing walls, bowling lanes, multi-screen cinema, an interactive games arena, cafés, restaurants and excellent shopping has made Xscape a highly successful leisure venture.

Happy to work with all sorts

Michael says that the attributes which are best for working at Xscape are 'friendliness, an outgoing personality, and an ability to interact with other staff and departments'. You also have to work with a broad client range:
- Daytime and school holidays – families
- Evening – mostly adults
- During term time – school groups and corporate clients

There are events to manage, too, such as SnowX competitions for mountain bikers, ski and skateboard competitions, and escapology shows.

You can carry out further research at www.Xscape.co.uk

Personal Protective Equipment (and Clothing) at Work 1992

This legislation – PPE for short – helps to ensure that when staff are working in noisy, dangerous or unusual conditions they have the use of protective equipment and clothing to minimise risk, and have been trained in how to use or wear it effectively. For example:

- climbing instructors need helmets, harnesses, ropes and other hardware.

- canoeing instructors need helmets, lifejackets, throw lines and spray decks, among other things.

66

---

activity

WHAT TO WEAR

What protective clothing, selected from the list below, would you prescribe for the following people working in the leisure industry?
- Mountain bike instructors
- Fencing coaches
- Sailing instructors
- Crew on a sea-going pleasure boat
- Hang-gliding teachers.
Clothing: crash hats, life-vests, gloves, face masks, body armour, elbow pads, knee pads, wetsuits, thermal suits, neoprene socks, waterproof jackets, lightweight boots, wellingtons, deck shoes, balaclavas.

Many special considerations have to be allowed for when prescribing the wearing of safety gear in the leisure industry. Some protective clothing can be heavy and cumbersome – a hockey goalkeeper's outfit, for example, can restrict movement. Football and hockey players often choose not to wear shin guards, and many cyclists do not wear helmets. As with other equipment, training in use, maintenance and checking for defects has also to be given.

Display Screen Equipment Regulations 1992

Staff in the leisure industry use computers for many purposes – booking systems, customer databases, mail shots, etc. These regulations ensure that organisations must provide equipment that complies with the minimum standards for visual display units (VDUs). They recommend that:

- Any employees who use a computer for more than an hour a day should have health checks.

- All workstations should be checked for sitting and reading heights, distance from the screen, glare and lumbar support.

- Staff should have several regular short breaks rather than few longer breaks.

---

activity

USING COMPUTERS SAFELY

Working with a partner, design a poster for staff in the busy group-bookings section of a tour operators, which gives them clear advice on the use of computers and also gives a suitable checklist of things to do and check.

Control of Substances Hazardous to Health Act 1994 (COSHH)

There are often large amounts of cleaning fluids, pool chemicals, caustic substances for clearing drains, pesticides, etc. on leisure premises. This would include swimming pools, premises with canteens and kitchens, multi-sports centres, theme parks, hotels and children's farms or visitor centres – which probably represents about two-thirds of the industry.

Following correct procedures in any of the examples above might mean saving someone from burns, skin or eye irritations, fainting, suffocation or bacterial infection. The Act requires staff to:

- Pass on any information about hazardous materials

- Assess risks to staff and customers carefully

- Store and handle the chemicals safely.

---

activity

RESEARCHING LOCAL EXAMPLES

Visit or contact some local leisure premises to find out how they control, handle and store any substances hazardous to staff or customers, and how they train staff to use it safely.

Reporting of Injuries, Diseases and Dangerous Occurrences Regulations 1995 (RIDDOR)

These require organisations and individuals to keep a record of and report any accidents or serious occurrences of ill health, so that:

1. Organisations can assess if there is a pattern or cause, and identify solutions.

2. If any claims are involved, a clear record of the incident helps decisions to be made fairly.

Examples of incidents in the leisure industry that would certainly require recording and reporting are:

- if someone has fall, or is injured by something falling, or

- if someone trips over an obstruction, or slips on a wet surface,

– but it is wise to ensure that all incidents are recorded (see below).

Injury	Disease	Accidents
Fractured limbs	Poisoning	Collapse of a structure e.g. a wall or fence
Burns	Contagious skin condition	
Electric shocks	Infections, e.g. hepatitis	Explosion
Unconsciousness		Release of chemicals

Examples of incidents that should be recorded

Within three years of an incident, customers (or staff) may make claims of negligence against individuals or the organisation, and if they are found guilty in court, compensation may have to be paid. In sports situations all injuries need to be recorded – in case the player claims in the future that their career prospects have been limited by the repercussions of the injury. Most organisations in the leisure industry have an incident book in which details are recorded.

activity
MULTI-PURPOSE INCIDENT FORM

Working with one or two others, design a form that could be used to gather the information you think would represent a comprehensive record of incidents. The form should be able to be used by anyone investigating a claim or incident, e.g. police, insurance company, fire service, medical expert, etc.

The Disability Discrimination Act 2000 (Note: Knowledge of the DDA Acts is not required for your assessment of this unit.)

The 1994 DDA, which tried to ensure equal working rights for disabled people, was amended in 2000 in response to criticism about difficulties of access and transport. The new legislation made it a requirement for all organisations with buildings and transport to take this into account. Consequently there was a great deal of activity up to 2003 – the deadline for the changes to be implemented:

- Ramps were built (as shown below)

- Parking spaces were widened

- Bus entries were lowered

- Reception counters were lowered

- Lifts were installed

- Toilets and changing rooms were adapted, with lower fittings.

The Disability Rights Commission has powers to conduct investigations into organisations which do not operate a proper policy on recruitment and access.

DISABILITY RIGHTS

Working with a partner, first find the websites of the Disability Rights Commission and the English Federation for Disability Sports. Then scan their pages for the six points they make which you feel are the most important ones for employers and activity leaders. Compile a display board illustrating the points.

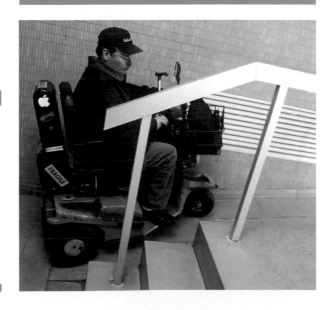

Legislation and regulations for specific situations

In the last topic we looked at general workplace legislation, which covered all premises and all people. In this topic we will look a little more closely at specific situations requiring extra regulations to help create safe working practices.

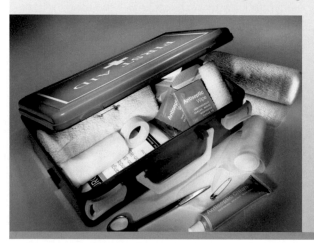

This type of legislation has been put in place over the years as organisations have experienced problems and the government has realised that clear guidelines were needed.

The Acts and regulations we will explore are:

- Health and Safety (First Aid) Regulations 1981
- Fire Safety and Safety of Places of Sport Act 1987
- Food Safety Act 1990
- Children Act 1989
- Data Protection Act 1998
- Working Time Regulations 1998

Health and Safety (First Aid) Regulations 1981

The dynamic nature of leisure activities makes these regulations very important to the industry, as bumps, scrapes, cuts, burns, fractures and concussion are quite common occurrences. Customers want to know that there are trained 'first-aiders' on hand as they take part in their recreation activity.

Organisations are required by the regulations to ensure that first aid provision is 'adequate and appropriate'. Each leisure situation will have different requirements of adequacy and appropriateness – for a busy leisure pool, for example, you don't just want a packet of plasters on hand! As with all the regulations, a risk assessment needs to take place to decide what first aid kit is needed and how many qualified staff need to be on hand.

Differing locations and numbers of participants help to determine the cover which is needed. Along the route of a marathon, for example, you are going to need many first-aiders, backed up by ambulances and doctors. Whereas, for a small amateur dramatics show, one first-aider and a first aid box, might suffice. Wherever possible, a first aid room should be provided (or perhaps a tent for outdoor events). This needs to be clearly marked, and all staff informed of its location and the whereabouts of the first-aiders on

duty. Quick access is the key here. For individually run classes – an aerobics group, for example – the instructor may well be a trained first-aider, but they should as a minimum carry a first aid kit. Whatever the scenario, organisations must ensure (under the regulations) that there are always trained first-aiders on hand.

First aid boxes and kits which are taken to away matches or on activities need to be checked before going, and restocked after returning if any items have been used (see Table 1). Quantities will vary according to how many people the box or bag is meant to cover. The contents will also vary depending on the nature of the activities to be covered. Some, for example, might need to include inflatable splints or breathing apparatus and sterilising tablets.

For the working environment, the regulations give clear guidelines – for example:

- Contents should be checked regularly for date and adequacy

- The boxes and bags themselves should be of a robust nature and clearly marked

- Dressings should be packaged so that they can be applied without the first-aider touching the wound directly.

Table 1 The basic contents for a permanent first aid box and a portable bag

A permanent first aid box should contain:	A portable bag should contain:
A card giving guidance on basic procedures	A card giving guidance on basic procedures
20 assorted individually wrapped sterile adhesive dressings	6 individually wrapped sterile adhesive dressings
2 sterile eye pads	1 large sterile unmedicated dressing
6 triangular bandages (sterile and wrapped individually) + safety pins	2 triangular bandages + safety pins
6 medium-sized sterile wrapped wound dressings	4 individually wrapped moist sterile wipes
2 large and 3 extra large individually wrapped unmedicated wound dressings	Disposable gloves

activity

UNTRAINED AND DANGEROUS?

Discuss with a partner what dangers there may be when untrained people try to use a first aid kit or apply first aid, and why there are no drugs or medicines listed in Table 1. You might want to consult a trained first-aider in your institution for some help.

Fire Safety and Safety of Places of Sport Act 1987

As a consequence of a number of football stadium and indoor event fires – e.g. Bradford City's horrific stadium fire in 1985 – the safety of spectators became a major concern, in many cases because of old grounds having wooden stands and poor evacuation procedures. The Safety of Sports Grounds Act of 1975 and the Fire Precautions Act of 1971 were modernised and improved to cover fire and safety at places of sport in 1987. The most important provision of the 1987 Act is the requirement for any ground with a stand for more than 500 spectators to have a safety certificate either for small one-off events or regular large ones, such as league matches.

The Football Licensing Authority was set up to monitor improvements and issue certificates, but much is done by local authorities now. With the arrival of this new legislation many clubs decided it was easier to build new stadiums than modernise old ones. Derby (pictured), Stoke and Sunderland were some of the first to choose this course of action.

Fire certificates are also needed by other types of leisure venue, such as night clubs, hotels and guesthouses, to ensure that they have proper provision for smoke, fire and evacuation situations.

Since 1999, risk assessments have had to be carried out by all leisure venues, so shops, theatres, museums and so on must carry out this process regularly. Non-compliance is taken as a criminal offence.

Fire and evacuation risk assessment

Factors to be taken into account include:

- Boxes or other obstacles (e.g. lockers) blocking passageways
- Frequency of fire drills
- Whether there is fire safety training for staff who act as evacuation controllers
- Records of any new installations changing fire safety considerations
- The occupancy levels of rooms and spectator areas
- Bottlenecks and the safety of assembly points.

activity

RISK ASSESSMENT FACTORS

Can you add three more ideas about fire and evacuation risk assessment from your own experience? If possible, get some ideas from an expert – perhaps someone in your local fire station or police station.

Food Safety Act 1990

For many organisations in the leisure industry the supply of food and beverages is a vital source of income, but before this 1990 Act standards of food storage, service, hygiene and quality in leisure premises were to say the least, varied. The regulations apply to all premises and all canteens, cafés, restaurants and food halls. The Food Standards Agency was set up in 1999 to monitor what goes on.

The legislation requires providers to ensure that:

- Food produced is fit for consumption, i.e. not contaminated or past its sell-by date

- The food contents are clear, e.g. to help us know what the meat or fat content might be, or whether the food contains substances likely to cause allergic reaction in some people

- If food is genetically modified we are informed

- Sourcing, preparation, storage and processing are done according to strict hygiene guidelines

- Handling, transport, packaging and presenting are all done with attention to hygiene codes too

- All staff are required to be trained in food hygiene practices and gain a food hygiene certificate.

The regulations are very specific in all of the areas above, and prescribe what cleaning should be done in particular locations – the materials to be used and the frequency for staff, rooms, utensils and surfaces.

As result of tighter regulations and higher customer expectations, eating areas have in most leisure places become a pleasure to visit. In private health clubs, cooling down after a workout in the comfortable bars and café areas is now all part of the experience (see above), and attracts valuable additional spending.

Children Act 1989

Children are great consumers of leisure activities. At some stage if you work in the leisure industry you are going to be involved with children, so you need to be aware of what this Act covers. Originally it was only intended to cover 'children at risk', but, unfortunately, today's society requires protection for all children. The Act requires authorities (mainly local authorities) to ensure that:

- adequate social services are accessible

- people providing child care and minding are properly qualified and certified

- information on child protection is circulated

- day-care facilities are registered and inspected, e.g. crèches at sports centres.

Police checks have also become more common for anyone working with children. Ratios of cover for children are set out, as are guidelines on types of equipment which can be used, the records which must be kept (an accident book, for example). Access for adults now has to be carefully controlled.

The taking of images (photographs and videos) which include children is now more strictly controlled, and so is the monitoring of the use of children's images for advertising and other promotional activities – quite often an important medium for leisure providers.

Most schools, leisure clubs and youth groups have developed their own code of practice on giving out data on their members, and will not give out any personal details on children.

The Football Association has a child-protection scheme built into its coach education programmes – each club should have a child-protection person and clear codes for players, officials and spectators. It also mentions (in the form of questions) some tell-tale signs and incidents that adults might see or hear, including:

- What would you do if you saw bite marks or bruises on a child's body?

- What would you do if a parent was shouting abuse at other children in a match?

- Do you know the background of the first-aider who attends children at matches?

- How would you check the credentials of coaches working at a children's football summer school?

Data Protection Act 1998

With the advent of the computer age and the ability of organisations to keep huge databases of information on people, there came the need for legislation to protect privacy and personal information. The Act does not ban the collection of the data, but it does give consumers the right to know if personal data is held about them and to check that it is fair and true, and if not to have it amended.

Leisure organisations are likely to hold quite a lot of personal data, such as addresses and banking details on their membership databases, so they must pay attention to the key points:

1. Data must have been obtained fairly and lawfully.

2. Data must only be held for the purpose it was given.

3. Data must not be 'sold' on to third parties unless this was made clear from the outset (this is usually contained in the small print of agreements).

4. Data kept should only be that which is required for the membership purposes and be wiped out after it is no longer necessary.

5. Data must be kept secure by electronic means (or physical means for manual databases).

Other types of information captured on video and CCTV are also subject to the same conditions.

Leisure organisations which fall under the Act have to register their systems and purposes on the Data Protection Register. They must also detail the sources they will use and to whom they will disclose the information. The Act currently in force stems from a 1998 EU Directive, and is a lot tighter than the original 1984 version, requiring much more information on the purpose of the data.

Working Time Regulations 1998

The original aim of the regulations was to ensure that staff would not be required to work excessively long hours, i.e. more than 48 hours in any seven days. But since these regulations were brought in there has been a great deal of debate about their usefulness. Many workers or services have opted out or are exempt.

The regulations had quite a large impact on the leisure industry because many staff work irregular shifts, some venues are open 24 hours a day, and in many locations staff work unsocial hours, e.g. in nightclubs. Shift patterns had to be changed to comply with the regulations, which had an impact on staffing rotas and wages.

Regular breaks are also a key focus of the regulations, requiring workers to take daily, weekly and annual breaks to keep them refreshed and motivated. Where this is not always possible, compensatory rests have to be given. This sometimes means staff working long shifts, but then having a number of days off.

Summer activity camps are a good example. Young staff work as activity leaders, supervise meal times and entertain and check children – all in a 24-hour period. Employers have to take on plenty of staff to cover these needs (as well as sickness).

Adult workers are entitled to 11 consecutive hours rest in any 24-hour period and at least 24 hours off in any seven-day period. This makes scheduling and staff rotas a key issue for managers who have to ensure that they have complied with the regulations but also have enough staff on duty. This can be a tricky task when a two-week long event such as the Edinburgh International Festival is on.

Working hours can be long at activity camps.

activity

PROTECTING CHILDREN

Working in a small group, devise you own guidelines that adults working with children, e.g. as coaches, could follow to ensure that they are protecting children in their care.

activity

OVERWORKING STAFF

List all the problems which might occur for the owner of a medium-sized hotel, if he:
a) works his staff for long hours
b) does not give proper breaks.

Topic 4 Risk assessment and implementation

As we have seen, some of the most important legislation affecting the leisure industry is now based on carrying out 'risk assessments'. It is clearly important that you understand how this process is done, so this will be the main subject of this topic. The final part of the topic will consist of scenarios in varied leisure contexts, where you can think about how you would go about setting up safety schemes and training. So this topic will be split into:

- Risk assessment terminology
- The six stages of risk assessment
- Applying legislation: scenarios for practice.

As with the legislation, you only need to build up your knowledge of the 'key intentions' of the processes and applications.

Risk assessment terminology

The generally accepted definition of a risk assessment is:

'making reasoned judgements about the risks and extent of these risks to people's health, safety and security, based on the application of information, which leads to decisions on how risks should be managed'

Hazards are anything that can cause harm, such as an injury to someone. Examples commonly found in the leisure industry would be slippery poolside tiles, equipment stored badly in corridors, or unfinished repair work.

Probability is the likelihood of something actually happening, given certain circumstances.

Severity is how badly people might get injured if something does happen.

Measures and precautions are the actions that can be taken to reduce risk.

Undertaking a risk assessment is a serious piece of work. By law, it must be carried out by employers and employees whenever the need arises. This might be part of regular checks, or an annual inspection, or prior to a major event.

Some hazards are predictable because they are easily seen, such as the ones mentioned above. Others are less predictable, but still have to be considered – even if you have to go looking for them. An example of this might be worn bolts on a basketball backboard, which show only up after a maintenance check. Risk in this context is the chance of something hazardous happening. Sometimes this risk can be high – such as beginners capsizing their canoes on their first river trip. Other times the risk is low – such as children getting chased by a bull during a country walk.

When hazards are identified, precautions have to be taken in order to eliminate, minimise or control the risk. These precautions are called health and safety measures. Examples would be the duty manager making sure that there are enough lifeguards on duty at a busy 'splash time' in a local pool; chefs wearing protective clothing in a busy kitchen; or a nursery owner ensuring that there are sufficient fire extinguishers in a children's playgroup housed in a temporary wooden building.

Some large leisure locations with many activities will be exposed to a wide range of hazards and will need to cover all their risk factors. In a theme park, for example, the hazards might include:

- Children getting lost
- Children falling off rides

- Equipment breaking off and hitting people
- Electrical failures
- Safety guards/bolts not tightened
- Discarded cigarettes causing a fire
- Machines leaking oil.

Using guidance supplied by the Health and Safety Executive (HSE) workers can carry out a range of risk assessments in the leisure industry. Besides carrying out a risk assessment in conjunction with employees, employers must also implement the measures recommended, perhaps in conjunction with experts. The people carrying out the risk assessment also have to weigh up what incidents could happen in future, the probability of the incident occurring, and how severe the consequences might be if the incident did occur. They must close the process by also ensuring that emergency procedures and training for such incidents is in place too.

The six stages of risk assessment

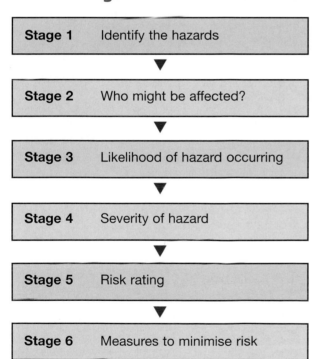

Stage 1	Identify the hazards
Stage 2	Who might be affected?
Stage 3	Likelihood of hazard occurring
Stage 4	Severity of hazard
Stage 5	Risk rating
Stage 6	Measures to minimise risk

Stage 1: Identify the hazards

The first stage of a risk assessment involves identifying the hazards in the workplace. This whole process should be recorded in a manual log or in report format, for future reference. The HSE guidance suggests that when carrying out a risk assessment: 'look only for hazards which you could reasonably expect to result in significant harm under the conditions of the workplace'. Here are some leisure industry examples:

- Poor lighting in sports store cupboards
- Slipping/tripping hazards – torn carpets or tiles sticking up
- Use of ladders
- Pressure systems on theme park rides
- Temporary wiring at outdoor concerts
- Hot food counters.

activity
LISTING HAZARDS

Select two rooms (or areas) in your institution and, working with a partner, make lists of their hazards. Discuss your findings with others in your class who looked elsewhere.

The range of hazards found in a leisure facility will obviously vary with its size, location, complexity and the nature of its use. You would not expect a cinema and theme park to have similar hazards, or an outdoor centre and a museum.

Stage 2: Who might be affected?

The HSE guidance suggests: 'There is no need to list individuals by name – just think about groups of people doing similar work or who may be affected'. Here are some leisure industry examples:

- Customers/players
- Office and admin staff
- Site maintenance teams and cleaners
- Suppliers and contractors on site
- Operatives and technicians.

You must also pay particular attention to some special groups – disabled staff and visitors, pregnant women, new personnel, and those who work alone or at night a lot – because they may be more vulnerable. The total numbers of all groups who are on the premises at any one time should also be considered.

activity
LINKING HAZARDS AND GROUPS

Working with a different partner, design a chart to record both hazards and associated 'groups' (e.g. children, elderly) who might be harmed in a combined shopping mall and leisure complex.

73

Stage 3: Likelihood of hazard occurring

Deciding the likelihood of a hazard resulting in an accident or incident means rating (estimating) the probability – weighing up how likely it is. Risk assessors might, for example, use three levels: Highly unlikely, Unlikely, and Likely. If the hazard is easily identified – unsupervised swimming by youngsters in a pond, for example – it is likely to cause a problem, pushing the probability rating high.

Stage 4: Severity of hazard

Judging severity means weighing up how dangerous it would be if an incident did occur. The severity factor is the degree of harm which could occur – everything from a cut finger to broken limbs, or worse. Assessors might use three levels of severity: Slightly harmful, Harmful, and Extremely harmful. Severity increases with:

- contact sports
- when large numbers are involved in an event
- increases in speed
- if one incident causes others, e.g. one collision causing a whole pile-up behind.

To help with judgements, previous occurrences can be taken into account – such as stadium fires, sports injuries, escape of gases. Managers of leisure facilities may seek help from each other, from professional bodies such as the ISRM or ILAM, or from government departments and agencies such as the Environment Agency, the fire service, or local authority environmental health departments. In all events the HSE guidance can be sought.

Stage 5 Risk rating

The rating for likelihood, combined with the rating for severity, gives the degree of risk – the risk rating. The diagram below shows how the three-part probability scale and the three-part severity scale , when combined, produce five levels of risk: Trivial, Tolerable, Moderate, Substantial, and Intolerable.

	SLIGHTLY HARMFUL	HARMFUL	EXTREMELY HARMFUL
HIGHLY UNLIKELY	TRIVIAL RISK	TOLERABLE RISK	MODERATE RISK
UNLIKELY	TOLERABLE RISK	MODERATE RISK	SUBSTANTIAL RISK
LIKELY	MODERATE RISK	SUBSTANTIAL RISK	INTOLERABLE RISK

LOW SEVERITY ➡ HIGH SEVERITY

LOW PROBABILITY ... HIGH PROBABILITY

The relationship between combinations of probability and severity

INCREASING PROBABILITY AND SEVERITY

As a class, brainstorm five ways in which probability and severity would be increased in these leisure contexts:
- a gorge walk
- a camping trip
- dry-slope skiing.

Stage 6 Measures to minimise risk

The outcome of the evaluations made go into the plan for covering the hazards and the risks. The actions which are needed, and the timescale to do them, are determined by the level of risk – the probability and severity – you allocate to the hazard. For example, if you were running a small yoga class for ladies, the likelihood of injury would be low, so you would take little action other than checking the first aid kit before the session. Precautions for a major triathlon, on the other hand, would need lots of action and plenty of time, to prepare for the hazards of hypothermia, drowning, crashes and injuries, with a high probability of some incidents happening.

The HSE guidance suggests you ask the following question: 'over and above the precautions we found in place – what more could we reasonably do for those risks which were found to be not adequately controlled?' Obviously you give priority to those risks which involve large numbers or severe harm. The following principles are recommended:

- try to remove the risk completely – by taking major action

- try a less risky option – by changing the event

- prevent access to the hazard by guarding it – by erecting barriers

- reorganise work to reduce exposure – change the equipment for safer versions

- issue personal protective clothing – gloves, garments for body protection

- provide support services for any outcomes – first aid.

EXAMPLES OF MEASURES

For each of the six principles of 'measures to minimise risks', listed above, think up an example to illustrate what might be done in a leisure context. Create a chart to present your ideas.

Recording the actions taken

The HSE requires all organisations with more than five staff to have written records of all significant findings and of the controls put in place to counter risk. Examples of such records would be:

1. Electrical installations in the staff restroom/kitchen – insulation, earthing, sockets and cables all checked and found sound. (Next check due in 3 months.)
2. Fumes from children's ride generator – exhaust and fan fitted. (Next check due in 3 weeks.)
3. New stepper bought and installed in gym – guidance on usage posted and staff trained in its use. (Check in 1 week.)
4. Frequent thefts from changing rooms – new lockers installed. (Monitoring ongoing).

The HSE say that assessments need to be: 'suitable and sufficient, not necessarily perfect', and that records should show that precautions taken are reasonable and that checks are made. From time to time, as situations or equipment or staff change, precautions will need to be reviewed and measures and training implemented to take account of any new significant hazards.

Triathlons involve a whole range of risks.

Applying legislation: five scenarios for practice

To create a safe working environment, managers often have to work with their staff to cover health, safety and security in a range of situations. Try these scenarios to see what *you* would do.

Scenario A. Implementing an inspection programme

Consider yourself the manager of a sports centre which has five tennis courts, one multi-play area, a large well-equipped fitness gym, two squash courts, a spinning room, a large sports hall and small side hall, plus a crèche and reception area. Most of the storage is off the main hall in large cupboards, while the changing areas are centrally located. You have to plan and implement a programme of inspection for each of these areas. This will involve a risk assessment, deciding on the frequency of inspections and the type of training staff will need to spot hazards. Design a risk assessment form (see example, below) for the findings in each area. Lay out your plans in a report format, and identify which legislation you might draw on, e.g. Protective Clothing; Manual Handling; First Aid; Health and Safety at Work.

Farber Leisure Services – risk assessment form
Assessors should follow the 6-stage process recommended by the Council.

This form must be completed by a competent assessor for any activity or programme before it is run and submitted to the Health & Safety Department. Reference to the Council's 'Risk Assessment Manual' is recommended (all leisure premises).

Activity/Location or Event/Programme being assessed:

Mountain Biking trip (novice group) in Danby Woods. 1 leader

Identify the hazards for this activity	Identify who might be affected	Likelihood of the hazard occurring	Severity of hazard	Risk rating	Measures to minimise risk
Collisions	Other bikers & walkers	Highly unlikely if group is controlled well	Harmful	Tolerable	Clear briefings about speed control & wearing of safety gear
Abrasions & cuts	Participants	Likely	Slightly harmful	Moderate	Headgear and padded clothing/gloves
Broken limbs	Participants	Highly unlikely if group is controlled well	Extremely harmful	Moderate	Clear briefings about speed control & wearing of safety gear
Concussion	Participants	Highly unlikely if group is controlled well	Harmful	Tolerable	Helmets worn at all times

Scenario B. Staff training and development

Consider yourself a supervisor at a busy town swimming pool with a group of ten staff who work under you, five permanent and five shift and 'on call' staff. You wish to update everyone on three subjects:

■ Child protection

■ Reporting of injuries, diseases and dangerous occurrences

■ Control of substances hazardous to health.

You need to prepare a training plan detailing how you will go about this. Your plan needs to contain a flowchart of sessions, the methods you will use to get the message over, and how you will assess if the training has been effective. As it is a staff development programme, you must include some 'fun and problem-solving activities' relevant to the topics you intend to include. Present your plan in a portfolio style, making sure you identify which legislation you might draw on.

Scenario C. Safeguarding the security of property and information

Consider yourself the safety officer for a private gym in a large city. The gym has a membership of 3,500 people, and over 40 staff. Just recently there have been some disturbing thefts of members' property and misuse of information held on the database. Two staff have been dismissed as a result. The owners have asked you to implement a 'safety and security programme' to prevent anything like this happening in the future. You need to prepare a proposal for consideration by the owners. Your proposal needs to cover the following areas of concern:

■ Reception   ■ Changing rooms

■ Pool area   ■ Workout zone

■ Dance studio   ■ Staff training

■ Offices.   ■ Coffee shop

Don't worry about the costs for this example, but do try to identify which legislation you might draw on.

Scenario D. Protecting staff and visitors from violence and abuse

At theme parks or football grounds, the safety and welfare of staff and visitors is a very important issue, and trained security staff are usually employed to prevent any violence or abuse. In this scenario you are a freelance expert, with experience in training staff in this sort of work. You have been asked to prepare two outline proposals – one for a small theme park, and one for a Conference-side football ground. Identify which legislation you might draw on, and prepare your outline proposals for presentation to the organisations. You need to give details on what threats might be faced, what kind of risk assessment needs to take place, the procedures you feel will be needed, and how you will train the staff.

Scenario E. Dealing with specific customer and staff issues

You are the owner of an event company which stages a range of events around the UK throughout the year, e.g. concerts, corporate fun days, 'it's a knockout' competitions. You have fifteen staff, but lately some of them have started complaining about their office environment, and others think that some of the tasks you set them don't follow proper guidelines. Their complaints include:

■ Desks and chairs are old and rickety

■ Storage is inadequate, and rooms are cluttered with boxes and files

■ There is no trolley for moving heavy kit

■ No one has ever had any first aid or fire training

■ Uniforms and other clothing are worn out

■ Computers are old fashioned, and many staff complain of headaches.

You know you must do something immediately or face major problems. Which of the EU regulations do you need to consult for guidance, and why?

How would you work with the staff to put things right?

In this topic and the next two we will review some of the quality systems which are available to most leisure organisations.

In exploring the schemes we will look at four main aspects:

- How they are managed in the UK
- Which organisations are eligible
- How organisations achieve the award
- The potential benefits to organisations.

Our first quality system, called Quest, is a framework for managing sport and leisure facilities or development schemes. We will start, however, by giving an overview of what quality systems are supposed to achieve, and how they came about as a management tool.

Quality systems

For the last decade and more, successive governments have wanted more efficiency and effectiveness in the management of public sector services – including leisure provision. The 'not for profit' organisations need to run themselves well too, for they are often on tight budgets. The result has been the adoption of more and more business-like methods of management – the methods used by the commercial sector.

In order for any organisation to survive and thrive today, they have to have efficient and effective systems. Leisure organisations must ensure that they provide a service or product that is enduring and satisfying, and attracts people back because of its quality.

Quality systems provide standards – set by national or international bodies – against which managers can measure the service delivery or operations of their organisation or individual departments. Many leisure organisations implement quality systems to help build an 'organisational culture', which includes excellence in customer service. At an operational level, staff and supervisors all know the levels they must reach and maintain. Evidence has shown that using a quality system as part of customer care usually leads to more

delegation of tasks and responsibilities to staff, but at the same time staff skills and capabilities are often better used. The drive for quality of delivery has to be supported by resources too, such as more investment in training.

The use of standards and quality systems began in the manufacturing sector of the industry – e.g. the production of rackets, balls and kit – where 'consistency' and 'few rejects' were the standards required. The service sector of the industry then adopted these principles – requiring high standards of 'customer care and satisfaction'. We now have

international standards such as ISO 9000 and Charter Mark, both of which we will cover in later sections.

To measure performance, a number of dimensions need to be tested to give a broad picture. Financial targets, of course, give clear figures for evaluation, but non-financial factors also give a good picture – e.g. customer satisfaction, staff morale, facility usage. You can also measure performance by comparing your facility with that of a very similar one. This is called 'benchmarking', and is used widely in the sports sector, particularly by retail outlets and local leisure centres. Managers can compare performance aspects such as numbers of users, levels of satisfaction, income and other spending to see how well they rank against each other.

Many companies with high standards will only do business with others who have similar high standards – and have a recognised award as proof. This is sometimes described as 'quality begetting quality'.

Continuous improvement of the organisation and its services is often the theme which drives many of the schemes, but the criteria for judging improvement vary across the leisure industry, from organisation to organisation:

- for some, such as local authority leisure centres, price and value for money may be important

- for others, such as theme parks, enjoyment might be most important

- some organisations, such as hotels, may value cleanliness and friendliness most.

Let's investigate the Quest quality system, which is operated in the sport and leisure sectors, to see which criteria are used there and what benefits it might bring an organisation.

The Quest quality system

With the varying standards that were being experienced in sport and leisure provision in the 1990s, and several different quality systems being adopted by the leisure organisations, it was felt by the UK Sports Councils that sport had some catching up to do. In conjunction with the British Quality Association, they set about the task, and in 1996 the outcome of their research was the Quest system for leisure services.

The current Quest scheme promotes good practice by providing the industry with standards, and encouraging their application and development in a customer-focused management framework. It is recommended by the British Quality Foundation for Self Assessment in Sport and Leisure Operations.

There are two distinct categories of Quest awards:

- Quest Facility Management – aimed at sports and leisure facilities, in the commercial, voluntary and public sectors

- Quest Sports Development – aimed at sports development units in local authorities, governing bodies and voluntary organisations.

QUEST: THE TWO TYPES OF CRITERIA

'Enabler' criteria (50%) (Aspects of management that help facilities to attain high standards)	'Results-oriented' criteria (50%) (Levels of achievement measured by results attained)
Leadership	
People management	People satisfaction
Policy and strategy	Customer satisfaction
Resources	Impact on society
Processes	Business results

How Quest is managed in the UK

Quest is designed by and for the industry to help managers enhance, improve and continue to improve the quality of service provided to customers. The scheme is endorsed and supported by the four home country Sports Councils, and supported by a wide range of industry-representative organisations who have played an important role in its development. Together, these Sports Councils and organisations make up Quest's Industry Policy Committee (IPC).

The IPC acts as the guardian of the scheme and is responsible for preserving its credibility, and for all policy decisions relating to Quest's implementation and future development. It is overseen and administered by an independent consultancy to ensure impartiality. The industry-representative organisations supporting Quest include:

- Local Government Association

- Chief Leisure Officers' Association

- Institute of Leisure and Amenity Management

- Institute of Sport and Recreation Management

- Leisure Management Contractors' Association

- Scottish Association of Directors of Leisure Services.

Which organisations are eligible?

All leisure organisations which run sports facilities or sports development schemes are eligible. Information from the management team explains:

'Currently there are 450 Leisure Centres/Facility Management sites registered under the Quest scheme, alongside 38 Sports Development Units. These range from huge multi-purpose centres such as Guildford Spectrum to smaller sites with just a swimming pool or dry-side facilities, and more recently golf clubs and university sports facilities. They are operated by a range of private contractors, local authorities and leisure trusts.'

You can access more information from their website, www.quest-uk.org

At the annual Quest conference, awards are made to centres under various headings. The sample shown below, from the 2004 awards, will give you an idea of the wide range of awards and winners.

How organisations achieve the award

Applicants can use either a self-assessment and improvement programme or submit themselves for an independent external assessment in their 'quest' for a Quest award.

Under self-assessment, organisations are able to assess their operation in comparison to the industry standards (which are to be considered as long-term aims) and 'best practice' information that is provided in the Quest 'Manager's Guidance Pack'. This enables managers and their teams to:

- make informed judgements about how they are performing against recognised industry standards
- identify their strengths
- identify their areas for improvement
- draw up their own plans of action to raise standards of service delivery to customers.

The scheme encourages managers and their teams to consider their operation from the customers' point of view, asking key questions such as: 'If it does not benefit the customer – why are we doing it?'

External validation is undertaken by trained 'Assessors' from the industry. The assessment will check the operation against industry standards, and provide a percentage score (see example, right).

Quest operates a grading system, based upon the following scores:

- registered – above 60%
- highly commended – 75% to 84%
- excellent – 85% and above.

For the Facility Management award, the external validation also incorporates a 'mystery visit'. This is a market research method employed by many organisations, whereby someone working for the organisation (in this case, Quest) visits the facility and acts as normal customer. Staff, of course, do not know who they are, so the mystery visitor will be able to rate how they really perform – in secret. It's a reliable way of finding out about an organisation.

A selection of Quest awards

- *Highest overall facility management score (joint) winners*
  Wyre Forest Glades LC and
  Lynnsport and Leisure Park East Anglia

- *Highest overall sports development score*
  Kirklees Leisure Development, Yorkshire

- *Highest dual-use centre*
  Magee College Sports Centre, Belfast

- *Highest dry-side score*
  Lynnsport and Leisure Park East Anglia

- *Highest wet-side centre scores*
  Bedale LC, North Yorks
  Hamilton Water Palace, Scotland
  Pendle Wavelengths, Lancashire

- *Highest first cycle sports development score*
  Sport England North East

- *Highest first cycle facility management score*
  Castle Place LC (managed by DC Leisure)

- *Most improved sports development score*
  Kirklees Leisure Development

- *Most improved facility management score*
  Saltire LC, Angus

Quest success: 70% rating

Quest has awarded Craven Swimming Pool a 70% rating. Centres have to achieve a 60% rating to get registered on the scheme, while the national average is 67%, so the manager Peter Chapman is very pleased. He says 'we are now among the top 25% of centres in the country (out of 430), which is especially pleasing because the staff are a new team'. Clearly much of the achievement is down to the staff, backed by support from the top. A recent survey gave them a 99% customer-satisfaction return, user levels are up by over 10%, and membership numbers exceeded their target by a mile – reward indeed for following the quality system route.

The frequency of assessments is based on a two-year cycle, with two visits made to monitor and maintain the registration. This frequency ensures that quality of service delivery is maintained in line with the Quest standards – and the standards themselves are continually updated.

The accompanying extracts from the assessment manual show the types of questions and scoring which goes in as part of the assessment process for housekeeping, maintenance of buildings, plant and equipment, and the best practice principles that assessors are looking for.

An extract from an assessment page for Facilities Operation, as shown on the pmpconsult.com website.

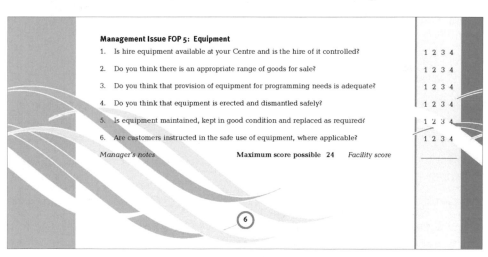

Management Issue FOP 5: Equipment

1. Is hire equipment available at your Centre and is the hire of it controlled?   1 2 3 4
2. Do you think there is an appropriate range of goods for sale?   1 2 3 4
3. Do you think that provision of equipment for programming needs is adequate?   1 2 3 4
4. Do you think that equipment is erected and dismantled safely?   1 2 3 4
5. Is equipment maintained, kept in good condition and replaced as required?   1 2 3 4
6. Are customers instructed in the safe use of equipment, where applicable?   1 2 3 4

Manager's notes   **Maximum score possible 24**   *Facility score*

6

Facilities Operation

Management Issue FOP 5: Equipment

Quest Best Practice

- Suitable, sufficient and well maintained equipment is available for use.
- A range of equipment is provided to allow programming variety.
- Safety in use is achieved.

Quest Best Practice Principles

1. Hire equipment is available and hire is controlled.
2. An appropriate range of goods is for sale.
3. Provision of equipment for programming needs is adequate.
4. Equipment is erected and dismantled safely.
5. Equipment is maintained and kept in good condition and replaced as required.
6. Where applicable, staff and customers are instructed in the safe use of equipment.

An extract from the Manager's Guidance Pack for Facilities Operation, as shown on the pmpconsult.com website.

Quest Best Practice Principles explained

1. Hire equipment is available and hire is controlled.

   Equipment provided for customers use and for use by staff should be maintained in good condition (see FOP 4: Maintenance). The scope of this requirement covers equipment for hire and sale, sports activity equipment, coaching course aids and special event equipment.

2. An appropriate range of goods is for sale.

   Goods should be available for hire or purchase during opening times. The Centre should recognise the potential to generate secondary spend and market this appropriately.

   Where possible, goods for sale should be displayed attractively at Reception or applicable sales points.

What 'quality gurus' advise

It is clear that attention has to be paid to certain aspects of running a centre to achieve the award. Business experts – 'quality gurus', as they are often called – writing on general good practice in management, give a few key ideas, which leisure organisations trying to achieve the Quest award might take note of:

- Objectives have to be set, and then actions targeted at achieving these.

- Don't accept things like poor timekeeping, poor workmanship, late deliveries or bad coaching – get it right first time.

- Don't buy the cheapest, and make sure that what you do buy has a guarantee.

- Train staff to track problems back to their source, and solve them.

- Create an atmosphere where everyone can express ideas and comments freely – build communication across departments.

- Stress the elements of pride, professionalism and highest standards.

The potential benefits to organisations

Quest ultimately benefits customers, the organisation, staff and other stakeholders or partners, in a number of ways:

Benefits for customers

- They enjoy ongoing improvement to service.

- They experience an increased focus on identifying and meeting their needs.

- Quest provides an independent assessment of the service that customers receive.

Benefits for organisations

- They are better prepared for Competitive Performance Assessments (CPA), formerly 'Best Value' (the local authority management system for public services).

- Quest gives a structured framework which supports the delivery of best practice in service delivery.

- It provides a great opportunity to have the leisure organisation publicly recognised, and endorsed to a UK-wide industry standard.

- It is a well recognised approach to managing a centre and/or team.

activity
WHY WE SHOULD GO FOR THE AWARD

Working with a partner, and using the material given in the previous paragraphs, together with some of your own ideas or research, prepare a concise proposal supporting the idea of 'your facility' going for a Quest award. The proposal should try to convince your steering committee that it is a good idea, pointing out all the advantages, such as better image, fewer customer complaints, etc.

Benefits for staff

- Quest gives staff improved motivation and understanding of their role, and their contribution within the organisation to meeting customers' needs.

- It contributes to improved continuous professional development, through a better understanding of the organisation's policies and objectives.

Benefits for other stakeholders and partners

- Quest lends greater support and recognition of the benefits of working together.

- It provides an improved understanding of shared values and objectives.

- It gives an independent assessment of the organisation's performance.

Long-term benefits

- Quest can help achieve good performance ratings for a CPA, through the external assessment and benchmarking of services against others.

- It can give a better framework for continuous improvement, service enhancement and reducing the costs of poor quality, e.g. time spent dealing with complaints.

- It can lead to cost savings and better financial performance, through a planned approach to income and expenditure.

- It actively encourages staff to take more ownership of their work.

Possible problems in implementing a quality system

Organisations following a quality system to improve working practices may find some problems when they implement the scheme. For example:

1. All staff have to get more involved – this might not suit many and they may leave, especially if they feel they are actually having to work harder or differently, but the new work is not linked to any pay rise or bonus.
2. Working and making no mistakes (zero tolerance) may be too tall a challenge for some staff, and their motivation may suffer. People do need to be forgiven the odd error.
3. Employees are expected to be creative and flexible, while sticking rigidly to a system of operation. This might prove difficult for some to understand – it may appear as a contradiction in terms.
4. 'Participative' management – where everyone's opinion is taken – is not a style that can be achieved overnight. Confidence needs to be built so that staff are not afraid to speak up.
5. The organisational culture may have to change, i.e. away from cosy old working practices.
6. To make it work, everyone from the top down needs to be involved – the board, committee and managers all need to show that they are fully behind the scheme.

ASSESSING GOOD PRACTICE

Imagine that you are a trainee assessor, and that your supervisor has asked you to make a report on good practices at a small local leisure pool. Using the eight numbered headings given below, explain how you would assess the pool – listing your questions, actions and observation activities for each heading.

Examples of good practice

Some practical examples of good practice, which would contribute to a good Quest assessment, will help to make the scheme clearer. Listed below are a sample of the ideas mentioned by delegates from all over the country at an English Institute of Sport conference in 2004. They include the sort of things that Quest inspectors are looking for, under a range of headings – the first eight are Quest assessment headings. (The activity above asks you to expand on these.)

1. CLEANLINESS
- Have a 'no outdoor shoes' policy in certain areas
- Promote cleanliness with effective signs and reminders

2. HOUSEKEEPING
- Arrange vending stock at heights suitable for young children to see what is there
- Have a cleaning schedule

3. MAINTENANCE
- Show an effective fault-reporting system
- Have an 'at a glance' maintenance year-planner

4. EQUIPMENT
- Outsource the cleaning
- Regular risk assessments

5. ENVIRONMENT CONTROL
- Use a waste compactor and recycle bins
- Define and monitor temperatures for different areas

6. CHANGING ROOMS
- Free shampoo
- Locker audit

7. HEALTH AND SAFETY MANAGEMENT
- Have external assessments
- Hold in-house training

8. CUSTOMER CARE
- First-time-visitor packs
- Interactive CD Rom for staff to do personal training on

Customer research
- Know local demographics and socio-economic groups
- Carry out some trend analysis

Customer feedback
- Fully kitted customer comment station
- User forums

Marketing and pricing
- Keep the marketing plan up to date
- Consider a flexible pricing system

Reception and admin
- Reception desk modified for ease of access for disabled and children
- Admission is controlled

Staff supervision and planning
- Holiday inducements for good performance
- A positive appraisal scheme

People management
- Three-day training scheme for Risk Assessment, First Aid and Child Protection
- Further qualifications scheme

Strategy and business planning
- Following a mission statement
- Using strategy documents for specific areas, e.g. play, marketing
- Managing by objectives
- Benchmarking against other organisations

Financial management
- Involve all staff in budget planning
- Set annual targets
- Review progress monthly and adjust where necessary

ICT
- Training in e-booking
- Online training
- Use thematic filing.

The Investors in People award

In the last topic we saw how a national quality award, Quest, is valued by leisure organisations running sports development schemes as a benchmark of achievement in management.

The 'Investors in People' (IIP) award follows many of the same principles, but it focuses on organisations attaining Standards for training and development of their staff.

We will explore aspects of the award under the following headings:

- How the award is managed in the UK
- Which organisations are eligible
- How organisations achieve the award
- The potential benefits to organisations.

We will start, however, with a brief overview of what staff training and development schemes should be all about.

Why training and development are important

Staff are central to many of the processes of service delivery in the leisure industry, and their training and development is very important. Developing staff is one of the basic roles for any manager – alongside leading, motivating and directing. With today's flatter, leaner organisations, the training of those staff at the core of the business is essential. Much training today therefore focuses on devolving responsibility down to the staff – and they become the quality controllers, instead of the manager. This new responsibility needs supporting with a development in confidence, and new systems to support them. So training and development actually become an integral part of the quality system itself. Sometimes a whole new kind of training and development culture has to be created to facilitate the use of a quality system, and old practices have to be done away with.

Training and development have many benefits, such as increased confidence, recognition and promotion prospects. The training can take place in many different ways – through electronic mediums, seminars, films and activities.

Whatever the method, there should always be:

- a clear commitment
- clear objectives
- styles of training and development to suit the staff.

The Investors in People award

INVESTORS IN PEOPLE

Investors in People is the national Standard, setting out a level of good practice for training and development of people to achieve the goals of the organisation they work for. It was developed in 1990 by a partnership between the National Training Task Force, leading national businesses, personnel, professional and employee organisations such as the Confederation of British Industry (CBI), Trades Union Congress (TUC) and the Institute of Personnel and Development (IPD) and the Employment Department. The Standard provides: 'a national framework for improving business performance and competitiveness, through a planned approach to setting and communicating business objectives and developing people to meet these objectives'. The four key principles are shown below. You can see that they would transfer into any leisure organisation, and later we will include some examples for you to study.

> **THE FOUR KEY PRINCIPLES OF THE IIP STANDARD**
> 1. **Commitment** – invest in people to achieve business goals, i.e. give them more training
> 2. **Planning** – show how the training will be done
> 3. **Action** – show how any action will move the organisation towards its goals
> 4. **Evaluation** – checking that what was planned has been achieved.

How the IIP award is managed in the UK

There are currently twelve 'Quality Centres' within the UK – nine in England and one each in Scotland, Wales and Northern Ireland. They are licensed by IIP UK on an annual basis. Their main role is to offer IIP assessment and recognition to organisations in their area and to 'quality assure' the process. They also work to get more local organisations involved in IIP.

Organisations which wish to be assessed contact their local Quality Centre, which then allocates an 'Assessor'. Assessors look for indicators and evidence under the four principles mentioned (see Table 2).

PRINCIPLES	INDICATORS	EVIDENCE
Commitment An Investor in People is fully committed to developing its people in order to achieve its aims and objectives	The organisation is committed to supporting the development of its people	Management can describe strategies that they have put in place to support the development of people in order to improve the organisation's performance
Planning An Investor in People is clear about its aims and its objectives, and what its people need to do to achieve them	The organisation has a plan, with clear aims and objectives that are understood by everyone	People can consistently explain the aims and objectives of the organisation at a level appropriate to their role, and are consulted about the organisation's aims and objectives
Action An Investor in People develops its people effectively in order to improve its performance	Managers are effective in supporting the development of people	The organisation makes sure that managers have the knowledge and skills they need to develop their people
Evaluation An Investor in People understands the impact of its investment in people on its performance	The development of people improves the performance of the organisation, teams and individuals	The organisation can show that the development of people has improved the performance of the organisation, teams and individuals

Table 2 Some examples of indicators and evidence
You can check out a fuller range of examples on the IIP website at www.iipuk.co.uk

> **activity**
>
> ## HOW WOULD YOU ASSESS?
>
> Working with a partner, and pretending you are assessors, decide what evidence in real terms you might want to see or hear to verify what was going on in a leisure centre, e.g. by examining paperwork or holding interviews, based on the evidence column in Table 2.

Which organisations are eligible?

Any organisation with more than five people on the staff can apply. Obviously they will first need to be sure they have all of the measures in place to meet the training and development Standards. Below is a description of how a Welsh leisure organisation prepared for the award, put in its submission for appraisal, and was successful.

Badgers Café was recognised as an Investor in People in 2001

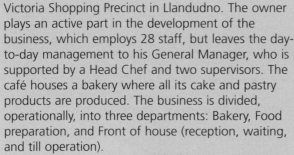

Badgers Café was established in 1997 by its current owner, in the Victoria Shopping Precinct in Llandudno. The owner plays an active part in the development of the business, which employs 28 staff, but leaves the day-to-day management to his General Manager, who is supported by a Head Chef and two supervisors. The café houses a bakery where all its cake and pastry products are produced. The business is divided, operationally, into three departments: Bakery, Food preparation, and Front of house (reception, waiting, and till operation).

The 'three Qs'

The café works hard to promote to its staff the importance of the 'three Qs'– Quality food, Quality service, and Quality surroundings. Great emphasis is placed on staff attitudes and their contribution. New recruits, for example, are offered a 4-hour introductory experience of working in the café before committing themselves to employment with the business. This allows them the opportunity to work alongside other members of staff and to compare the reality of the café to their own work expectations. Most training and development is in-house, but staff also have access to external training, and some are working towards NVQs.

The owner and General Manager, who attended a briefing meeting on the Investors in People Standard, felt that working towards recognition would be an objective way of measuring the café's performance, would help them identify any further development action, and would benefit the business. They invited an external consultant to talk to the staff about the Standard and help them in identifying development activity necessary to achieve recognition.

Meetings and job rotation

Feedback forms were put out on every table, inviting customers to rate the business against the 'three Qs'. Results were tracked on a quarterly basis, with a view to improving standards, where necessary. Regular meetings, involving all staff, reinforced the teamwork approach, and allowed individuals to discuss issues that affected different departments. Monthly supervisors' meetings were also introduced to support this process.

A programme of job rotation was introduced to allow employees the opportunity of understanding the demands of different departments. It also broadened the skills and flexibility of staff, enabling them to work in other areas when the business required. The General Manager spent time working in all departments to gain full understanding of their working practices, and to understand at first hand the demands placed upon staff.

Setting targets

Individual review meetings were introduced for supervisors, settings targets for achievement within their work areas and reviewing ways in which training or development could help. Objectives for the business were set down on paper and shared with staff, so that everyone was clear about what was expected of them and their teams, but were also aware of the support available.

Staff were supported in developing their skills internally, through observation and feedback, and external training was provided in key areas such as customer services (through the Welcome Host scheme) and food hygiene.

Successful outcomes

- The business has doubled its profitability.
- The café has been recognised by Taste of Wales and the Wales Tourist Board, who awarded it a Quality Crown for superior customer service.
- It was voted 'Best Newcomer in 2000' by the Les Routieres guide.
- It also received the 'Best Tearoom in Wales' accolade, and is rated amongst the 'Top 10 Tearooms in the UK' by the Tea Council.
- The General Manager won the 'Tourist Manager of the Year' award in a competition run by the Wales Tourist Board.

Information courtesy of the IIP

SELLING THE PROCESS

Discuss, with others in a group, what lessons other leisure organisations could learn from the Badgers Café example, and summarise these into no more than six points. Then present them (using visual displays) as if you were talking to staff from a leisure organisation that was thinking about being assessed, and needed to know more about the process.

SELLING WITH A FLOWCHART

Working with a partner, use the bullet points (below, left) to develop a flowchart which sums up the stages the café went through. Put key words only in each box. Again, try to imagine you are making a presentation to staff from a leisure organisation that is contemplating going through the process.

How organisations achieve the award

In general terms, the process to achieve the award is as follows:

Whoever is leading the project must:

- Understand the Standard and its strategic implications for the organisation

- Undertake a review against the Standard, to identify any gaps in current practice

- Make the commitment to meet the Standard, and communicate that commitment to all the staff

- Plan and take action, to bring about change

- Bring together the evidence for assessment against the Standard.

If an organisation wishes to be assessed and accredited as an Investor in People organisation, they must first contact their local Quality Centre and complete an assessment application form. Specific organisational data will be required, including a full list of employees – their names, job title, length of service, working hours and whether they are in a trade union. This is so that the Assessor can select a balanced sample of employees to ensure that the views of all groups are represented, and that the outcome is impartial and unbiased.

Chessington World of Adventures

Our second example of a leisure organisation which has followed this process is Chessington World of Adventures, which is part of the Madame Tussaud's Group, and employs 200 permanent and 800 seasonal staff.

The company aims to encourage new and repeat business through providing excellent customer service and an ongoing commitment to developing staff. A 'total quality management' (TQM) philosophy is being adopted throughout the organisation. The most important elements of the company's plan are:

- a clearly defined framework for training and development

- improvement in processes and investment in people

- ensuring that customers enjoy their Chessington experience by having staff who are trained to provide excellent service

- funding to aid preparation and progress of the action plan

- training for those people involved in training other staff, to help them conduct appraisals and interviews

- evaluation of training and development needs to ensure that business objectives are achieved and maintained.

By adopting this strategy, the company has seen significant benefits in performance, including:

- an effective induction programme resulting in greater staff effectiveness and lower staff turnover

- training programmes integrated with business objectives and priorities

- specific training and development needs identified

- improved quality of service to customers

- teamworking and interaction

- improved staff appraisal system.

The potential benefits to organisations

The IIP organisation itself, looking at all businesses, not just leisure organisations, is clear about the benefits of its work. The following information (and the HF Holidays example) is paraphrased from its website.

Over the past 12 years independent research has consistently shown that the Investors in People Standard provides real business benefits to organisations of all sizes, across all sectors.

There are currently over 34,000 'recognised' organisations in the UK, employing over 27% of the total workforce, and every one of those organisations is benefiting from the Standard in one way or another. With a 90% retention rate, we must be doing something right!

The practical benefits of working towards and achieving the Standard are many, including:

- Improved earnings, productivity and profitability. Skilled and motivated people work harder and better, improving productivity.

- IIP organisations help employees become customer-focused so that they meet customer needs at a profit.

- Through greater involvement, personal development and recognition of achievement, motivation is improved. This leads to higher morale, improved retention rates, reduced absenteeism, readier acceptance of change and identification with the organisation beyond the confines of the job.

- Skilled and motivated people constantly examine their work to contribute towards reducing costs and wastage.

- Investing in people significantly improves the results of quality programmes.

- IIP adds considerable value to the 'Excellence Model', ISO 9000, BS 5750 and other total-quality initiatives.

- IIP organisations develop a competitive edge.

- IIP status brings public recognition for real achievements measured against a rigorous national standard. Being an Investor in People organisation helps to attract the best quality job applicants. It may also provide a reason for customers to choose specific goods and services.

Employees in organisations which have achieved the Standard may see benefits such as:

- Good quality training when required

- Improved job satisfaction

- Better communication

- Skill and career development opportunities

- Increased responsibility and involvement

- A better working environment

- Health and safety gains.

activity

SCEPTICAL STAFF SCENARIO

As with any quality system there are negative aspects or costs to consider. Discuss, with one or two others, what implementation difficulties there might be for a manager who has sceptical staff. List the objections you might hear and set out any resource implications that might need considering.

HF Holidays was recognised as an Investor in People in 1995

HF Holidays is the world's leader in walking and special-interest holidays. Owning nineteen country house hotels in the British Isles, and providing holidays in other centres throughout the world, HF has come a long way since its beginnings more than 80 years ago, providing affordable open-air holidays for people from inner-city areas. HF remains a non-profit seeking organisation, owned by its members, but competes in very demanding holiday markets, entirely on a commercial basis. The recruitment, training and other functions operate from attractive premises in the hills above Penrith in Cumbria.

Key benefits

HF were first recognised as Investors in People in 1995; key benefits from assessment and recognition included:

- Confirmation that the work to transform staff skills and involvement 'is on the right lines' – by reference to a rigorous national standard
- Increased motivation and pride in the company on the part of all staff – including seasonal workers and part-timers
- Assessor feedback giving useful ideas to support continuous improvement
- Indications that some seasonal staff are choosing to work for the company because Investors in People shows it is 'a quality employer'
- Greater guest satisfaction, resulting in higher turnover and improved bottom line results
- Using the discipline of re-assessment to ensure Standards are kept up and continuously improved.

Sue Chandler, Recruitment and Training Manager says 'in this highly people-oriented industry, IIP sounded interesting right away and since we are committed to guaranteeing a quality holiday experience for all our guests, we can only do this by having skilled, committed people throughout the organisation, with good plans, resources and systems to back them up.'

Support from the top

Chief Executive Peter Chapman backs this up fully: 'It is fundamental to the success of an IIP programme that support comes from top management. Commitment from the top is essential if you are going to have success, because if you are not willing to be involved and set the Standard, then others will not follow. Our team approach allows 100% participation and as a result, a two-way support to drive improvement forward.'

HF Holidays use the Investors in People logo extensively on marketing, booking and recruitment literature. 'Investors' plaques are displayed at all the hotels and 'our members (who are very frequently our customers) are very proud of what's been achieved'.

Keeping up the momentum

HF Holidays staff stress how important it is going to be to keep up the momentum of continually improving customer service, staff skills and involvement. Nobody is complacent about competition or the increasingly sophisticated demands from customers. Investors in People re-assessment is being used as an essential tool in this continuing improvement process.

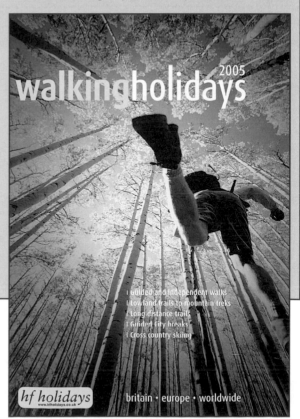

activity

SUMMARISING AND SELLING THE IIP AWARD

Working with one or two partners, and using the examples provided in this topic, sum up what you feel are the important aspects and benefits of achieving IIP status. Transfer your findings into a poster or a leaflet which could be used by IIP for promotional purposes.

ISO 9001, Charter Mark and Clubmark

In the last two topics we looked at a quality system (Quest) and a training and development scheme (Investors in People) both of which clearly offer leisure organisations good benefits. But these are not the only ones, so it is important that you understand the key points of some other quality systems that the industry uses. This topic investigates three that are common in the leisure industry:

- ISO 9000/9001 – created by the International Standards Organisation
- Charter Mark – used by public sector organisations and awarded by government departments
- Clubmark – a grassroots sports scheme award supported by the Sports Councils.

ISO 9000/9001

The International Organisation of Standardisation (ISO) is a worldwide organisation which develops many different kinds of standards. ISO 9000 is the name for a whole 'family' of standards, including ISO 9001 – the one that we are concerned with here. ISO 9001 is the series of documents that give requirements for the 'Quality Management System Standard'. ISO 9001 applies to all types of organisations – whatever size they are or whatever they do. It can help both product- and service-oriented organisations achieve standards of quality that are recognised and respected all around the world. A leisure organisation going for this award must meet the requirements to become 'ISO 9001 Registered'. The full name of the current version is ISO 9001:2000 because it was revised in 2000. Past versions are no longer in use. ISO 9001 places emphasis on process management (how things are done) and resource management (how materials, equipment and people are used) throughout the organisation.

Why do companies want ISO 9001?

Many organisations decide to implement ISO 9001 and obtain registration because it assures customers that the company has a good Quality Management System (QMS) in place. An organisation with an effective QMS will typically meet customer expectations better, and many organisations require their suppliers to have ISO 9001 registration too.

Some organisations implement ISO 9001 because they can see their competitors achieving better operations, improved performance, and improved profitability.

What do leisure organisations have to do to achieve the award?

The first (and biggest) step in obtaining ISO 9001 is looking at the organisation's current processes, and redesigning them to address all of the requirements in the standard. There are requirements about establishing a quality system, promoting quality, satisfying customers, reviewing management, and providing quality resources and personnel. Once organisations have modified or developed their day-to-day processes to meet the standard, they have to write out what they are, for all employees to follow. The required processes and written procedures have to be in place for three months before an assessor comes to visit (see box, above right).

What will the ISO 9001 assessor look for?

- Documents – such as communications between departments or locations – showing clarity, accuracy and an integrated approach.

- A clear sign that managers are committed to the process, through evidence such as policy statements, high standards, clear objectives and performance measurements.

- Evidence of appropriate training and evaluation (e.g. a manual or log book) adequate facilities, resources and support services (e.g. office equipment and guidance) appropriate workspace and layouts – with attention to health, safety, security and environmental requirements.

- Evidence of the required monitoring, inspection and test activities for product/service acceptability.

- Evidence that staff and customer satisfaction are measured and continuous improvements made, and that the organisation conducts internal audits to determine product/service/system effectiveness (e.g. records of meetings, and action plans completed with objectives met).

- Evidence of corrective/preventive action being carried out.

activity
YOUR SIMPLE GUIDE TO ISO 9001

Working in small groups, first prepare a brief guidebook which staff working in a swimming pool or theatre could use to help them prepare for ISO 9001 assessment. Also produce a bullet-pointed list of things you might find that they do not do well. Discuss what difficulties these two types of organisation might have in achieving the award.

Charter Mark

CUSTOMER SERVICE EXCELLENCE

Charter Mark is an easy-to-use quality system for the public sector, designed to help everyone in an organisation focus on, and improve, customer service. Organisations achieving the standard have the right to display the prestigious Charter Mark logo – something much sought after by leisure services in the public sector.

Charter Mark can be attained by any pubic sector institution, department or organisation, e.g. a swimming pool, sports centre, indoor bowling facility, stadium or track. It can also be achieved by a primary school, a Jobcentre, or a museum. Voluntary organisations serving the public (directly or indirectly) such as Citizens Advice Bureaux, scout groups or sports clubs, can also apply. But to be successful they have to provide evidence of meeting the key criteria, which set standards based on what the customer wants. At the heart of Charter Mark criteria is the fundamental question: 'what does the customer expect or hope for from the services you offer?'

No leisure organisation can be sure how it is performing without consultation and feedback from users. To achieve a Charter Mark, an organisation must show that it listens, acts and delivers choice to the customer. Charter Mark holders have to demonstrate that:

- they offer choice to their customers so that a wide range of needs are catered for, e.g. children, single parents, and the elderly using a leisure centre

- they promote continuous improvement, e.g. new targets are set every year at a slightly higher level or lower cost

- the benefits of new technology are maximised, e.g. a computerised booking system, or environment control for a swimming pool

- users and staff are consulted on where choices can be made, e.g. surveys are used

- communities have a say in the design and delivery of local services, e.g. focus groups are organised.

The publicity material from the Cabinet Office (who monitor the award) says that 'Charter Mark is more about achieving a change of culture than winning a trophy – and change and improvement must be ongoing. Complaints, compliments and suggestions from the customer and staff help improve service.'

Research has shown that people on the 'front line' of a leisure organisation – such as receptionists, dealing with the public daily – are often the best judges of what needs to be done to improve service. To achieve the award, organisations have to show that staff are involved in the planning of services, and are encouraged and empowered to put things right wherever possible.

For Charter Mark to be a worthwhile investment of time, effort and money it must have the potential to at least recover the assessment fee and the set-up costs, and it must compare well with other quality initiatives. The benefits to the organisation, however, should be worthwhile:

- less time spent on dealing with complaints

- less effort by staff to put things right
- happier customers, meaning greater usage and more income.

For those aiming to achieve the Charter Mark standard in the future, the Cabinet Office and Save the Children have been working together, looking at the way in which children and young people's needs are taken into account. They have produced a guide, including practical ideas, to help organisations using the Charter Mark criteria to focus on children and young people as service users.

To give you an idea of the range of current leisure organisation holders look at the examples below, which are taken from across the country.

The Cabinet Office maintains a database of good practice examples as part of its wider Public Sector Benchmarking Service (PSBS). The purpose is to highlight the many good things that are being done in public services in a way that allows others to learn from them. This database has a short description of each example and, most importantly, details of a person to contact to help others to learn. Use of the database, which contains over 1,250 examples, is growing rapidly. You can visit it at the Public Sector Benchmarking Service (PSBS) website: www.benchmarking.gov.uk.

A sample of Charter Mark holders

Amber Valley Leisure, East Midlands region

Littlehampton Swimming and Sports Centre, South-east region

Stour Leisure, South-east region

Waves Water Fun Centre, North-west region

Grundy Park Leisure Centre, East Anglia

Leisure Services Sports Development, East Anglia

Festivals and Entertainment Division, Cheltenham and Gloucester

---

activity
WHY IS IT NOT MORE POPULAR?

The government are obviously keen to have very many voluntary or public sector organisations take up the challenge of Charter Mark. Discuss why this might be so, and why you think many local authority leisure services departments have not taken it up or achieved the award. Maybe you could ask at your local centre – is it cost, time, knowledge, lack of incentives?

Clubmark

The aim of Clubmark is to provide more and better opportunities for children and young people to participate in sport in their local communities. The scheme, led by Sport England, working with governing bodies of sport, local authorities and other partners, provides a nationally adopted set of standards for national governing bodies of sport (NGBs). The affiliated clubs have to set and meet standards that will lead to better quality sports club provision for children and young people. Clubmark has been developed through Active Sports, which is funded through the National Lottery.

The scheme enables parents, carers and young people to quickly recognise a club that is committed to providing a quality experience.

This new important quality mark, which is also supported by the Child Protection in Sport Unit and Sports Coach UK, is promoted at local levels all around the country.

Clubmark has a range of criteria indicators and good practice standards, which clubs have to achieve. *Criterion 1: Set standards and perform well*, for example, includes:

- Children and young people are regularly involved and supported, e.g. in designing their own playground.

- The organisation benchmarks itself against others showing good practice, and makes changes where better practice is found.

In addition, Clubmark sets out standards for:

- Duty of care and child protection
- Coaching and competition
- Sports equity and ethics
- Club management.

To apply for Clubmark, clubs need to first contact their relevant NGB, such as the British Canoe Union, English Basketball Association or Rugby Football Union. Sport England also produces a resources pack for clubs trying to get accredited. The accreditation can be renewed annually through a simple self-certification scheme, showing that standards remain at the same level.

Sport England also produce a Clubmark factsheet to help those wishing to go for the award. Out-of-school clubs, for example (now used by nearly half of all children) are keen to get involved because the award gives them a good image with parents.

The importance of the award

Reports of some recent Clubmark awards are given below, to show how important they are to the clubs concerned and their local communities

Netball clubs awarded Sport England Clubmark honours

Tibberton, Shrewsbury and Drayton Junior Netball Clubs are the most recent of Shropshire's junior clubs to receive the much-coveted Sport England Clubmark awards.

The Clubmark scheme recognises clubs as safe, effective, child-friendly and committed to providing a quality experience. The award also includes recognition by the All England Netball Association CAP's accreditation programme, which is a method of examining, maintaining and improving the provision of junior club netball.

Tina Owen, organiser of Shrewsbury Netball Club, commented that the club had undertaken the accreditation process, because they felt it was important to let parents know that their children were going to get a good quality experience, and also said that it had proved a very useful learning experience for the volunteers who help out at the club.

Canoe clubs gain prestigous award

Four BCU canoe clubs have recently been awarded the Sport England Clubmark and revised BCU Top Club awards.

The Clubmark and Top Club awards recognise clubs that are safe, effective, and child-friendly and provide a varied programme of activity for young people.

Congratulations go to :

Chelmsford Canoe Club – the first to achieve both Top Community and Top Performance Club in England.

Elmbridge Canoe Club – first to achieve Top Performance Club in London and South East Region

Macclesfield and District Canoe Club – first to achieve Top Community and Clubmark awards in the North West

White Rose Canoe Club – first to achieve the Top Community and Clubmark awards in Yorkshire.

There are currently 63 BCU clubs working towards the awards.

Sutton & Epsom RFC success

Sutton & Epsom RFC has become the first sports club in Surrey to receive two awards in recognition of their junior set-up. The club was presented with the Clubmark and Seal of Approval awards at the BAA Gatwick Surrey Youth Games.

The Rugby Football Union is one of twenty national governing sports bodies to have introduced quality 'kitemarks' to assess and improve junior sports clubs.

Sutton & Epsom RFC boasts around 1000 members, two-thirds of them young people, and has twenty-two teams competing in all sorts of competitions, from local small-sided festivals to London Division One, the league below national level.

The club worked closely with officers from Surrey Rugby, Epsom & Ewell Borough Council and the Surrey Sports Partnership (SSP) to meet the criteria laid down.

Campbell Livingston, SSP's club and coach development officer, said: 'Sports clubs like Sutton & Epsom RFC are very important to the local community, and it is important that they should be recognised for their good practice.'

Holcombe Hockey Club wins two awards

Holcombe Hockey Club has been awarded the prestigious Sport England Clubmark Award and the England Hockey Clubs 1st Award to cap a season when their men's first team won promotion to the National League. Clubs achieving the Clubs 1st Award are recognised as working towards providing a safe, effective, and child-friendly hockey environment.

activity

THE BENEFITS OF CLUBMARK

Working with a partner, use the four case studies given, or some you have researched, to create a list of benefits for clubs who might be applying for the Clubmark award.

Topic 8 | Systems for stock control

Working systems are usually devised and put in place to provide information for managers, and to provide staff with procedures to follow. The information provided guides the managers' decision-making, and gives more control of daily aspects of the organisation such as sales of goods or how much stock to order.

Information technology has made such working systems easier, helping organisations to increase business efficiency and meet customer demands more effectively.

This topic will look at some stock control systems in leisure organisations, under the following headings:

- Stock control, including purchasing and sales
- Stock count
- Valuation of stock
- Electronic systems.

Stock control, including purchasing and sales

When a leisure organisation purchases goods (such as tennis rackets) or materials for manufacture (such as racket string), the quantity of purchase will normally be recorded in the stores (stock) records, e.g. '24 Wilson tennis rackets'. The individual stores records which carry this information are sometimes called 'bin cards'. Whatever form the stores records take, for each type of good, a stores record will be created, which shows the quantity purchased each time a delivery arrives, the quantity issued as sales, and the balance – the quantity now in storage.

For example – If a sports shop buys and supplies standard T-shirts for school training sessions, the stores record for March 2005 for the small size might look like the one on the right.

Stock count

At the end of an accounting period each item of actual stock must be physically counted and listed, and the amount is

then compared to the stores records. If there is a difference (variance) between the actual amount of stock and the balance on the stores record then this must be investigated. The difference will often be due to errors in the recording of purchases or in the issue of the stock. However, if there is less stock than according to the records, care should be taken to check that the stock has not been stolen.

The process described above is known as the 'stock count' and will normally take place several times a year (not just at the year-end) in order to keep control over the stock. You can probably remember not being able to shop sometimes while the retailer is 'closed for stock-taking'. The year-end stock count, however, is the most important as this is the one that will provide the stock figure that will appear in the final accounts, where overall profits (or losses) are calculated.

Before the stock can be valued, any differences between actual and recorded stock must accounted for. This is done in the form of a

T-shirts, small			Code 01335
Quantity stored at the start of the month			
Date	Purchases	Issues	Balance
1 March	Balance B/Fwd		140
4 March		60	80
10 March	100		180
15 March		80	100
24 March		40	60
27 March	100		160

Quantity of goods received

Quantity of sales made

Quantity stored at end of month

closing stock check which hopefully finds a balance, or 'reconciliation'. You can see how this process happens in the example below:

At 31 March 2005 our sports shop carried out a stock count and compared the quantity of each line of stock to the stock records. In most cases the stock quantity agreed with the stores records, but for two lines of stock in the school PE range, the shop owner found differences:

	Green T-shirt, Large	Blue T-shirt, Medium
Quantity counted	48	150
Stock Record quantity	54	126

She checked the stock records and documentation carefully and discovered the following variances:

- On 26 March, 6 green large T-shirts had been returned to the supplier because they were damaged. The value of these is due to be given back to the shop as a credit, (see page 99) but a note of this has not yet been received, and the record of them having been returned (the dispatch note) had not been recorded in the stock records.

- On 30 March, a 'goods received' note showed that 40 blue medium T-shirts had arrived from a supplier, but this had not yet been entered in the stock records.

- On 28 March, she had taken 16 blue medium T-shirts out of the stock in order to process an urgent order, and had forgotten to update the stock record.

Using these facts, she now prepares her closing stock reconciliation (see below).

Closing Stock Reconciliation 31 March 2005	
Green T-shirt, Large	**Quantity**
Stock record	54
Less: Returned to supplier	(6)
Counted	48
Blue T-shirt, Medium	**Quantity**
Stock record	126
Add missing order note 30 March	40
Less: Urgent order requisition	(16)
Counted	150

She can now use her closing stock quantities to prepare her closing stock valuation.

Valuation of stock

Once each line of stock has been counted and checked, and the quantity recorded, then each line of stock can be valued:

Quantity x Value per item = Value of stock line

Accounting procedures dictate that stock should be valued at whichever is the lower – the cost, (the full cost of replacing the stock to current levels, including delivery charges) or the net realisable value (the expected selling price of the stock, less any further costs to be incurred, such as selling or distribution costs).

An example will help. A sports top, for instance, would normally be purchased from the supplier for £30, and then resold to a customer for £40. In this case the stock will be valued at cost of £30. If, however, it is known that the sports top (which may now look out of date) could only be sold for £25, then valuing it at £30 would be overstating the value of the 'asset' (something which many companies have been accused of recently in order to increase their share price). The accounting process expects the shop to take a more prudent approach and value the sports top at the lower value – the £25 net realisable value, rather than the £30 cost. The swimming pool example, below, will show how this works in practice.

| Valuing stock at a swimming pool |

A small local swimming pool has just three lines of stock: goggles, children's floats, and shampoo. The total cost and total net realisable value (NRV) of each line is given below:

	Cost (£)	NRV (£)
Goggles	125	200
Floats	140	120
Shampoo	110	190
Total	**375**	**510**

Although the total cost of £375 is lower than the net realisable value of £510, this is not the value of the closing stock of the business. The cost and net realisable value must be compared for each individual line of stock, as follows:

	Cost (£)	NRV (£)	Stock value (£)
Goggles	125	200	125
Floats	140	120	120
Shampoo	110	190	110
Total	**375**	**510**	**355**

The stock should therefore be valued at £355, which is the total of the lower of the cost and the net realisable value for each line of stock.

STOCK CONTROL CALCULATIONS

Let's see how effective you would be at doing your stock control calculations, if you had your own small leisure business.

1. Your business has 120 units of an item of stock at the year end which cost £25.80 plus delivery charges of £1.00 per unit. This item can be sold for £28.00 per unit, but must be delivered to the customer at a further cost of £1.10 per unit.
   a) What is the cost and the NRV of this item of stock?
   b) At what value would these 120 units appear in the final accounts?

2. A small local cinema has four different stock lines:
   A – popcorn
   B – crisps
   C – cartons of drinks
   D – bags of mixed sweets
   (Each unit represents a box of 20)

Stock line	Units in stock	Cost per unit (£)	Selling price per unit (£)	Selling costs per unit (£)
A	80	12.90	20.30	0.30
B	65	14.60	15.00	0.80
C	90	19.80	30.20	0.90
D	30	17.50	18.20	1.00

What is the correct value of the closing stock?

Electronic systems

Larger leisure businesses tend to use electronic systems for stock control. Stock control has been renamed 'logistics management' by many of the top companies as part of 'supply chain' management from supplier to shop to customer. Many leisure goods are now held centrally in a warehouse and called up electronically to the points of sale, e.g. catalogues items from Argos or Index.

The whole purchasing, transport, delivery and sales sequence (logistics) has been greatly improved through electronic means:

■ Organisations with products in storage, e.g. sports goods, know exactly what is in their warehouse, where it is, and when to restock it.

■ Effective transport control keeps costs down – journeys can be planned, using software to calculate the best routes for fuel and time efficiencies. This particularly benefits companies who are making frequent deliveries, e.g. suppliers of electrical goods for home-based leisure.

■ Storage space is maximised through computer-based plans.

■ Inventories are accurate, and items can be ordered in the right quantities, with no guesswork from the staff.

■ Efficiency and customer satisfaction are both high because processes are faster and consistent.

These logistical benefits represent a powerful argument for changing from paper-driven procedures to electronic systems. But there are other business benefits too. Electronic systems can link stock control systems not only to front-office administration but also to head office, who can then monitor stock

Features and benefits of the Accord integrated logistics system

- Stock can be moved out or sold on a 'first in, first out' (FIFO) basis, movements can be tracked, and low-stock alerts given, e.g. sale of football strips.
- The speed (turnover) of fast moving goods (FMCs) and slow moving goods (SMCs) can be given, e.g. cans of soft drinks.
- Barcode technology can be employed for price and code labelling – as you see in nearly all DIY stores.
- 'Best-before dates' can be recorded, and stock removed as appropriate.

- An ongoing inventory of stock is created, and the right amount of reordering can be made – just as stocks run low.
- Self-adjusting levels of reordering can be activated – and stock control computers can be linked to suppliers' computers so that stock is replenished automatically.
- The forecasting of demand can be tracked, and reordering activated to meet the trends identified.
- Radio frequency and 'voice-activated pick ups' and orders can be made for drivers and stock workers at the warehouse.

activity

CHIPS FOR EVERYTHING

In the leisure industry, the efficient distribution of food and drink can be crucial. List five benefits that software applications can bring to the process.

turnover. Printouts, reports and the current state of stock (position statements) can all be run off at the press of a switch. Read about the Accord system (above) and the Mikrofax system (right) to help develop your understanding.

Electronic systems seem ideal for organisations who manage stock of various kinds in any volume – such as vending machine operators, fast food outlets or catalogue companies.

Uncontrolled, unbudgeted or unauthorised spending on stocks (and internal purchases too, such as maintenance supplies and consumables) can cost leisure organisations millions of pounds each year. So a software system would give much more control, offering time and money savings by automating tasks.

activity

SYSTEM FOR A SPORTS SHOP

Carry out an online search for a system of stock control that would suit a sports shop, and list the features it offers.

Features and benefits of the Mikrofax system

The entire purchasing process can be automated with the Mikrofax software system, including eProcurement. The software has been developed over 18 years, and is able to create:

- electronic requests for supplies – reminders that new stock is needed
- online approval to purchase – staff are authorised to buy in more stock
- request pages for quotes – quotes can be given for commodities
- catalogues – can display the goods pictorially
- optional website interface – links to a website can be made
- invoice processing – bills are prepared
- accounts payable details – statements of what is due are issued
- an asset register – a list of company assets can be kept.

Accounting and accounting systems

Finance is such an important part of running any leisure facility, whether it be private, public or voluntary. You need to know how financial systems work in general, and how people working in the industry account for income coming into the organisation and for payments going out. Accounting involves:

• recording business transactions in financial terms

• reporting financial information to the owner and managers of the business and other interested parties (such as shareholders or the tax man)

• advising the owners/management how to use the financial reports to assess the past performance of the business, and to make decisions for the future.

This topic will look at some accounting systems in leisure organisations, under the following headings:

■ Keeping accounting records

■ The accounting system

■ Payment methods, including direct debits, credit cards, cash and cheques.

Keeping accounting records

Financial accounting records are kept in handwritten form and, increasingly now, on computer. Computer accounting systems are sensibly backed up by handwritten records, in case of computer disasters such as total loss of data. The main record in a handwritten system is the ledger which, at one time, would be a weighty leather-bound volume, neatly ruled, into which the bookkeeper would handwrite each business transaction into individual accounts.

Computers are now relatively cheap and are used by even the smallest leisure business. The major advantage of computer accounting is that it is a very accurate method of recording business transactions. The word 'ledger' has survived into the computer age but, instead of being a bound volume, it is used to describe data files held on a computer disk.

Financial records should be maintained so that they are:

■ accurate and up-to-date

■ confidential – not revealed to people outside the business (unless authorisation is given), and revealed within the business only to those who are entitled to the information.

KEEPING ACCOUNTING RECORDS

With a partner, analyse the last two bullet points, and say why they might be important to a leisure company, e.g. a private gym.

The accounting system

The flow chart (far right) illustrates the five main stages of the accounting system. As you read through the sections that follow, referring back to the chart will remind you where you are in the whole process.

Prime documents

Business transactions in the leisure industry usually generate documents. This is often referred to as the 'paper mountain'. Computers have not really solved the problem because we still need to obtain print-outs or receipts for most financial transactions.

Sales and purchases – the 'invoice'

When a business sells goods or services it prepares an invoice (see example, above right) stating:

■ the amount owing, and when it should be paid

■ details of the goods sold or the service provided.

STEPHENSON'S SPORTS SUPPLIES
Suppliers of rackets, balls and clothing for every sport

15 High Street
Barkerville
B016 5XT

INVOICE

Invoice number: 6324
Date: 16 March 2005

Barkerville Tennis Club
Pentagon Square
Barkerville B2 3QZ

To supply of 6 tubes of competition tennis balls
@ £9.22 per tube (inc. VAT) £55.32

To supply of 3 'Winner's Cup' trophies
@ £12.80 per cup (inc. VAT) £38.40

TOTAL   £93.72

Please pay within 30 days

An invoice is prepared by the seller for:

- cash sales – where payment is immediate, whether by cash or by cheque. Note that not all cash sales will require an invoice to be prepared by the seller – shops, for instance, normally issue a 'receipt' for the amount paid.

- credit sales – where payment is to be made at a later date – normally within 30 days.

A 'debtor' is a person who owes you money when you sell on credit.

A 'creditor' is a person to whom you owe money when you buy on credit.

Return of goods – the 'credit note'
If the buyer (e.g. a sports shop) buys goods on credit from a supplier but then returns them (because they are faulty, for example) the supplier will prepare a credit note and send it to the buyer, reducing the amount of money now owed. The credit note, like the invoice, states the amount, and the goods to which it relates.

Bank transactions – 'cheques', 'BACS'
All leisure organisations need to pay in money, draw out cash and make payments. Paying-in slips and cheques are used as prime documents for bank account transactions as are documents generated by the BACS inter-bank computer payments system (e.g. for direct payments into the bank).

When all these documents have been entered into the different records, the 'final accounts' are prepared, which show how the organisation has performed.

The five main stages of the accounting system

PRIME DOCUMENTS (sources of accounting information)
- Invoices – sales and purchase
- Credit notes – sales and purchase
- Bank paying-in slips ⎫ important to record
- ⎬ detail on the
- Cheques issued ⎭ counterfoils
- BACS documents

BOOK OF PRIME (ORIGINAL) ENTRY (gathering and summarising accounting information)
- Day books (for recording sales, purchase invoices, and credit notes)
- Journal (for 'one-off' items)
- Cash books (see also double-entry)

DOUBLE-ENTRY BOOKKEEPING (recording the dual aspect of business transactions in the accounting system)
- Sales ledger – accounts of debtors (customers)
- Purchases ledger – accounts of creditors (suppliers)
- Nominal ledger – accounts for sales, purchases, expenses, capital, loans, etc and also accounts for items such as assets (things owned by the businesses)
- Cash books
    - cash book for bank and cash transactions
    - petty cash book

TRIAL BALANCE (arithmetical checking of double-entry bookkeeping)
A summary of the balances of all the accounts, which is then 'extended' to produce the final accounts

FINAL ACCOUNTS (a statement measuring profit (or loss) for an accounting period and a statement of assets, liabilities and capital at the end of an accounting period)
- Profit and loss account
and
- Balance sheet

Final accounts

The final accounts of a business comprise the 'profit and loss account' and the 'balance sheet'.

Profit and loss account

INCOME *minus* EXPENSES *equals* PROFIT

The profit and loss account of all leisure businesses calculates the profit due to the owners of the business, after the cost of purchases and other expenses (such as wages and delivery costs) have been deducted from the sales income.

The figures for these calculations – sales, purchases, and expenses of various kinds – are taken from the ledgers for sales, purchases, and cash transactions. The records are kept in a 'double-entry' system where amounts are entered twice – once as the 'receiving' transaction and once as the 'giving' transaction. This allows cross-checking at later stages – when profits and losses are being calculated, for example.

Profit and loss accounts, are always presented in a vertical format:

	income	£
minus	expenses	£
equals	profit	£

Balance sheet

The balance sheet is so called because it 'balances' in numerical (money) terms:

ASSETS *minus* **LIABILITIES** *equals* **CAPITAL**
(what a business owns) (what a business owes) (how the business has been financed)

The double-entry ledger system contains figures for:

Assets – items the business owns, which can be:
• fixed assets – items bought for long-term use in the business, e.g. premises, vehicles, computers
• current assets – items used in the everyday running of the business, e.g. stock, money owed by customers (debtors), and money in the bank.

Liabilities – items that the business owes, e.g. bank loans, and money owed to suppliers (creditors).

Capital – money or assets introduced by the owners of the business; capital is in effect owed by the business to the owner.

Balance sheets – like profit and loss accounts – are usually presented in a vertical format:

	assets	£
minus	liabilities	£
equals	capital	£

This concept is known as the 'Accounting Equation'.

P&O Interim Results 2004-05
Group profit and loss account

Group profit and loss account
for the six months ended 30 June 2004

	Six months to 30 June 2004 £m	Six months to 30 June 2003 £m	Year to 31 Dec 2003 £m
Turnover: Group and share of joint ventures (note 2)	1,673.5	1,823.1	4,137.9
Less: share of joint ventures' turnover	(554.2)	(762.4)	(1,846.9)
Group turnover	**1,119.3**	**1,060.7**	**2,291.0**
Net operating costs	(1,051.5)	(1,026.0)	(2,192.1)
Group operating profit	**67.8**	**34.7**	**98.9**
Share of operating results of: joint ventures	17.0	(6.0)	40.8
associates	28.3	16.4	35.0
Continuing operations			
Total operating profit before goodwill amortisation and reorganisation and impairment charges	121.8	48.7	221.1
Goodwill amortisation	(8.7)	(9.4)	(18.4)
Reorganisation and impairment charges	–	–	(39.8)
	113.1	39.3	162.9
Discontinued operations	–	5.8	11.8
Total operating profit (note 3)	**113.1**	**45.1**	**174.7**
(Loss)/profit on sale of fixed assets and businesses (note 5)	(72.1)	13.2	16.6
Profit on ordinary activities before interest and taxation	**41.0**	**58.3**	**191.3**
Net interest payable and similar items (note 9)	(47.1)	(55.0)	(111.3)
(Loss)/profit on ordinary activities before taxation	**(6.1)**	**3.3**	**80.0**
Taxation (note 10)	(20.7)	(8.8)	(20.8)
(Loss)/profit on ordinary activities after taxation	**(26.8)**	**(5.5)**	**59.2**
Equity minority interests	(6.5)	(3.5)	(9.2)
(Loss)/profit for the period attributable to stockholders	**(33.3)**	**(9.0)**	**50.0**
Dividends on equity and non-equity share capital	(23.8)	(34.8)	(102.5)
Retained loss for the period	**(57.1)**	**(43.8)**	**(52.5)**
Basic and diluted (loss)/earnings per £1 nominal of deferred stock (note 11)	(4.8)p	(1.6)p	6.5p
Headline earnings/(loss) per £1 nominal of deferred stock (note 11)	6.2p	(1.7)p	12.4p
Dividends per £1 nominal of deferred stock	3.0p	4.5p	13.5p

Summary Balance Sheets
as at 31 March 2004

	Group 2004 £'000	Group 2003 £'000	Company 2004 £'000	Company 2003 £'000
Fixed assets	416,212	436,809	56,963	56,963
Current assets	126,515	107,513	87	87
Creditors: amounts falling due within one year	(101,817)	(95,628)	(627)	(627)
Net current assets/(liabilities)	24,698	11,885	(540)	(540)
Total assets less current liabilities	440,910	448,694	56,423	56,423
Creditors: amounts falling due after more than one year	(57,179)	(40,666)	–	–
Provisions for liabilities and charges	(739)	(616)	–	–
Net assets	382,992	407,412	56,423	56,423
Capital and reserves				
Called-up share capital	33,715	33,715	33,715	33,715
Merger reserve	566,560	566,560	–	–
Capital redemption reserve	23,248	23,248	23,248	23,248
Other reserves	18,700	18,840	–	–
Profit and loss account	(259,231)	(234,951)	(540)	(540)
Shareholders' funds	382,992	407,412	56,423	56,423

COMPARING PERFORMANCE

All large companies have to publish their accounts every year. Find summary reports for three large leisure corporations (in your library, or go online) and compare their performances in terms of profits or losses.

WHAT'S HAPPENED HERE?

The table below sets out account balances from the books of another leisure business, just starting up.

The columns show the account balances on six dates – Date 1 to Date 6 – resulting from a series of transactions that have taken place over the time. You are to compare each set of adjacent columns, i.e. Date 1 with Date 2, then Date 2 with Date 3, and so on, and state, with figures, what accounting transactions have taken place in each case.

	Date 1 £	Date 2 £	Date 3 £	Date 4 £	Date 5 £	Date 6 £
Assets						
Equipment		2,000	2,000	2,000	2,000	2,000
Van				10,000	10,000	10,000
Bank	10,000	8,000	14,000	4,000	6,000	3,000
Liabilities						
Loan			6,000	6,000	6,000	3,000
Capital	10,000	10,000	10,000	10,000	12,000	12,000

Payment methods

Leisure organisations need to have good control over cash flow – the payments into and out of the organisation. A business cannot make payments for goods received, for example, if it has no receipts to check amounts against, and it must also exercise control over the monies received for sales. The systems used for such transactions are designed to keep control and prevent loss by accident or theft. Money received (called 'receipts' by accountants) must be recorded and banked promptly, because

- Unrecorded money can be misused.

- A cheque can be stolen, and is no use until it has been paid into the bank account.

- The records can be checked to supporting documents (e.g. remittance advice) to ensure that all receipts have been recorded.

One way of preventing loss through accident or theft is to split up duties that staff carry out with respect to finance. One person banks the money received, for example, but a separate person records it.

Till receipts

Cash registers or 'smart tills' are used in many leisure locations, where the money is handed over directly by the customer when the transaction takes place, e.g. fast food outlets, shops and entertainment venues. Most retail outlets have electronic cash registers, often registering the details of items sold using barcode readers, e.g. Beefeaters.

BALANCING THE BOOKS

Complete the missing figures for this gym:

	Assets (£)	Liabilities (£)	Capital (£)
Year 1	20,000	0	....
Year 2	15,000	5,000	....
Year 3	16,400	....	8,850
Year 4	....	3,850	10,250
Year 5	25,380	....	6,950
Year 6	....	7,910	13,250

Money received from customers

The types of money received (receipts) from customers in a leisure venue can vary, as can the timing of when it is actually paid, but all need to be 'receipted', first, for the customer as 'proof of purchase' in case the item needs to be returned, and secondly, for accounting purposes later within the organisation.

The most common types of money received are cash, cheques or plastic cards. Depending on the type of business, there are other, less usual, forms:

- Standing orders – set up with the customer's banks who automatically pay for them, e.g. for a monthly membership fee. The amount of a standing order can only be changed by the payer (the customer).

- Direct debits – payments requested by organisations from the customer's bank account, which the customer has authorised. The amount can be changed by the receiver as well (so is suitable where payments change, e.g. phone bills).

- BACS – automated banking payments, e.g. salary payments.

The timing of the 'receipts' of a business will depend on the type of business, the type of sales (credit/cash or both) and seasonal trends.

---
activity

WHAT SYSTEMS FOR THESE BUSINESSES?

Consider these three different kinds of leisure business and the receipts (payments) they would expect on an average day. Discuss what type of system would suit them best.
1. Newsagent: 500 receipts at an average of £1 each. Total = £500
2. Football merchandising shop: 50 receipts at an average of £20 each. Total = £1000
3. A leisure consultancy: 3 receipts at an average of £1500 each. Total = £4500.

Types of sales and payments

For receipt of payments by cheque, it is best to follow the procedure shown, above right.

Paying by plastic card is a convenient method and has become enormously popular. In the leisure industry plastic cards are used primarily by individuals, rather than by companies (although companies do own credit cards which are allocated to members of staff to pay their business expenses such as petrol).

Most retail outlets now use EFTPOS (Electronic Funds Transfer at Point of Sale). However, some small shops still use manual processing.

A credit card payment has three stages (see right), and involves three parties: the supplier of the goods, the cardholder and the card issuer.

---
activity

CREDIT CARD CONDITIONS

Obtain a credit card statement and assess the numerous complex conditions that apply.

Payment by cheque: checklist

Step 1
Examine the cheque. Are the following correct?
- Date (including the year)
- Payee name (person receiving the amount)
- Amount in both words and figures

Step 2
Make sure that the cheque is signed by the drawer (person signing the cheque)

Step 3
Compare the signature on the cheque with the signature on the cheque guarantee card

Step 4
Check the details on the cheque guarantee card:
- Guarantee limit and expiry date
- Name, account number and sort code

Step 5
Write the following on the back of the cheque:
- Cheque guarantee card number
- Guarantee limit and expiry date

The three stages of credit card payments

• *Stage 1. Purchase of goods from a supplier by a cardholder*

On producing his card for a supplier of goods or services, the cardholder can obtain what he requires without paying for it immediately. The supplier uses a telephone link to the card issuer to verify the authenticity of the card and the available credit level. The card issuer then authorises the supplier to proceed with the transaction.

• *Stage 2. Payment of supplier by card issuer*

The supplier recovers from the card issuer the price of the goods or services, less a commission – which is the card issuer's profit margin.

• *Stage 3. Payment of card issuer by cardholder*

At monthly intervals the card issuer sends to the cardholder a statement. The cardholder may either settle interest-free within 28 days or he may pay interest on the balance owing after 28 days. He is required to make a minimum payment, however, which differs between card issuers.

Credit card fraud is major problem for customers and suppliers. As a result, when a leisure business rings for authorisation, credit card companies may sometimes ask to speak to the customer to carry out security checks. Usually, however, verification can be done electronically very quickly.

New generation 'chip and pin' credit cards have the customer's details in an electronic chip embedded in the card. Customers no longer have to sign vouchers, but now key their PIN (personal identification number) into a terminal in order to complete a transaction.

The term 'charge card' covers such systems as American Express and Diners Club. The differences between charge cards and credit cards are:

	Credit card	Charge card
Cost	Issued free or with an annual 'membership' fee.	Enrolment fee, plus annual 'membership' fee.
Payment	Monthly or by instalments, with interest.	Full balance must be cleared monthly. No further credit.
Credit limit	Set individually, according to customer's circumstances.	No limit (in theory).

Charge cards are popular for paying business expenses so are more likely to be used by company directors. The main advantage is that they overcome the problem of the limit on cheque guarantee cards (often £50) or spending limits on credit cards (which could come into play for a business trip to a leisure conference in the USA with air fares, hotel expenses, meals, etc). The procedure for accepting payment by charge card is the same as for credit cards, except that the authorisation process is not needed.

In-house store cards are issued and operated by large retail chains such as Debenhams, Boots, Marks & Spencer, etc. where you might buy sports or leisure clothing. The cards operate in the same way as a credit card but they tend to be more expensive for the customer due to their higher interest rates, which are not always well publicised.

Debit cards are designed for customers who like paying by plastic card, but who do not always want credit. The process is usually:
1. The customer signs a voucher at the point of sale.
2. This is then processed either through a system similar to the credit card system, or through an EFTPOS system.
3. The amount of the transaction is deducted directly from the customer's bank account.

---

activity

EXPLAINING THE VARIOUS METHODS

Imagine that you are employed in the three different leisure businesses, as detailed below. In each case, a potential customer telephones you with a query about how payments may be made. State what you would say to the customer, making any assumptions about the policies of the organisation which you consider appropriate. You should explain your reasons as part of your response.
1. A city gym. The customer's query:
'I am a regular customer, and receive a bill from you each quarter. I want to continue to pay quarterly, but I don't want to go to the trouble of writing out a cheque or making a special trip (for example to my bank or the club) to pay the bill. However, I do need to know how much the bill is going to be before I am due to pay it. What method of payment would you suggest?'
2. Mail order company. The customer's query: 'I want to place an order with you for a garden swing. I don't have a bank account, building society account or credit card, so I suppose that I'll need to send you the amount due by cash through the post. Is that OK?'
3. DIY retailer. The customer's query: 'I want to call in to your store to buy a strimmer costing £34 for a friend's husband's birthday. I know that you accept cheques supported by a cheque guarantee card. If my friend makes out and signs the cheque and gives me her cheque guarantee card, could I bring the cheque and card in when I collect the machine?'

Project planning

The leisure industry is such a dynamic industry that it always has many examples of new and ongoing projects – new white-knuckle rides, new stadiums and new visitor attractions. Some projects may be quite small in scale, such as a local fair, exhibition or a fun run for charity. Whatever their size, however, all these projects need a plan to follow. The plan will have aims and objectives, a strategy for using people and resources, and a timescale for completion. The larger projects will have every last detail worked out by professionals, while the plans for the smaller ones, often run by amateurs, may be more basic.

The emphasis in this topic will be on the things that make projects work, and, bearing those things in mind, how to prepare for a project. The essential components which we will explore are:

■ Setting the parameters and aims for a project
■ Testing the project's feasibility
■ Creating a plan
■ Evaluating projects.

Setting the parameters and aims for a project

The leisure industry can boast many different examples of projects. Some are buildings, some are events and some have a mixture of elements, such as attracting participants, creating new facilities and fundraising. Examples include:

■ The new Wembley Stadium – a long-term facility project

■ London's 2012 Olympic bid – a long-term sports project

■ Sheffield Ski Village's new 'Frontier land' for children – new facilities

■ Your school or college sports day – focusing on participants

■ An annual scout camp – an occasional project for children

■ A fun run – a fundraising event for a good cause.

Before you can undertake a project of any sort, you need to gather together some basic information:

■ an aim for the project

■ what ideas might work, i.e. some options

■ the basic parameters like timescale, budget, resources and people involved.

Most projects in the leisure industry are run by a team of people, who meet regularly. The first meeting of the 'project team' will discuss the aims, options and basic parameters – perhaps in the form of a brainstorming session.

activity

YOUR FIRST PROJECT

Try this exercise with some of your classmates. You are a small events company and have been asked to stage a fashion show for a new clothing store opening in town. What would your aim be? What (realistic) objectives would you set yourselves? How long do you think it would take to plan it all? Don't worry about budgets and resources as yet.

After tackling the previous activity, compare what you decided to some of these aspects of project planning:

- An aim needs to give a clear overview for the whole project – did yours?

- Objectives need to be measurable, such as tickets sold or take-up of seats – were yours done in quantities like these – were they 'SMART'?

- Your timescale would have to be at least 3 months to allow for printing of posters, booking the venue and models, and all the logistics on the day – was yours shorter?

This type of planning needs to have two more elements added – budgets and resources – before you can really assess its viability. In any project, proper attention needs to be paid to the costing, for that will guide what the budget limits must be. At this stage some projections or forecasts would suffice, but you will eventually need to calculate detailed and accurate financial outgoings and income for the project, as part of your business plan.

You would also have to decide on what kind of resources the project needs. At this stage, an estimate of 'how many' and 'how you would find them' would suffice, e.g. if the project was to build a new changing room at a sports ground, you would have to decide on how much would be needed of everything – from the tonnes of concrete for the foundations, to the number of clothes hooks on the walls.

Professional project managers analyse all the tasks to be done and then put them into the most logical, efficient order. This process (called critical path analysis) results in a precise, detailed sequence of steps to be taken (the critical path).

Testing the project's feasibility

With your project idea agreed, now comes the task of finding out if the idea is feasible. The research tasks are best split up between the project team to cover:

- How it will be financed. There are many sources which could be used, such as a bank loan, development grant, private funding, fundraising. Your final business plan will need accurate figures.

- How much it will all cost, including materials, people and any interest payments on loans.

- What marketing will be needed, and how much it will cost.

- The costs of any administration and support systems needed for the lifespan of the project, such as temporary offices and site managers.

- What legal aspects need covering, such as insurance and safety measures.

- Financial projections of the revenue that the project will bring after completion, from the various 'income streams' – ticket sales, memberships, etc.

Researching the feasibility of a project will take some time – phoning round for quotes, contacting suppliers, trying to cover every detail, working out the costs of various tasks and estimating likely customer figures. This is not an easy task, and some large leisure projects have got it very wrong, and gone out of business as a result – Sheffield's music museum, for example. Another example, the national rock climbing centre at Ratho in Scotland, was so far over budget that it was put into receivership on the day it opened! It has, however, got a future of some sort (see below).

> ### Rock Climbing Centre fights to survive
> The centre hosted the Inter-University and UIAA World Championships in 2004, assuring wide publicity and extra customers. But whether this will help the centre meet its break-even targets is the banks' decision. Based in an old quarry outside Edinburgh, the centre is a diverse leisure venue – if somewhat remote. It creates a spectacular impression, with walls of glass and several spectator viewpoints over the mixture of quarry walls and artificial climbing walls. There is a restaurant, bar, performance rooms, an outdoor-equipment shop, and accommodation too. It's not yet clear what aspect of the project soaked up the money more than it should have, or whether someone just miscalculated visitor numbers, but clearly the centre will have to diversify to survive – or become a great white (glass) elephant of a project gone wrong!
>
> Sources: *Scottish Mountaineer* June 2004 (paraphrased) and author's visit

Decision time

The real test of feasibility is when all of this information comes back and is collated. The team must then sit down and decide whether the project is going to meet the aims, objectives and logistical parameters of the project, as set out at the start. To do this, each member of the team usually presents their resource needs, with their costs. It is likely that a great deal of debate will take place, as the resources and costs are trimmed to suit the budget and the project's objectives.

Finally, the team has to decide whether the project:

1. Is feasible, and can go ahead

2. Is not feasible, and must be dropped

3. Needs to be changed, to make it feasible

4. Has too many risks attached, and needs its parameters to be more closely defined.

Project managers will often use a 'decision tree' to help with this process (see below).

If the outcome is that the project is feasible on the basis of the preliminary research, then the next stage is to develop a project plan, which has every detail in it. The financial projections must be accurate for they may become the basis of a business plan for the future running of the facility created.

Creating a plan

A project plan is not really a complex thing. It is just a clear description of how you are going to reach each objective en route to the final completion. The plan needs to be flexible, because tasks can be delayed and deadlines not met. It should also have as much detail as possible – vague plans allow poor interpretation of what is wanted. Some sort of breakdown of tasks needs to be made, using planning aids such as flow charts, schedules, or network charts (see examples, right).

Unit 2 Working Practices in Leisure

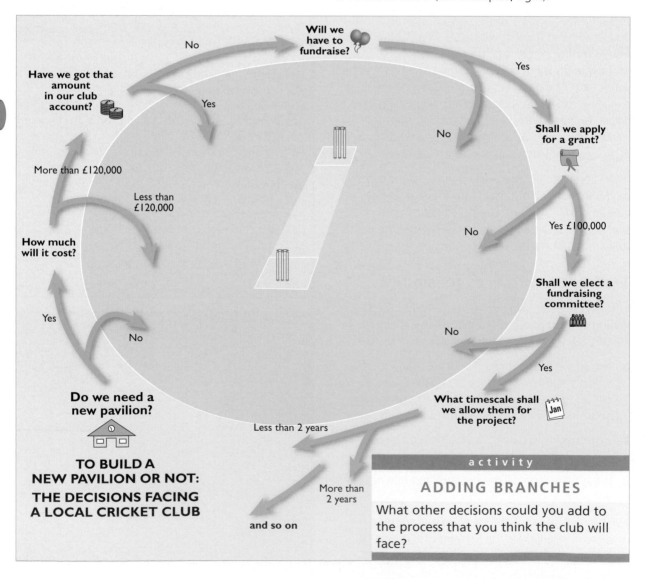

Will we have to fundraise?

No   Yes

Have we got that amount in our club account?

Yes

More than £120,000

Less than £120,000

How much will it cost?

Yes

No

Do we need a new pavilion?

TO BUILD A NEW PAVILION OR NOT: THE DECISIONS FACING A LOCAL CRICKET CLUB

Shall we apply for a grant?

No

Yes £100,000

Shall we elect a fundraising committee?

No

Yes

What timescale shall we allow them for the project?

Less than 2 years

More than 2 years

and so on

activity

ADDING BRANCHES

What other decisions could you add to the process that you think the club will face?

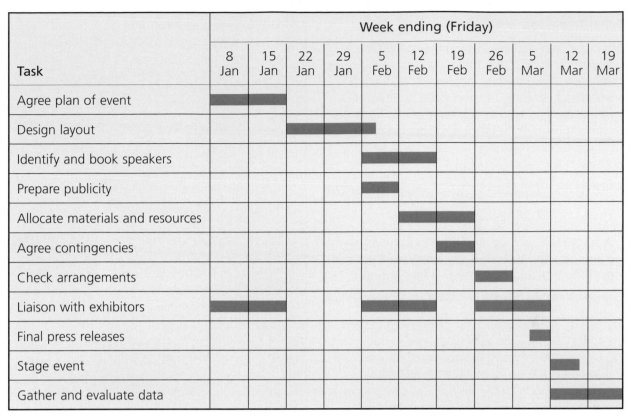

Task	Week ending (Friday)										
	8 Jan	15 Jan	22 Jan	29 Jan	5 Feb	12 Feb	19 Feb	26 Feb	5 Mar	12 Mar	19 Mar
Agree plan of event	██	██									
Design layout			██	██							
Identify and book speakers					██	██					
Prepare publicity					██						
Allocate materials and resources						██	██				
Agree contingencies							██				
Check arrangements								██			
Liaison with exhibitors	██	██			██	██	██	██	██		
Final press releases									██		
Stage event										██	
Gather and evaluate data										██	██

A schedule for a leisure industry careers event

A network chart, showing the timetabling of tasks leading up to an event

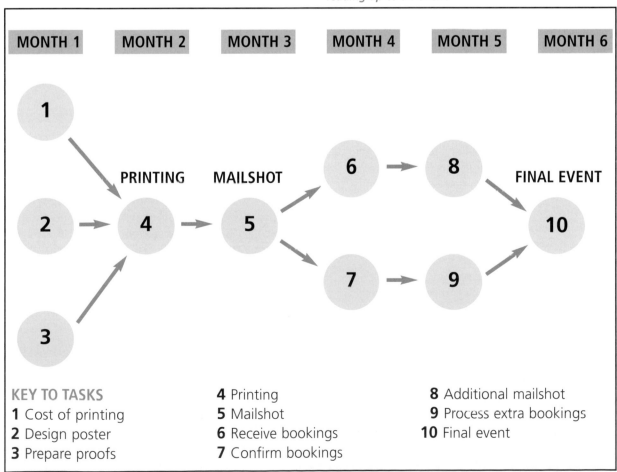

MONTH 1 **MONTH 2** **MONTH 3** **MONTH 4** **MONTH 5** **MONTH 6**

PRINTING MAILSHOT FINAL EVENT

KEY TO TASKS

1 Cost of printing	**4** Printing	**8** Additional mailshot
2 Design poster	**5** Mailshot	**9** Process extra bookings
3 Prepare proofs	**6** Receive bookings	**10** Final event
	7 Confirm bookings	

Scheduling and costing

It is common practice to allow some 'buffer time' between tasks, for things that run over schedule to be completed before the next phase starts. Extra time costs money, however, and you don't want project workers waiting round for someone else to finish, so this aspect needs to be carefully monitored to keep the progress continuous on as many fronts as possible.

activity

YOUR PROJECT PLAN

Working with a partner, and using one of the planning aids illustrated, try to create a project plan for a Christmas show or a camping trip.

Once you have your plan, with timescales and tasks allocated to people, detailed costs need to be calculated. You can carry forward the costs you researched at the feasibility stage, probably just double checking that they still hold true. Most good project managers include a 10 per cent additional amount to cover 'contingencies' – things that may happen, but cannot be predicted.

Costs can be of two types:

- Fixed costs – which are not affected by increases or decreases in activity or outputs, e.g. rents and business rates for the building

- Variable costs – which change as the activities or outputs change, e.g. more exercise classes needs more instructors.

It is easy for income calculations to be over-optimistic. Realistic estimates and careful costing are needed from the start, followed up by ongoing monitoring.

The technique of 'marginal costing' uses costs to forecast profits from the sales levels expected in the future. It is based on calculating the difference between the final selling prices of the goods or services and the variable costs needed to produce them. The formula is simple and shows the final 'contribution' that each unit – seat, bed, fee, or product – will make to the profits.

> CONTRIBUTION *equals* SELLING PRICE (per unit) *minus* VARIABLE COSTS (per unit)

The example (see box) shows how marginal costing would work in practice.

Marginal costing example

A manufacturer making skateboards decides to extend their premises through a £16,000 building project, to allow them to make an extra 3,000 boards per year, selling at £24 each. With variable costs of £15 per unit, and fixed costs of £10,000 per year. We can deduce that:

Contribution is £24 - £15 = £9. Therefore for each board sold, £9 can go towards paying off the fixed costs and the building costs.

The extra sales revenue will have to cover building costs, fixed costs, variable costs and give a profit as well – once the break-even point has been passed. To calculate this break-even point, the organisation has to:

divide the building costs plus fixed costs by the unit contribution.

$$\text{Break-even point} = \frac{\text{total costs}}{\text{unit contribution}}$$

In our case £16,000 + £10,000 = £26,000 divided by £9 = 2889 skateboards.

The sales value at the break-even point is 2889 x £24 = £69,336. In other words, if the company makes its extra 3000 boards and sells 2889 of them within the first year, it will earn enough to pay for those boards' variable costs, the fixed costs of producing them and the cost of building the extension. If it sells all 3000, then the extra sales will help to produce a modest profit. The real profit, however, will come in the second and subsequent years, when there will be no building costs to pay for.

activity

PRACTISE MARGINAL COSTING

Read through the marginal costing example, and then make similar calculations for a company called 'Awards' which makes sports trophies and medals for sale to shops around the UK. It is hoping to extend its factory at a cost of £20,000, and to sell an extra 3,000 awards per year as a result, at £10 per award. Its variable costs are £6 per unit and its fixed costs are £4,000 per year. Will the extension be viable and give them a profit – is it worth doing?

These are quite simple cost calculations – but many smaller leisure businesses do not make them at all, or they make them badly. As a result their project fails to make money, or fails completely – and may even put the organisation out of business.

There are many software packages available to help owners and managers predict the 'risk' that is inherent in this type of project. For very large projects a framework is created, using computer programmes such as PRINCE 2. For projects in the leisure industry with multiple aspects, such as a waterside development or a regeneration scheme, there are software packages available that are designed to deal with several related projects.

During the implementation phase of the project, constant 'monitoring and control' must be carried out – checking that actual costs are in line with projections. Most of the sub-areas of a project will have their own budgets, with someone monitoring and controlling spending. Adjustments might have to be made within a sub-area – by substituting cheaper materials, for example, or adjustments might have to be made on a larger scale – by moving money from one sub-area to another. Despite all this monitoring, overspending on projects is all too easy, even on the best planned projects, such as the Millennium Dome or the new Wembley Stadium.

Evaluating projects

The success of a project is judged by assessing whether the objectives that were agreed at the beginning of the whole process have been met. This is partly why the objectives had to be 'measurable' – so that they could eventually be compared with the actual outcomes. A project will have different kinds of outcomes, concerning:

■ finance

■ tasking

■ use of resources

■ teamwork.

The financial evaluation, the most important, should be relatively clear. When the completed project is up and running, all the actual costs, revenues and profits can be compared with the original estimated, forecast and projected figures.

Evaluating whether the tasking has been a success involves deciding whether all the tasks allocated to teams or individuals were completed. Where a task was not completed well or on time, further analysis may produce lessons that will make things easier next time.

Evaluating the use of resources really means judging whether the resources were used 'effectively'. Were they all used well – or was there some wastage, and if so, why? Likely explanations for wastage or shortfalls might be found in the original calculations of what was needed, or in the figures for breakages and losses.

Teamwork is probably the least tangible outcome to measure. There are, however, observable signs of effective teamwork:

■ Communication is good

■ Decisions are reached quickly and amicably

■ Tasks are completed on time

■ There is a pride in the work done.

Signs of ineffective teamwork include:

■ Arguments and absenteeism

■ Tasks are incomplete or poorly completed

■ Standards are not met.

---

activity

PLANNING SOME EVALUATIONS

Decide, in conjunction with a colleague, how you would evaluate the following leisure projects:
• The building of a new multiple games area (a MUGA)
• The refurbishment of an old theatre
• A sports development project for disadvantaged children
• An Easter parade in a small town.

To wind up a project, a 'final report' is usually submitted. This sums up the performance of the project, reporting on each stage, each element, all the outcomes and a final evaluation. Analysis of what did not go well is included – allowing teams to learn from their mistakes and improve on their project management next time round.

Membership and ticketing systems

Many leisure organisations with a base of regular 'members' (such as theatres, football clubs or golf clubs) have installed electronic membership and ticketing databases. A database allows the organisation to monitor usage, detect trends and carry out mailshots more effectively – all part of the organisation's marketing activities.

A number of firms have software packages on the market which will carry out a range of membership and ticketing tasks. This topic investigates a few of these systems, highlighting their capabilities, user-friendliness and any issues with training or installation, under the following headings:

■ Membership systems – key features, advantages and disadvantages
■ Ticketing systems – key features, advantages and disadvantages

Membership systems

Membership systems for small clubs may just be paper records, such as the players' names and addresses kept in a book, but as the size of the club increases there is a point at which electronic records become more effective. Most large organisations in the leisure industry switched to electronic systems long ago, and in this topic we shall take a mostly electronic view of membership and ticketing systems.

Club managers who use membership systems (and therefore know a lot about their clients) are at a great advantage over their rivals, because they can use this information to maintain and even increase business. Research shows that:

■ each year, as many as 40 per cent of customers are likely to not renew their club membership

■ it costs six times as much to get a new customer as it does to keep an existing one.

Customer retention is therefore the foundation of successful leisure and sports organisations today. Happy members are also likely to recommend the club to their friends and family, and it has been shown that even a small increase in members (as little as 5 per cent) can double some clubs' profits.

Reasons why members or fans leave

1. Failure to receive enough attention, guidance or benefits (e.g. weight loss or fitness)

2. Lack of proper support in use of the club or equipment

3. Poor maintenance, design, equipment, facilities, food, or parking

4. Unfriendly atmosphere – too many children, too little entertainment, boring matches

5. Little value added to their experiences, health or enjoyment.

The key to all of this is customer satisfaction. The critical time for any leisure organisation operating a membership scheme is the first year of membership – or the first few games for a fan. This is the period during which they will decide whether to stay and renew their membership, or let it lapse and move on. Those who decide to give up usually do so for a reason (see box above).

The FitLinxx membership system has a feature called 'Attrition Urgency Ranking' which identifies those members in need of attention before they give up, ranking members as high, medium and low risks.

A membership system has to be able to capture customers' needs, wants, habits and preferences, while the manager has to have the ability to interpret the information, and to produce products and services that will meet with a positive customer response.

A membership database is, in effect, a 'customer profiling system' which should enable operators in the leisure industry to develop and maintain a personal relationship with their members. This 'relationship marketing' is clearly a key tool in any marketing strategy.

activity

RELATIONSHIP MARKETING

Through a class discussion, identify other sectors of the economy which try to build relationships with their clients.

Key features

What can be achieved through the combination of a membership database and marketing strategies will depend upon two things – what information can be gathered, and how that information can be used.

In 1995 two researchers, Irwin and Sutton, suggested that there are four important features that a customer profile system (CPS) needs to develop, which still hold good today:

1. Addressability – the CPS provides communication with every identifiable customer.

2. Consumer purchasing histories – attendance patterns and purchasing behaviour can be monitored.

3. Flexibility – customers can be 'segmented' for targeted mailshots.

4. Accountability – the number of members, customers or fans can be quantified.

After building the database, the leisure organisation can soon start creating a marketing strategy. This might include surveys, focus groups, promotion of events, tracking of purchases and habits, and giving the organisation some benchmark or baseline figures. The membership database then becomes part of the quality system for the whole organisation.

With the correct kind of management it can go on to be used for increasing business, by:

- introducing new programmes or events and products

- determining why current products or services are not selling or being taken up

- gaining more information about existing customers and tracking down reasons for non-renewals.

Electronic membership systems can easily be linked, via the internet, to the whole new electronic business world. The growth of 'eCommerce' or 'eBusiness' presents a new selling and buying medium, particularly for leisure goods and services. Powerful search engines can connect potential customers with a range of leisure organisations worldwide who are 'eMarketing' their products and services.

Advantages

The advantages in general are speed, accuracy, reliability, the volume of information that can be held, flexibility, quality assurance and control of access. In addition, a staff database can also be created.

A review of the electronic membership schemes currently available highlights a number of advantages for leisure organisations:

- Software can be made specific for certain types of leisure organisation. For example, the 'Enterprise' range includes packages for golf clubs, among others. This gives tailored solutions for subscriptions, member profiling, account histories, letters and email.

- The frequency and quality of internal members' communications can be much improved. For example, how you communicate with captains, committee members, teams and players can be made different for every type of sports club.

- Many systems also include tracking capabilities, access control or ID-card production.

- Filters can be installed which give you birthday/anniversary data for special mail outs or offers.

- Clubs can provide an online match service through internet links to members and fans.

- 'Smart card' season tickets can be created.

- Databases allow more interesting ways of presenting information, e.g. through graphics.

- Software can crunch numbers faster.

- Lapsed clients can still be contacted from time to time

- The organisation can respond to changes in the market much more quickly.

111

Topic 11 Membership and ticketing systems

One club which has upgraded its system (Romsey Golf Club), reports that it can now run its subscription renewals at the touch of a button – for 400 members. The club is also linked to six other clubs and they have reciprocal playing arrangements, which can be booked online in Hampshire, Dorset, the Isle of Wight, East Sussex and Oxfordshire.

Disadvantages

For many small and medium-sized leisure organisations the initial cost can be a formidable barrier – the costs of purchase, installation and training, including the cost of staff time. Organisations must decide at what point it becomes more economical to make the change from paper to an electronic system. Having decided, many managers may have to 'sell' the system to their staff, some of whom may not be 'computer literate'. Some staff may even feel slightly threatened by a new system.

The manager then has to be able to make the software gather what they need and then be able to

Systems can't do everything

Forrester Research reports that almost two-thirds of customer relations systems did not work effectively, because managers were over-reliant on the software and did not always address the wider business issues. It must be remembered that systems and software are only tools – they won't, by themselves, turn dissatisfied customers into happy ones.

The recommendation from GJA Communications is to give the organisation's whole customer relationship programme (CRP) a 'health check' itself, from boardroom to operatives. A good CRP should appear throughout the organisation – at all levels and in many forms – in the organisational culture, its mission statement, and its procedures.

Some of the common problems that trip up CRPs are 'the lure of technology', inappropriate applications and poor internal communications. CRPs should be about using common sense and giving a good service. The interface with customers is crucial – not through an electronic interface, but person to person. Examples might include: at reception, in classes, even chance encounters, or when dealing with complaints and problems.

Source (paraphrased): *Leisure Management*, April 2002

interpret it correctly. Much time (and money) can be lost if this task is not right first time around.

Some online connections may not be entirely secure, and access will have to be controlled to prevent information being misused. The Data Protection Act allows all people (including customers) to know and correct information that is stored about them.

Leisure organisations also have to take care that they do not 'depersonalise' their operations when switching to electronic systems (see report, below). Talking to members 'face to face' is going to become even more important, rather than having staff tucked away in an office working on their PCs. Leisure, after all, is a people-focused industry.

Ticketing systems

Ticketing systems have been widely taken up by leisure organisations across the industry – stadiums, cinemas, theatres, event venues – anywhere where large crowds are to be involved and their access controlled. UCI cinemas is one example (see right).

Theatres are keen to have electronic ticketing systems which can be linked to membership systems, as well as manage the box office. Most of these systems are called 'venue management' packages, and would be equally appropriate for stadiums. Most new stadiums

have this type of technology linked to their security systems too, e.g. in Newcastle and Hull, and the new Arsenal and Wembley stadiums.

Operators can also 'outsource' their ticketing operations if the installation, training and set-up costs are too great.

Key features

Most of the ticketing systems are compatible with the other systems already used by leisure organisations – membership databases, accounting systems, etc. Key features include:

- Seating plan display
- Single and season ticket sales
- Monitoring of reserved and general admissions
- Booking over the internet
- Ticket printing and re-sales.

Advantages

Like any electronic system, ticketing systems are fast and reliable, and can handle vast volumes of information. Possibly the greatest advantage is the connection to internet sales and eBusiness. Audiences, fans and visitors now expect to be able to buy tickets direct on the internet. The savings on operating costs (e.g. mailing) are easy to identify, and the systems bring access to new markets too. All this should lead to greater customer satisfaction and eventually more profit.

---

activity

ELECTRONIC SYSTEMS IN USE

Working with a partner, try to identify or visit a local cinema, theatre, stadium or entertainment venue which has an electronic system and assess its capabilities. Ask the staff how easy it is to use and compare your findings with those of other partnerships.

> ### Automated ticketing system for UCI
>
> UCI cinemas, jointly owned by Paramount and Universal, is one of the leading cinema chains in Europe. As part of its strategy for continuing customer service improvement, UCI decided to opt for an automated ticketing system, for 'thefilmworks' in Manchester. A reliable and well tested system was needed which could facilitate the purchase and collection of tickets and the fully automated approach fitted well with the ethos of the modern multiplex venue. They selected a self-service, point-of-sale system which is located in terminals, using a software package from 'Smart Media'. The system consists of:
>
> - an automated till, with integrated credit and debit card authorisation software
> - integration with the existing UCI system
> - installation and operational servicing
> - remote monitoring devices
> - the capability to be upgraded and developed.

A website presence linked to a ticketing system reinforces brand awareness, and gives the ticket buyers:

- real-time access and purchasing (no delays)
- a seating plan, or even a virtual tour
- a chance to ask questions.

For the venue, a website brings a global presence (important for the largest venues hosting the biggest stars, e.g. Sheffield or London Arenas, the SEC and NEC, Albert Hall or Cardiff's Millennium Stadium).

Disadvantages

Many of the points made in the disadvantages section of memberships systems would apply here, but if we include the disadvantages of the internet connection a few others can be highlighted:

- Not everyone has access to the internet
- Systems can crash, leaving you with no service at all
- Online sales transactions may be open to fraud.

---

activity

ANY MORE DISADVANTAGES?

Can you add three more disadvantages to the list which could affect a small venue such as a football club in a lower division, a country museum or a visitor attraction?

How UNIT 2 is assessed

This unit is externally assessed. The format will be a 1½-hour written exam, using a question-and-answer booklet. The booklet, provided by Edexcel, will consist of short-answer and longer-answer questions. You should aim to be ready to sit the exam in January and/or June.

The Edexcel website – edexcel.org.uk – will have more guidance on external assessment, including specimen papers and example answers, or you can get more information from your school or college.

The exam will use case studies relating to the three areas that the unit focuses on – safety, quality, and business systems – which go together in the leisure industry to make 'effective working practices'.

Knowledge, understanding and competence will have to be shown in a practical way, so you will need to have first-hand experience of the relevant aspects in real working conditions.

To prepare for your assessment you will need to research a range of aspects about working practices and keep a record of your findings – in a 'revision portfolio' perhaps – in such a way that they will be easy to revise as the exam date approaches. The headings (right) should help you organise your revision portfolio.

1. Safe working practices

You need to be aware of the 'key intentions' of the following acts, how they are 'implemented' in a facility, and 'who enforces them'.

Key intentions
- Health and Safety at Work Act 1974 – general safe practices
- European Directives 1992 (the six-pack) – specific safe practices
- COSHH Regulations 1994 – for handling dangerous substances
- RIDDOR Regulations 1995 – for reporting accidents and diseases
- Health and Safety (First Aid) Regulations 1981– for situations at work
- Fire Safety and Safety at Places of Sport Act 1987 – for halls and stadiums
- Food Safety Act 1990 – in canteens and cafés
- Children Act 1989 – while on sports activities
- Data Protection Act 1998 – for personal information
- Working Time Regulations 1998 – for employees.

Implementation issues
- Inspections – of premises
- Training and development – for staff
- Security of property, possessions and data – on premises
- Staff and visitor safety from abuse and violence
- Risk assessments – all areas of a facility.

Enforcement
- The Health and Safety Commission – who make the regulations
- The Health and Safety Executive – who inspect
- Local Authorities and other public services – Environmental Health or the Police who enforce.

You must also keep up to date with new legislation that might supersede older Acts, e.g. Information Act 2005 and Age Discrimination Act 2006.

Paper Reference (complete below)
Centre No.
Candidate No.
Surname
Initial(s)
Signature

Examiner's use only

Team Leader's use only

Paper Reference(s)
6967
Edexcel GCE
Leisure Studies
Advanced Subsidiary
Unit 2: Working Practices in Leisure

Time: 1 hour 30 minutes

Question Number	Leave Blank
1	
2	
3	
4	

Materials required for examination
Calculator

Items included with question papers
Nil

Instructions to Candidates
In the boxes above, write your Centre Number and Candidate Number, your surname, initial(s) and signature.
The Paper Reference is shown at the top of this page, check that you have the correct question paper.
Answer ALL the questions in the spaces provided in this booklet.

Information for Candidates
There are 12 pages in this question paper. All blank pages are indicated.
The total mark for this paper is 90. The marks for individual questions in the parts of questions are shown in round brackets, eg (2)

Advice to Candidates
You are reminded of the importance of clear English and careful presentation in your answers.

Total

Turn over

This publication may only be reproduced in accordance with London Qualifications Limited copyright policy.
©2004 London Qualifications Limited.

Printer's Log No.
N0001A

N 0 0 0 1 A

edexcel

UA015763 – Specimen papers with mark schemes – Edexcel GCE in Leisure Studies (Single Award) – Issue 1 – October 2004   1

Specimen exam papers are available from the Edexcel website – edexcel.org.uk

2. Quality systems

You need to be aware of a 'range of awards and standards' , their 'fundamental requirements' and have working examples of 'organisations and practices'.

Range of awards and standards and fundamental requirements

- Quest – for customer standards
- Investors in People – for staff and business performance
- ISO 9001 – for products and services
- Charter Mark – for local authorities
- Clubmark – for sports clubs.

Organisations and practice

For all of these awards and standards you need to be able to report on organisations that have achieved them, how the process is managed and the benefits to the organisations from achieving them.

3. Business systems

You need to know 'how systems work' and their 'operational functions', and 'carry out some calculations' yourself.

The systems and how they work

- Systems for Financial accounting – how they work and what they are for
- Stock control – particularly electronic versions for purchasing and sales
- Payment methods – both electronic and paper for credits, debits and paper transactions
- Project planning methods – for forecasts of outgoings and incomings.

(In your exam you will be required to complete some simple financial tasks.)

Operational practices

- Membership systems – the range and operational capabilities
- Ticketing systems – key features and operational capabilities.

You may also be asked about the advantages and disadvantages of both.

Be prepared

Over and above these requirements, you need to know what the format, structure and duration of the test will be, and any rules or regulations which apply. Use and understanding of appropriate terminology will be important, and you will need to plan your revision to be ready for the exam. Your school or college should help you with all of these aspects by arranging visits and work experience to support your research.

They should also help you clarify the marking criteria for the assessment, but this will always be based on:

Knowledge and understanding: 25–35%

Application of knowledge, skills and understanding: 25–35%

Research and analysis: 20–30%

Evaluation: 10–20%.

The main focus for any leisure organisation will always be ensuring that customers want and, therefore, buy its products and services. This means first working out who their customers are, and then identifying their needs and expectations. This applies whether the organisation operates to make a profit or is non-profit making.

Leisure organisations are continually striving to improve their products and services in order to meet the changing needs of their customers. One of the main ways organisations encourage customers to come to them, rather than a competitor, is to provide excellent customer service.

This unit explores the various ways in which leisure organisations identify and meet their customers' needs. It also looks at the ways in which they continually strive to improve their level of customer service. In particular we will investigate:

■ The leisure customer
■ Operational aspects related to the leisure customer
■ Marketing activities related to the customer
■ Dealing with leisure customers.

Customer service is very much a team effort, and it is vital that all team members recognise the important contribution that they are expected to make. This is why many leisure organisations provide staff with training in customer service skills. If you have a part-time job in the industry you will probably have received training and will, therefore, be aware of some of the important aspects of customer service.

Providing excellent customer service is of particular importance in the leisure industry where, with many organisations providing similar products or services, it is often the quality of customer service that distinguishes one from another. Good customer service leads to customer loyalty, which in turn increases repeat business as customers will want to come back again, as well as encouraging their friends to visit.

Before you go on to the first topic consider the following ideas:

■ What makes you want to go back to an organisation that you have used?
■ To what extent are the staff a part of your desire to return?
■ What would put you off using an organisation again?

The Leisure Customer

Topic 1 Customer service and quality

The term customer service refers to all elements of the customer interface and includes all direct and indirect contact with the customer, as well as the products, services, systems and strategies that support the customer service process. In this context it involves the concept of 'customer care' or 'caring for customers'.

The attitude and behaviour of staff is the foundation for all excellent customer service. This means that staff really have to care about their customers and try to anticipate and satisfy their needs. It is also vital that the leisure organisation has a clear idea about the quality of the service that it offers to its customers.

In this first topic we explore what is meant by the term 'customer' and the importance of quality in customer service. In particular we look at:

- **Internal customers**
- **External customers**
- **Customer service quality**

Internal customers

We begin by looking at how staff should treat each other. This is because the way in which you treat your internal customers has a direct bearing on the quality of service that the 'paying' (or external) customer receives. Internal customers are members of staff or outside suppliers who contribute towards the service provided to external customers. They include:

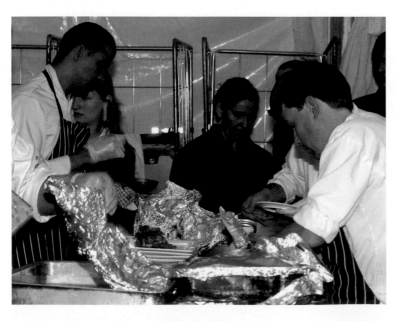

- **Colleagues.** These are the people with whom you work directly and who have a similar status to you.

- **Management and supervisors.** Most employees have a direct line manager in the organisation – a supervisor, head of department or manager.

- **Staff teams.** These are groups of staff who form a team to undertake specific functions or jobs. For example, a leisure centre may have a health and safety team comprising staff from different departments. Many hotels have a fire evacuation team who work together to evacuate the building if the fire alarm sounds.

  - **Employees.** If you are in a supervisory position you will have staff for whom you are responsible.

  - **Staff** in other functional departments or organisations who do not work directly with you but who contribute to the job that you do. For example, the personnel, finance, administration and maintenance departments in a local authority provide services to employees in the authority's leisure facilities.

- **Outside organisations.** Many leisure staff rely on other organisations to provide services that contribute to the overall product and service offered. For example, a hotel will have a number of outside suppliers who provide food, beverages, cleaning materials, linen, etc. Maintaining a good relationship with the supplier's staff is an important part of good internal customer service.

It is important for organisations to be able to provide effective customer service to internal customers, in order to establish good working relationships between all of those involved in providing products and services to external customers. The most successful leisure organisations are those that have a reputation for treating their staff well. Staff who are treated well will feel valued and will be more motivated to do their job effectively, which means that external customers will receive a far higher level of service. In addition, staff are more likely to remain loyal to their organisation, which in turn reduces the costs incurred by a high staff turnover.

---

activity

TERMS AND CONDITIONS

Below is a description of some of the terms and conditions offered to all part-time staff at a national chain of fast food restaurants.

- All part-time staff are guaranteed a set number of hours per week on the same days/shifts and issued with a contract stating this.

- Free uniforms are provided.

- Staff are entitled to set breaks with free food and a drink.

- Staff who work later than 10:00 p.m. are entitled to a free taxi home if they do not have their own car.

- All staff receive 20 days paid holiday per year.

- Full training is given before and during employment – with a wage increase being awarded once staff have completed all of the company's training programme.

- There is an 'Employee of the Month' scheme, which provides a £25 bonus to the employee who has demonstrated the best customer service.

Ask all members of the group who have or have had a part-time job to list the terms and conditions that they were offered. As a group, decide which of their employers provided the best internal customer service.

External customers

External customers are the people who actually buy or use an organisation's products and services. There are many ways of categorising external customers, depending to a large extent on the type of organisation and the nature of its business. Common methods of categorising types or groups of customers include by:

- individual
- group
- age
- culture
- language spoken
- specific needs, such as wheelchair access, sensory disabilities and people with young children.

In the next topic we will look at the specific needs and expectations of each of these types of customers. Before we do this, it is helpful to explore what is meant by each type.

Individuals and groups

When distinguishing between types of customers, it is common to classify them according to whether they are on their own or form part of a group. Some leisure organisations, such as fitness centres, are clearly going to attract more individuals than groups. However, it is important to recognise that although customers may use a product or service on an individual basis, they may also become part of a group. For example, some customers going to an aerobics class may hope to meet and socialise with others, whilst others may appreciate the fact that they are on their own and prefer to be treated individually. The huge increase in spa facilities and resort hotels has been particularly popular with individual customers who appreciate the opportunity to spend time on their own being pampered. Likewise, businessmen and women tend to be individual customers.

Other leisure products may predominantly attract groups rather than individuals. Few people go to a theme park on their own, preferring, instead, to go with friends or family or as part of an organised excursion.

Many organisations try to identify the specific types of individuals and groups using their products and services in order to provide a level of service that meets their needs and expectations.

People of different ages

Many leisure organisations promote specific facilities and services for people of different ages. For example, theatregoers tend to be in the 45+ age bracket, whereas young people are targeted through many council-run sports courses during the school holidays. The age of customers can be broken down into:

- children: babies, toddlers, older children, teenagers;
- adults: young adults, middle-aged adults, senior citizens.

However, it should be remembered that customers will often be in the company of friends or relatives, so that a group may comprise a combination of ages. Some common combinations are:

- parents with young children and/or babies
- parents with teenage children;
- adults with grandchildren
- adults with senior citizen parents.

Different cultures

It is often important to recognise types of customer by their cultural background in order to provide them with effective customer service. Cultural background influences people's traditions, tastes, preferences and opinions and it will therefore have an impact on the type and level of service they need and expect. For example, some cinemas show films in different languages to cater for the demands of large ethnic populations in their areas.

As with different age groups, the cultural background of customers is useful in identifying their needs, but it is equally important not to make assumptions based on culture. At best, this may result in customer dissatisfaction; at worst, it may offend and upset the customer.

Language

Foreign visitors are becoming an increasingly important part of the UK leisure market. Many such visitors may speak little or no English, but will expect staff to be able to deal with their needs despite the language barrier. Large organisations often employ multi-lingual staff to communicate with non-English-speaking visitors.

Specific needs

Some customers have specific needs that may require special customer service in addition to that provided to meet the general needs of customers. These include:

- sensory disabilities such as visual impairment, hearing impairment or speech impairment.

- mobility problems such as the need for a wheelchair, zimmer frame or walking stick.

- literacy and/or numeracy learning difficulties.

- dietary requirements such as vegetarianism, nut allergies or religious restrictions.

- people with babies or young children.

Following the introduction of the Disability Discrimination Act (1995), it is now a legal requirement for all organisations to provide appropriate products and services for customers with a disability. However, most leisure organisations have always welcomed customers with specific needs and tried to ensure that their needs are met.

activity

TYPES OF CUSTOMERS

Look at the leisure organisations listed in the table below. In pairs, complete the table by listing the main types of customers that use each organisation. You will find that some of them attract a wide range of different customers.

ORGANISATION	TYPES OF CUSTOMERS
Manchester United Football ground	
Marriot hotels	
Legoland	
Ascot racecourse	
Pizza Hut	
Madame Tussaud's	
Vue cinemas	

When you have completed the table discuss the following:

1. Which organisations are likely to deal with the most non-English-speaking visitors and why?

2. Which organisations are unlikely to attract many individual customers and why?

3. Which organisations are likely to list families with young children amongst their main types of customers and why?

4. Which organisations are likely to attract individual businessmen and women and why?

5. In what situations would each of the organisations need to be concerned about customers with food allergies?

Customer service quality

When considering the issue of quality in customer service, it is important to realise that the term 'quality' does not mean 'the best'. Quality means that the products and services provided meet the standards that the organisation sets and that the customer expects. In this way, a small privately owned visitor attraction can be equally as successful in meeting their quality standards as a major attraction like Thorpe Park. Three issues are particularly important in terms of quality:

1. The organisation should have a clear idea about the quality standards that they are aiming to achieve.

2. These standards should be clearly communicated to the customer.

3. The organisation should continually monitor service delivery to ensure that the standards are being met.

In later topics we look at some examples of service level standards and the ways in which leisure organisations monitor quality.

activity

THE STANDARDS YOU EXPECT

Think of three different leisure organisations that you use. Explain:

1. What standards you expect from each in terms of customer service.

2. The extent to which these standards are always met.

3. Examples of when the standards have not been met.

Topic 2 | Providing for different types of customers

In the previous topic we identified the different types of customers who buy leisure products and services. We now look at the specific needs of each of these types of customer and how leisure organisations provide a service that meets their needs:

- individuals
- groups
- people of different ages
- people from different cultures
- non-English speakers
- people with specific needs

Individuals

People use leisure products on their own for a variety of reasons:

- They may have no option: a single person going to the cinema on their own.

- It may be a conscious choice: personal time spent visiting an art gallery or having a quiet drink in a pub.

- It may be a natural part of another activity: a businesswoman using a hotel's leisure club whilst staying there on business.

- It may even be unintentional: being stood up by friends after arranging to meet at a restaurant.

To a large extent, the reason why a customer is on their own will determine their needs and expectations. Those who are on their own through choice will often expect to be left to enjoy their own company – although this does not mean that they will not expect good service! Being able to judge when a customer wishes to be left alone is as important a part of customer service as being able to identify when they require service. A guest avidly reading a newspaper in a hotel lounge, probably does not want the waiter who brings his coffee to launch into a long conversation about the weather.

Conversely, customers who are not on their own through choice may welcome a higher level of social interaction. For example, an elderly widow taking an evening class in pottery might expect the tutor to spend time chatting to her and to introduce her to other members of the class.

A further consideration with many individual customers is that they may feel apprehensive about being on their own. This may be due to inexperience: an elderly person taking an exercise programme at a sports centre for the first time may worry that he will not know what to do, what to wear or what the other customers and staff will be like. Customers with these sorts of concerns need a lot of patience and reassurance as well as accurate and helpful information.

Other customers, a businesswoman staying on her own in a hotel for instance, may have concerns about safety and security. Many hotels have recognised this problem and now provide facilities such as 'women only' bedroom floors, peep-holes in bedroom doors and close monitoring of telephone calls to individual women's rooms.

activity
CUSTOMER NEEDS

You work as a receptionist in a sports centre and the customer described below has come to you to book an exercise class. Identify what you think are the main needs and expectations of the customer and how you could meet them.

Linda Balham (48 years old) has recently separated from her husband, and her three adult children have all moved away from home. She has decided that she would like to start going to an exercise class to get fit and meet new people. She has never been to a class before and is embarrassed that she does not even know what many of the classes, such as Tai Chi and Spinning, involve. She is also concerned about the safety aspect of using the car park during the dark winter evenings.

activity
THE THACKRAY MUSEUM

The Thackray Museum in Leeds is an interactive museum based on the history of health, disease, and treatments. It offers a number of educational days to schools and colleges, such as the one described below.

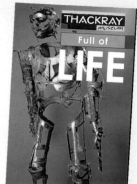

In pairs, discuss what you think the needs and expectations of a group of 20 primary school children and three teachers would be. Then identify any individual needs and expectations that the staff at Thackray might need to deal with.

Victorians Alive!
A taught session available for
Key Stages 1 & 2
Spend your day as a Victorian character at the Thackray Museum. Explore time packages of objects relating to six of the characters from the streets of 1840 Leeds. Build up a picture of their lives from the artefacts and documents. Discover where you live and work. What happens when you become ill and decide whether to see a doctor, chemist or the quack? And can you afford your treatment? Return to the present day and see what your decision, treatment and fate would be now.

Groups

One of the problems encountered when dealing with groups of people is satisfying all of their individual needs, for although they may have chosen to experience a leisure product or service as part of a group, customers may also expect some personal recognition and attention. For example, a visitor on a guided tour of a stately home may well have particular interests and questions that the tour guide will need to deal with on a personal level. Likewise, children on a football coaching week will expect the coach to speak to them personally and answer their specific questions. Members of staff must try to deal with the general needs of a group by providing advice and information, whilst also recognising the individual needs of members of the group.

People of different ages

Generally speaking, the formality of the way in which customers are dealt with increases with age. Saying, "Hi, young man that's a great smile!", is appropriate for a 3-year-old boy, but hardly fitting for a 60-year-old man! However, we need to be careful not to make assumptions about customers' needs and expectations based purely on their age. A 13-year-old may be equally offended by being offered a children's menu as an active 70-year-old who is offered a bridge class when he was hoping to take up karate!

Most leisure organisations recognise that customers of different ages will have different needs. Providing for the needs of families with young children is a key issue and, consequently, many organisations make clear provision for this particular group.

Provision for families with young children, at Chessington World of Adventures

- Child wristbands with contact details – in order that in the unlikely event that your child becomes temporarily separated from you, you can be quickly reunited – are available on request at Admissions, Guest Service and the Medical Centre.

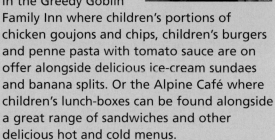

- Baby food and milk can be purchased from the Park's Medical Centre.

- You can heat baby food at the Alpine Café, Guest Services or the Medical Centre.

- Great toddler food options can be found in the Greedy Goblin Family Inn where children's portions of chicken goujons and chips, children's burgers and penne pasta with tomato sauce are on offer alongside delicious ice-cream sundaes and banana splits. Or the Alpine Café where children's lunch-boxes can be found alongside a great range of sandwiches and other delicious hot and cold menus.

- Nursing Mothers & Baby Changing Facilities are located in the Land of the Dragons, Market Square, Pirates Cove (Nursing Mothers only), Transylvania (Baby Changing only) and the Forbidden Kingdom (next to the Medical Centre).

- Nappies can be purchased from all Baby Changing Facilities and the Medical Centre.

- Toilets with family cubicles (offering a large space and a wall-mounted seat, should a parent wish to attend to two toddlers at the same time) are located in the Ladies at North Admissions, Transylvania and Market Square and in the Gents at Forbidden Kingdom.

activity

YOUR EXPERIENCE

Select a leisure facility that you are familiar with and identify the facilities and services they provide for families with young children. Make any suggestions as to how these could be improved.

People from different cultures

Dealing with people from different cultures can give rise to a whole range of challenges. Variations in what and how they eat, dress, meet and greet each other and communicate, create the potential for accidentally offending someone if you do not get it quite right. Certainly one of the main differences between many cultures is the way in which body language is used. The extract below is from the website www.executiveplanet.com, and illustrates some of the differences between different cultures.

DIFFERENT CULTURES, DIFFERENT WAYS

The Chinese
- Consider it rude to make expansive gestures and unusual facial expressions.
- Do not use their hands when speaking, and will become annoyed with a speaker who does.
- Do not smile as noticeably, since there is a heavy emphasis on repressing emotion.
- Consider pushing and cutting ahead in queues acceptable.

The Indians
- Consider pointing with your finger to be rude; Indians prefer to point with the chin.
- Think winking is either an insult or a sexual proposition.
- Consider grasping the ears signifies sincerity or repentance.
- Consider feet as unclean, so never point your feet at another person. You will be expected to apologize whenever your shoes or feet touch another person.

The Swedish
- Think that if women must cross their legs, it must never be ankle over knee
- Consider that in public, formal is always better than informal – no gum chewing, slouching, or leaning against things.
- Believe a toss of the head means, 'come here'.
- Tend to stay slightly farther apart than North Americans.
- Never speak with their hands in their pockets.

Non-English speakers

In an ideal world there would be staff who could communicate in the native language of all of their customers. However, even if you are not proficient in other languages there is still a great deal that you can do to help the communication process, such as:

■ using gestures, especially when pointing out directions

■ using diagrams and pictures

■ keeping copies of dictionaries so that you can translate key words.

and

■ making the effort to learn a few simple phrases in some common languages. Being able to say 'hello'; 'goodbye'; 'please' and 'thank you' in two or three foreign languages will please your foreign guests and show that you care enough to make the effort.

You should not forget that even foreign visitors whose native language is English may still have difficulty in understanding some words. For example, Americans have a range of different words and phrases from us, which can lead to confusion.

The Turkish

• Keep both feet flat on the ground when sitting. Displaying the soles of your shoes or feet to someone is insulting. It is impolite for women to cross their legs while facing another person.
• Consider it rude to cross your arms while facing someone.
• Keep their hands out of their pockets.
• Indicate 'yes' by nodding their heads up and down; the gestures for 'no' are different. Raising the eyebrows in a subtle way indicates 'no'. This arch look may be accompanied by the sound 'tsk'.
• The US gesture for 'no' [wagging the head from side to side] is a Turkish gesture for 'I don't understand'.

The Italians

• Stand much closer to you than you are used to or even feel comfortable with. Italian personal space is smaller than that of northern Europeans and significantly smaller than that of Americans.
• Do not consider queue-jumping the crime that it is in other countries. Italians are very tolerant of people who take advantage of the lack of strict queuing to get served first.
• Maintain direct eye contact, which is the way Italians show their interest. Be aware that looking away may be perceived as a sign of boredom or outright rudeness.
• Consider placing the hand on the stomach to signify dislike, usually for another person.

People with specific needs

It is important to remember that when dealing with customers with special needs they do not want to be made to feel different; they simply have different needs that may require additional service.

The following extract is from the Disability Etiquette Policy from www.Tameside.gov.uk, and includes some useful advice on dealing with people with specific needs.

LANGUAGE

It is important to gain a general understanding of words and phrases that may give offence to people with disabilities. There are no hard and fast rules; it is far better to try to keep in touch with disabled people and respect their preferences, which may change over time.

DO NOT SAY "Victim of............crippled by ....suffering from .... afflicted by ...."

DO SAY "Person who has / person who experienced ...."

DO NOT SAY "Invalid". This equates disability with illness and can be construed as "not valid".

DO NOT SAY "Wheelchair bound" or describe someone as "confined to a wheelchair". Remember that a wheelchair represents freedom to its user.

DO SAY "Wheelchair user" or "person who uses a wheelchair".

DO NOT SAY words like "spastic" – "cripple" – "retarded" – "defective" or phrases like "blind as a bat" – "deaf and dumb" – "mentally deficient", as they are often used in general conversation as terms of derision or abuse or as jokes. This reinforces damaging and inaccurate images of disability. Such words and phrases should never be used, whether a disabled person is present or not.

MEETING PEOPLE WITH DISABILITIES

People who are deaf

Do not make assumptions about a person's ability to communicate or the ways in which they do it. Always ask the person to tell you. Remember that those deaf people who use sign language find this the easiest method of communication. If an interpreter is present, speak to the person you are meeting, rather than to the interpreter. When you are speaking directly to a person who is deaf, remember that shouting does not help.

Do not assume that everyone who is deaf can lip-read. Always ask the person when you first meet them. If they do lip-read, remember that this skill is never wholly reliable. It requires intense concentration and is very tiring.

When meeting a person who is lip-reading: Look directly at them and speak slowly and clearly.

Face the light and keep hands, cigarettes and food away from your face while speaking.

Wheelchair users

When talking for more than a few moments to someone in a wheelchair, try to put yourself at their eye level to avoid stiff necks.

Speak to the person in the wheelchair and not their companion.

Push the wheelchair only with the permission of the user.

People with visual impairment

First identify yourself clearly and introduce anyone else who is present.

When offering a handshake, say something like "Shall we shake hands?"

When help is needed on unfamiliar ground, say "Let me offer you an arm". This will enable you to guide rather than propel or lead the person.

When offering a seat, place the person's hand on the back or arm of the chair.

Do not leave someone talking to an empty space. Say when you wish to end a conversation or to move away.

As we mentioned before, the Disability Discrimination Act has meant that organisations must make their products and services accessible to customers with a disability. There are many good examples of how this is achieved, including the Vue Cinemas 'Disabled Access Programme' as described in its policy statement below:

Pioneering provision for disabled film fans
Vue, the UK's leading operator and developer of state-of-the-art multiplex cinemas, is committed to the provision of various pioneering facilities that are designed to either meet or exceed the requirements of the Disability Discrimination Act and improve access to cinema for people with a wide range of disabilities.

Access to information
Vue Cinemas has launched a new website designed specifically for the visually impaired. Utilising the latest online developments, this text-only site provides a full range of information on all the films Vue is showing, as well as upcoming features, reviews and an innovative online booking service, all in a more easily readable format.

Physical access
All Vue Cinemas are fully accessible for physically disabled guests and we are continually reviewing our buildings to ensure that they provide the best access possible – this often involves working with local disabled groups. Moreover, once inside an auditorium, Vue is committed to ensuring that wheelchair-using filmgoers have the best viewing position possible.

Sensory access
Vue has already installed the most modern subtitling and audio-description technology systems in 25 of its 42 multiplexes. Audio description allows people with sight problems to visit the cinema and receive an audio-described narrative of the film, through individual headphones. This narrative provides an additional description woven around the film's soundtrack using pauses in dialogue to fill in details about facial expression, body language, actions, scenery and costume. Vue is now able to offer this service at any performance of the film shown in an equipped screen.

There is also a new film subtitling captioning system. Historically, Vue was dependent on the distributor making a subtitled copy of their film. Last year just five films were produced in this format. Due to the limited availability of the subtitled print, each cinema would only have the copy of the print for one night. Now, this new technology enables Vue to honour its commitment to providing regular subtitled shows.

Staff training
Vue has one of the best staff training programmes in the industry. We include as part of this specific training to make sure our staff offer all our guests the best cinematic experience and that the introduction of these new services and facilities is as successful as possible.

People with speech difficulties

Give your whole attention to a person with a speech difficulty. Be encouraging and patient. Do not correct or speak for the person. Wait quietly while the person talks and resist the temptation to finish their sentences.

Where possible, ask questions that require short answers or a nod or shake of the hand.

If you have difficulty understanding, don't pretend. Repeat what you do understand and the person's reactions will guide you.

Remember, at all times treat
Registered **D**isabled **P**eople with
Respect, **D**ignity and **P**atience

Customer service procedures

In previous topics we have examined how leisure organisations and their staff provide customer service that meets the needs of their customers. In this topic we explore how organisations ensure that customer service levels are set and maintained. In particular we look at:

■ Mission statements, codes of conduct and customer service charters
■ Customer service procedures.

Mission statements, codes of conduct and customer service charters

Many leisure organisations outline their customer service aims or strategy in what is known as a mission statement, a customer service charter or a code of conduct; in fact many organisations will have all three of these.

Mission statements

Generally speaking, a mission statement (also known as a vision statement) sets out in broad terms what a customer can expect from an organisation and its staff. It usually consists of no more than a couple of sentences.

The Youth Hostel Association
'To help all, especially young people of limited means, to a greater knowledge, love and care of the countryside, particularly by providing hostels or other simple accommodation for them in their travels and thus to promote their health, rest and education'

Customer service charter

Whereas a mission statement outlines a general idea, a customer service charter provides more detailed information on the aspects of service that are prioritised. The customer charter of the National Museum of Photography, Film & Television in Bradford, is a particularly good example.

The National Museum of Photography, Film & Television
helps the public understand and enjoy the history and contemporary practice of photography, film and television. We aim to inspire, enlighten and educate.

We Promise
Excellent care for the National Collection and research facilities

Displays and events that are accurate, stimulating and enjoyable

A high quality educational service

Up-to-date information about the Museum

A prompt and helpful response to enquiries to the Museum

A warm and courteous welcome

A safe, clean and comfortable Museum

Service to all parts of the community

Opening hours which reflect your needs

Cinema admission charges which offer value for money.

There is no specific length or format for a customer charter and some adopt a different style (see below).

Cannons Health Clubs

Mission

To be the best health and fitness operator in Europe.

Purpose

Satisfying people who take the time and have the courage to come to our door.

Values

- we're in this together ...one team
- we treat everyone as we'd like to be treated ourselves
- no question is stupid, ask any question
- simplicity drives our success
- work smart ...have fun
- WOW the member.

Codes of conduct

A code of conduct sets a minimum standard of service that the organisation guarantees to achieve. Codes of conduct are often set by regulatory bodies, and members are expected to abide by them. A key issue for many leisure organisations is child protection, and many have implemented codes of conduct such as not allowing any photography of children. The extract below outlines the reasons the British Amateur Rugby League Association (BARLA) introduced a formal child protection code of conduct.

British Amateur Rugby League Association

It is recognised that child abuse is a very emotive and difficult subject; however, everyone in Rugby League has a duty of care towards young and vulnerable performers and can help to protect them from abuse. Rugby League's approach to child protection is based on the principles recognised within UK and International legislation and Government guidance. The following have been taken into consideration:

- The Children Act 1989
- The Protection of Children Act 1999
- Working Together to Safeguard Children and Young People 1999
- The Human Rights Act 1998.

Many leisure organisations have a range of internal codes of conduct to cover different aspects of their operations. For example, Active Surrey issues the code below to all of its coaches.

ACTIVE SURREY

CODE OF CONDUCT FOR COACHES

- ✔ Set a good example, which others can follow.
- ✔ Arrive in plenty of time to set up your activities and ensure safety.
- ✔ Children play for pleasure, and winning is only part of the fun.
- ✔ Keep yourself informed about sound coaching practices and the principles of children's growth and development.
- ✔ Be reasonable in your demands on children's time, energy and enthusiasm – they need other interests too.
- ✔ The successful coach invests in the well-being and interests of their players, not their win/loss record.
- ✔ Teach your team that honest effort is more important than victory so that the result of each game is accepted without undue disappointment.
- ✔ Never ridicule or shout at a child for making a mistake or losing.
- ✔ Teach players to be fair and to follow the rules.
- ✔ Divide your time equally between all standards of players.
- ✔ Ensure you and your players have respect for their opponents, the officials and opposing coaches and supporters.
- ✔ Follow advice from a professional when determining if an injured player is ready to play or train.
- ✔ Take responsibility for the young people in your care until they have safely left the activity.

---

activity

FIND SOME EXAMPLES

In pairs, see if you can find three examples of mission statements, charters or codes of conduct in leisure organisations. Brochures, the internet and personal visits to organisations are all good sources of information.

Customer service procedures

In addition to codes of conduct, most leisure organisations also have specific internal procedures as to the ways in which they operate. Such procedures will cover activities like:

- Communications with customers
- Health and safety
- Accidents
- Complaints.

Health and safety is often a key issue for many providers who implement laid-down procedures. Like most providers, The Dome in Doncaster has a set procedure to deal with any incidents that may occur, including an accident report form (see below).

Many providers have set procedures for answering the telephone and replying to customers' letters, as shown in the example from Allerdale Council below.

When you contact us by telephone

- We will answer your call within 5 rings and with a standard greeting: "Good Morning / Afternoon, Allerdale Council" followed by "Name of Section or Officer".
- We will ring you back if you ask us to.
- We will give you our name and if you need to contact us again, our direct telephone number and/or email address.
- We will try to give you all the advice and information that you need.

When you contact us in writing/by email

- We will give you a meaningful response in 10 working days to letters.
- We will give you a meaningful response in 5 working days to emails.
- We will let you know when a full response can be provided if we cannot respond in this timescale.
- We will reply in plain English.

Source: www. allerdale.gov.uk

Accident form for The Dome

SOP 302   page 1

THE·DOME
DONCASTER
LEISURE PARK

Accident Form

all white boxes to be completed

copy passed onto Duty Officer   tick ☐

Part A

To be completed immediately by the person who dealt with the incident

1. About the person who had the accident

2. About the person who treated the casualty

Forename

Surname

D.O.B.

Sex (tick) | Male | Female |

Signature

Forename

Job Title

Where the leisure provision involves physical activity, the provider will normally have a procedure to ensure that customers are sufficiently fit and healthy to participate.

Part of a health assessment questionnaire from East Riding Leisure Services – for customers applying for membership of the gym.

To be completed by all customers

TITLE	SURNAME	FORENAME

ADDRESS

TOWN	COUNTY	POSTCODE

TELEPHONE	TELEPHONE (MOBILE)

DATE OF BIRTH	OCCUPATION

EMAIL ADDRESS

EXERCISE OBJECTIVES - PLEASE TICK YOUR **MAIN** OBJECTIVE

STRENGTH TRAINING ☐   CARDIOVASCULAR FITNESS ☐
GENERAL FITNESS ☐   WEIGHT LOSS ☐
MUSCLE TRAINING/BODY BUILDING ☐

EMERGENCY TELEPHONE NUMBER

EMERGENCY CONTACT NAME

Complaints

Complaint handling is another area where there are usually procedures in place to ensure that complaints are dealt with efficiently and in a uniform way. Procedures vary considerably between different organisations. Some may train all of their staff to handle complaints, whereas others may have a policy of referring all complaints to a supervisor or manager. Some organisations specify standards in terms of how quickly they will respond to complaints and what recompense the customer can expect. Many providers also use standard complaint forms to ensure that they have all of the relevant details needed to deal with the complaint, such as the example below.

activity

WRITE A PROCEDURE

Imagine that you are working in a theme park. Write a procedure for one of the following:
1. Dealing with lost children
2. Responding to a written complaint
3. Dealing with an accident
4. Dealing with a booking from a school group.

**THE ACADEMY
CUSTOMER COMPLAINT FORM**

NAME

ADDRESS

CONTACT NUMBER

DATE:	TIME:

DETAILS OF COMPLAINT

DOCUMENTED BY	DATE

OFFICE USE ONLY

ACTION TAKEN

FURTHER ACTION FOR HOD	YES/NO	NAME OF HOD

FURTHER ACTION REQUIRED

HOD COPIED	YES/NO
GENERAL MANAGER COPIED	YES/NO

This form can be found on the "s" drive - Forms/General

Customer Complaint form from the Academy in Harrogate

Training programmes

It is rare to find a leisure organisation that does not provide significant staff training in customer service. Whilst most organisations strive to employ new staff who have the right attitude and behaviour to provide good service, most recognise that additional training is almost always necessary. In this section we will focus on the key areas of training that an organisation might provide including:

■ Initial assessment
■ Induction
■ Ongoing training
■ Remedial training.

Initial assessment

Most organisations endeavour to employ staff who they feel will be able to provide good customer service. Some go even further and make an assessment of customer service skills an essential part of the interview procedure. For example, McDonald's has a number of targeted questions that interviewees are asked (see examples, right); their responses are graded on a scale of 0–17. Failure to reach a minimum number of points means that the applicant is not offered a job.

Interview questions from the McDonald's 'Staff Selection Guide for Managers'

You are cleaning up in the dining room of a restaurant you work in. You overhear a customer complain that the food they ordered arrived cold. What would you do in this situation?

You work at the counter of a local information centre. You are having a very busy day. While serving a person who wants restaurant information, another person comes up to you and says, 'I'm in a hurry. I need information on what films are showing tonight' What would you do in the situation?

You work in a café. Earlier in the day you ran out of hot chocolate. The manager ordered more but it hasn't arrived yet. A customer orders hot chocolate. What would you do?

You and your friend work at a local quick service restaurant. There are no customers to serve. The manager asked you both to clean the area when there are no customers. You start to clean but your friend is doing nothing. What would you do in this situation?

activity

WHAT WOULD *YOU* SAY

1. Work out how you would reply if asked each of the above questions at an interview.
2. As a group, discuss why you think each question is being asked and what type of response is expected.

Induction

Induction refers to the initial introduction and training that a new member of staff receives on joining an organisation. Depending on the organisation, induction may last anything from a few minutes to several days or even weeks. Effective organisations will include customer service training within the induction period. This is vital to the success of the organisation because the customer will rarely know whether the member of staff who deals with them is new or highly experienced. Whether face-to-face, on the telephone or in writing, the customer will expect the same high level of service that they have always received. Many organisations – as the example from Warwick Castle (right) shows – provide new staff with clear information about the training they will receive at induction and throughout their employment.

Ongoing training

Of course, the initial induction training is rarely all the customer service training that members of staff will require. Continuous training is usually necessary for any or all of the following reasons:

- The job is complex and takes time to master, therefore training is phased over an extended period of time.

- Changes to information and procedures may result in update training being necessary.

- Individual staff are keen to progress and therefore learn skills at a higher level to enable them to apply for promotion.

- Organisations may encourage 'multi-skilling', where staff acquire skills in other areas so that they are more flexible in terms of where they can work. This is particularly popular in the hotel industry where a receptionist may be trained in bar and restaurant work in addition to their usual reception duties.

We are committed to the continuous training and development of all of our staff, and provide induction training for all new starters. We also conduct six-monthly appraisals to help us to identify additional training/development needs.

Induction for new starters

For new starters we offer a two-day induction programme. The first day provides an insight into our aims and objectives as an organisation and the chance to become familiar with our customer service standards. Staff are also given the opportunity to become more familiar with the layout of the Castle and surrounding grounds through the completion of a treasure hunt!

The second day of induction training provides a thorough introduction to individual departments and specific training needs.

Further development

Both seasonal and permanent staff are invited to attend training which will assist them within their job roles, such as customer service training.

Permanent staff

Having identified training needs within the six-monthly appraisal system, further development and support is provided in a wide range of areas, including professional qualifications.

Source: www. warwickcastle.co.uk

Much of this ongoing training may be provided 'in-house' – in other words it is delivered by the organisation's staff in the workplace. However, customer service training is increasingly being organised by external providers. Colleges offer a range of customer service qualifications on a part-time or distance-learning basis, and NVQs in customer service can be assessed and achieved in the workplace. In addition, regional tourist boards offer a one-day 'Welcome Host' qualification (see overleaf), which provides staff within the leisure and tourism industry with an introduction to the key elements of effective customer service.

Welcome Host is a one-day training programme that concentrates on improving customer care skills. It is part of a high-profile national initiative that can help your organisation to:

- increase sales and profitability
- build repeat business
- provide higher standards of service for visitors and local residents
- enhance customer satisfaction
- reduce complaint levels
- improve staff understanding of customer value.

The training is aligned to the NVQ Level 2 in Customer Service and provides valuable underpinning knowledge.

Welcome Host can help employees acquire new customer service and communication skills, as well as improving their knowledge of local facilities and services. It will benefit new and more experienced staff working in:

- accommodation and catering
- travel and transport
- leisure and entertainment
- retailing
- public sector and voluntary organisations
- other service sector businesses.

Course Content

The Welcome Host programme involves group work and discussion to ensure skills learnt are relevant to each participant.

- Welcoming customers
  - The value of excellent customer service
  - Why are we here?
- Understanding your customers
  - The customer experience
- Delivering service excellence
  - Key elements of customer service
  - Customer service trends
  - Setting and maintaining standards
  - First impressions
- Communicating successfully
  - The communication process
  - Types of communication
  - Are you listening?
  - That's a good question…
  - Telephone techniques
- Providing information and advice
  - Presenting information to customers
  - Knowing your local area
  - Giving directions
- Meeting specific needs
  - Providing an accessible service
  - Language and cultural diversity
  - Welcoming customers of all ages
- Dealing with difficult situations
  - I'm the nice customer
  - The causes of dissatisfaction
  - Handling complaints
  - Resolving problems
- Boosting business
  - Using customer service to boost business
  - Improving quality

Source: www.welcometoexcellence.co.uk

Remedial training

In an ideal world, effective recruitment, induction and ongoing training would ensure that customer service would be faultless. In reality we know that this is not always the case. The biggest single cause of customer complaints in the leisure industry is poor customer service. Occasionally this will involve experienced staff who have received extensive training, but often the nature of the complaint will be outside the control of individual members of staff, and be due to personal illness, equipment failure or unavailability of products. Sometimes a complaint may focus on the attitude of a member of staff or their inability to deal with a

situation – in other words, a personal failing of that particular staff member. In such situations, many organisations will offer what is known as 'remedial training': remedying the situation through further training for the individuals involved. For example, a theme park receiving a number of complaints about safety standards being disregarded by their ride attendants, would be likely to implement some immediate remedial training for all staff involved. Likewise, a customer complaining to a theatre that they received unsympathetic treatment when they arrived in a wheelchair, would be likely to engender some substantial staff training in disability awareness.

It should be stressed that remedial training is not always the solution; sometimes a member of staff simply does not have the right attitude, skills or personality for a job. However, responsible leisure organisations will always attempt to provide additional training to enable their staff to carry out their jobs effectively and meet the organisation's objectives.

The importance of training staff in customer service cannot be stressed too highly. However, the nature of the training will vary according to the type of organisation and the needs and expectations of its customers (see activity below).

WHAT TRAINING WOULD THE STAFF NEED?

Read the description below of activities for special needs school parties in the North York Moors National Park. In pairs, describe what training you think would be required for the staff coordinating these activities or dealing with enquiries about them.

Activities for Groups with Special Needs

The National Park Education Service is keen to work with people with special needs and to establish links with school and community groups of all ages.

Activities can be provided at the Moors Centre and at Sutton Bank National Park Centre or it may be possible for our staff to visit your group.

The following activities have worked well with special needs groups recently and we are always keen to develop new ideas for helping people to enjoy and understand the National Park.

FUR AND FEATHERS

Most people rarely get a close look at and may never touch a wild animal or bird, but we have a collection of stuffed wild animals and birds, which are an invaluable way of enabling people to feel closer to wildlife. We can explain how an animal lives, what it eats and how it is adapted to surviving in its habitat and then people can touch and handle it and observe it in close detail. For some birds we can also provide sound effects.

Age range: This tactile experience is suitable for any age group and the level of detail can be varied according to the abilities of the group members.

Duration: Length of session can be varied to suit the requirements of the group.

ART IN THE PARK

This session, based at the Moors Centre, involves visiting a habitat in the grounds of the centre such as woodland or a small pond and then using the experience to inspire art work. Our artists can work with your group to create a mural, mobiles or sculptures which can either be displayed at the Moors Centre or taken back with you.

Age range: This practical session works well with any age group from Key Stage 2 groups up to adults. Following discussions with group leaders our artists will select projects and techniques appropriate to the abilities of the group members.

Duration: Session length can be varied depending on the project and the requirements of your group, but a minimum of four hours is generally required to

produce satisfying masterpieces!

FACILITIES

The following facilities are available at the Moors Centre to assist people with special needs. Please let us know your requirements in advance.

Manual wheelchairs and electric wheelchair buggies can be borrowed free of charge for use around the grounds.

Wheelchair-accessible trail around Crow Wood with listening tapes.

Stair lift and ramps to first-floor classrooms.

Ground-floor toilet accessible with wheelchairs.

Monitoring customer service delivery

For most leisure organisations, setting standards and training their staff to enable them to provide excellent customer service is not the end of the process. The organisation will also continuously monitor their levels of customer service to ensure that it is meeting and, hopefully, exceeding their customers' needs and expectations. Once an organisation has identified the quality criteria on which it is going to monitor and evaluate its customer service it then needs to decide how to go about it. In this topic we are going to explore:

■ **The ways in which organisations monitor customer service**
■ **Mystery visits**
■ **The ways in which customer service is evaluated and improved.**

The ways in which organisations monitor customer service

There are a number of feedback techniques that organisations use to evaluate whether their customers are happy with the level of customer service. These include:

■ informal feedback
■ surveys
■ suggestion boxes
■ focus groups
■ mystery visits.

Informal feedback

All staff in leisure organisations will receive informal feedback on a daily basis. They may overhear customers talking or customers may voice their opinions directly to staff. Alternatively feedback may be from other staff, management or even people who are not customers but voice an opinion about the products and services offered. For example, someone passing by a tourist attraction may comment on how untidy the outside is looking and how the plants need watering.

This type of informal feedback is very important to organisations in helping them to monitor and evaluate the service that they offer. Many customers feel more comfortable making informal comments and may not have the time or inclination to complete formal questionnaires. Of course, informal feedback can also be positive and it is just as important to listen to this. Positive feedback tells an organisation what it is doing right and allows them to develop these areas to continue to satisfy customers' needs and expectations. Efficient organisations will have some mechanism to ensure that all informal feedback is fed back to management. For example many hold regular staff consultative meetings where different departments are represented by a member of staff. The agenda will often include the opportunity for staff to relay customer feedback.

Surveys

Many leisure organisations use formal feedback methods such as surveys and customer comment cards – often referred to as questionnaires. In Topic 7 of this unit we look at marketing research in more detail and the use of questionnaires. Questionnaires are very useful in terms of highlighting where any particular problems may be developing – or identifying a particular customer who is dissatisfied. Many organisations include questions on their customer service as part of a general customer questionnaire such as the two examples below.

Center Parcs adds up the scores from their customer questionnaires every month and the staff in the facility (i.e. restaurant, shops, sporting venues, etc) with the highest score receive an award. This is a good

Longleat Forest Questionnaire

1. Villa number / apartment number

2. Arrival date

General

3. What is your overall opinion on your stay at Longleat Forest in general?

	++	+	−	− −
	☐	☐	☐	☐

4. Please give your opinion on the following aspects of your stay.

General impression

	++	+	−	− −
Arrival lodge/check-in procedure	☐	☐	☐	☐
Helpfulness of Village Square Information Team	☐	☐	☐	☐
Helpfulness of Pre-arrival Booking Team	☐	☐	☐	☐
Leisure booking facility (on village)	☐	☐	☐	☐
Speed of response to faults reported	☐	☐	☐	☐

Accommodation

	++	+	−	− −
Cleanliness of accomodation	☐	☐	☐	☐
Maintenance of accomodation	☐	☐	☐	☐
Comfort of accomodation	☐	☐	☐	☐

General impression

	++	+	−	− −
Child friendliness	☐	☐	☐	☐
Sense of security	☐	☐	☐	☐
Tidiness of village	☐	☐	☐	☐
Natural environment	☐	☐	☐	☐
Tranquility at the village	☐	☐	☐	☐

Subtropical Swimming Paradise

	++	+	−	− −
Facility in general	☐	☐	☐	☐
Quality of Staff Service	☐	☐	☐	☐
Cleanliness of facility	☐	☐	☐	☐

---

incentive for staff to provide excellent service, although it has created a tendency for staff to constantly remind guests, 'Don't forget to give us two stars if you were happy with our service'!

Suggestion boxes

Some leisure organisations provide suggestion boxes for their customers. As with informal feedback, this has the advantage that many customers may not want to spend the time filling in a lengthy questionnaire but would like to make a brief comment on the service that they have received. A variation on the suggestion box concept is to have a visitors' book where customers can write comments. Visitors' books are particularly popular at tourist attractions to the extent that for many visitors they have become an enjoyable part of the experience. For example, in the Anne Frank Museum in Amsterdam, visitors queue, not only to write their own comments, but also to read the moving messages from visitors from around the world.

The Royal Pavilion Visitor Questionnaire

Date: /   /2004

Please spare a minute to answer the following questions and leave your comments.

1. **Where do you come from?**

☐ UK   Postcode_____

☐ Spain	☐ Netherlands	☐ Belgium	☐ North America
☐ France	☐ Germany	☐ Australasia	☐ South America
☐ Italy	☐ Scandinavia	☐ Japan	☐ Other_____

2. **What is your main reason for being in Brighton today?**

| ☐ On holiday | ☐ Visiting friends/family | ☐ Studying | ☐ Other_____ |
| ☐ Live here | ☐ On business | ☐ Day trip | |

Focus groups

A focus group is a meeting involving a group of people who are encouraged to discuss their opinions and feelings about a particular organisation, product, service or topic. It has the great advantage that the information collected is very detailed because customers can explain their feelings and opinions in depth. For example, a sports centre may hold a focus group discussion to identify how customers view the customer service that they get when booking facilities or attending a class.

Mystery visits

An increasingly common method of evaluating customer service is to employ a 'mystery customer' (usually known as a 'mystery guest' in the hospitality industry). This is someone employed by the organisation, but not known by the staff, who visits the facility as a customer and analyses the extent to which service levels meet quality criteria. A mystery customer may look at a wide range of different aspects of customer service such as staff appearance and attitude, length of time it takes to be served, quality of products offered, information and advice provided by staff and displayed on the premises and the ability of staff to deal with unusual requests or specific needs. The visit will usually include evaluating benchmarked standards such as stated queuing time or adherence to stated company procedures.

The mystery customer will usually have a checklist covering what needs to be looked at. For example, McDonald's restaurants operate a mystery customer system known as 'The Moment of Truth'. Outlets receive mystery visits several times a month and receive the results some weeks later. The performance of each outlet and its management team are judged on the results of the mystery visit with under-performing outlets having to produce action plans for improvement.

KayBurgers — How are we doing?

Assignment No: 759453   Restaurant: Croybury   Date: 26 Jan 05   Meal type: Lunch

Summary	Possible	Actual	Food bought
A Food quality	30	22	Double Kayburger
B Counter service	10	7	Medium Fries
C Cleanliness	10	9	Diet Cola
Total	**50**	38 = 76%	

Food quality
1a. Rate the temperature of your burger	0	[Hot: 5	OK: 4	Anything else: 0]
1b. Rate the taste	4	[Great: 5	OK: 4	Anything else: 0]
1c. Rate the appearance	4	[Great: 5	OK: 4	Anything else: 0]
2a. Rate the temperature of your fries	4	[Hot: 4	OK: 3	Anything else: 0]
2b. Rate the taste	3	[Great: 4	OK: 3	Anything else: 0]
2c. Rate the appearance	4	[Great: 4	OK: 3	Anything else: 0]
3a. Was your drink the right temperature?	2	[Yes: 2	No: 0]	
3b. Did your drink taste OK?	1	[Yes: 1	No: 0]	

Counter service
1a. Did the staff member greet you?	3	[Hello, Hi, etc: 3]
1b. Did they make eye contact/smile?	0	[Both: 3 One or none: 0]
2a. Did they listen to your order?	2	[Yes: 2 – but must not be distracted]
2b. Did you get what you ordered?	2	[Yes: 2 – but must get items/sizes ordered]
3a. How long did you have to queue? [not part of rating]		4 mins

Cleanliness
1a. Entrance/queuing area	2	[No litter: 3 <5 pieces: 2 Anything else: 0]
1b. Tables	2	[Clean: 2 Dirty/littered, unless being cleared: 0]

To be effective the mystery visit system needs to be carried out by someone who can pass for a standard customer and therefore receive the typical level of customer service that regular customers experience. For example, a visitor attraction may employ a couple with young children as mystery customers and ask them to evaluate customer service from the perspective of a young family. Alternatively a person in a wheelchair might be used to assess the extent to which the organisation is able to meet specific needs of those with mobility impairment. For extended mystery visits, such as an overnight stay in a hotel, the mystery customer may have a series of pre-set requests that they are required to make whilst there to judge the extent to which they are effectively met, as the following extract from a hotel mystery visit shows.

15. Outcome and evaluation of ordering room service meal late at night

Description of situation

At 1.30 a.m. I rang the room service number and requested a beef and horseradish sandwich, half a bottle of house white wine and a portion of strawberry cheesecake. I asked how long it would be, and was told 20 minutes.

Evaluation of service provided

The phone was answered promptly using the standard company greeting. The member of staff was efficient in taking my order but forgot to ask whether I wanted white or brown bread. The meal was delivered 35 minutes later but the waiter apologised for the delay. The tray was laid correctly but did not include a napkin or salt and pepper cruet. The room-service waiter offered to pour my wine. The wine had not been sufficiently chilled and the wine glass had smears around the rim. The standard of food was good. I left my tray outside the bedroom door for collection but it was still there the following morning. I noticed that there were a number of other used trays in the corridors.

---

activity

PLANNING A MYSERY VISIT

In pairs identify a local leisure organisation that you could visit as a mystery customer. Write a list of ten aspects of the customer service that you are going to evaluate during your visit. The aspects should include all of the following:

- Staff appearance and attitude
- Information provided and displayed at the facility
- Speed of service
- Quality of products and services provided
- Ability to meet the needs of individual customers.

Ways in which customer service is evaluated and improved

An evaluation of customer service seeks to ensure that the level of customer service is meeting the quality criteria, and that these quality criteria are, in turn, satisfying customer expectations. Some organisations, such as McDonald's, use a mathematical process to evaluate. The total scores are added up from each mystery visitor checklist, with a minimum score being set as acceptable.

Other organisations use a comparison of the levels of complaints as one method of evaluation. For example an increase in the number of complaints about a certain aspect of service such as provision of information would signify a problem.

Finally, having monitored and evaluated the level of customer service, an organisation will be in a position to make recommendations as to how the service could be improved. Remember that this is not always a negative process – i.e. putting right the mistakes.

activity

NOTHING BUT COMPLAINTS

The privately owned Gemini Health Club and Gym does not collect any formal feedback from customers or use mystery guests. However, the owner rates customer service and good complaint handling as extremely important to the business's success. This year complaints have risen by 23% compared to last year. Most of the increase comes from customers using the facilities at the weekend. Strangely, the number of customers at these times has risen by 37% over the same year. Discuss the following questions:

1. What do you think could be the reason for this apparent contradiction?
2. Is it sufficient to evaluate the level of customer service purely on the basis of complaint letters – if not, why?
3. What other methods of evaluation might be useful?

Sometimes it may be a question of identifying what the organisation does really well and doing it even better.

activity

CARRYING OUT YOUR MYSTERY VISIT

In pairs visit a local leisure organisation. Taking the role of a mystery guest evaluate the organisation on the basis of five criteria that you have decided are important. For example: prompt service, friendly greeting, good product knowledge, etc. Then report back to the rest of the group about how the organisation could improve its customer service.

One of the key issues in customer service delivery is the provision of information and advice to customers. This means that staff need to have a sound knowledge of the organisation and the products and services it offers. In this topic we examine:

- Providing information
- Providing advice
- Knowledge of the range of products and services offered by an organisation.

Providing information

Most leisure customers will expect an organisation and its staff to be able to provide them with information about the products and services it offers. Providing information is important in ensuring that customers can select products or services that meet their needs. The type of information that staff need to provide will largely depend on what the customer requires. They may want to know about the suitability of products or services in terms of meeting their needs and expectations. Alternatively, they may need information on what prices include or directions on how to get to somewhere. Many organisations include detailed directions and/or location maps in their promotional materials – an example of this is shown, right.

Naturally, no one can be expected to know the answer to every question. What *is* expected, however, is that staff members know where to obtain the information to answer customer queries. There is usually a wide range of sources available, including:

- manuals
- brochures and leaflets
- guide books
- tourist information centres
- recorded telephone information lines
- computerised information systems.
- maps
- reference books
- timetables

Beaulieu is in the heart of the New Forest, 14 miles from Southampton, 23 miles from Bournemouth, 85 miles from London. By road: London to Beaulieu, via M3, M27, A326, less than 2 hours. There is plenty of free parking. By rail: London Waterloo to Brockenhurst, then a taxi ride.

THE NATIONAL MOTOR MUSEUM
PALACE HOUSE AND GARDENS
ABBEY AND EXHIBITION
RIDES AND DRIVES

Beaulieu

John Montagu Building, Beaulieu, Brockenhurst, Hampshire SO42 7ZN

Telephone 01590 612345
e-mail: info@beaulieu.co.uk
www.beaulieu.co.uk

IMPORTANT INFORMATION
Open every day except Christmas Day, 10 am – 6 pm May to September, 10 am – 5 pm October to April
* Free re-entry is non-transferable and valid for six days following the original visit, except on days of major or separately charged events. Only one free re-entry is permitted per person. Free re-entry tickets are not issued on days of major or separately charged events. Offer closes March 2005. Not all rides, drives and features operate throughout the year and times vary by season (check on your day of visit). Height/age restrictions apply to some features.
The Abbey audio visual exhibition will be on show from Easter 2004.
The Mini exhibition commences on 29th May and runs until the 1st November 2004
The James Bond Experience was created in association with the Ian Fleming Foundation - www.ianfleming.org and runs until December 2004.

Giving advice

Giving customers advice is often an extension of providing them with information but, whilst information may be purely factual, advice requires you to make appropriate recommendations and suggestions. For example, a theatre booking clerk may give a customer information by providing a copy of the current events programme such as the one shown on the right.

In addition, a customer may ask for extra advice on what would best suit their particular needs; which productions would be suitable for their elderly parents or how the auditorium is equipped to accommodate people with mobility problems. It is important for advice to be impersonal, accurate and objective. In other words, it should be based on the customer's needs and not merely the opinion of a member of staff as, whilst the latter might consider the musical *Fame* to be excellent entertainment, a retired couple might prefer *The Nutcracker* or *The Play What I Wrote*.

will be sent pre-holiday advice about when and where to check-in for their flight, along with information about baggage allowances, insurance and so on. Once they arrive they will usually be given advice on health and safety issues such as the use of chairs lifts, ratings of different slopes, and emergency procedures.

Many leisure products and services are complex. A first-time customer can often find this quite confusing and their enjoyment of a product may be spoilt if they have difficulty understanding how it is delivered. As a result, one of the issues that many leisure organisations have to deal with is giving their customers sufficient advice on the ways in which services are delivered and used. For example, customers going on a winter sports holiday

Knowledge of the range of products and services offered by an organisation

In order to provide information and advice, staff need to have a sound knowledge of the range of products and services offered by their organisation. They should be able to dispense product information that meets their customers' needs and expectations and ensures total satisfaction. The sort of information that staff may need to be able to supply will vary according to the organisation and its customers. However, typical product knowledge might include:

- Knowledge of the company and its operating divisions

- The main features of all products and services offered

- The suitability of products and services for different types of customers

- Prices (including special offers and discounts)

- Location and directions

- Staffing

- Health, safety and security procedures

- Other local information (such as nearby attractions, medical facilities, transport, etc).

In any customer service situation, product information should be impersonal, accurate and objective.

- *Impersonal* means your own tastes and preferences should not limit or restrict the sort of information you give. For example, a customer visiting a cinema expects to receive product information about films that they would prefer, not ones that the member of staff would like to see.

- *Accurate* means making sure that everything you say is true. If you are not sure about something, say that you will check the information and then let the customer know the full picture. For example, telling customers that a visitor attraction is suitable for wheelchair users when you are not really sure, could result in some very dissatisfied customers.

- *Objective* means including all the information that customers need to know even if you think that it might put them off buying the product. This may occasionally mean referring potential customers to a competitor; however, the reputation that you gain for good customer service would mean that they are likely to come back.

Impersonal, accurate and objective information is important in all situations if you are to satisfy

customers' needs and ensure that they return. Sometimes, giving the wrong information can have serious repercussions; incorrect information about the level of fitness required for a particular exercise class could result in personal injury.

As we said at the beginning of this topic, staff cannot be expected to instantly know the answer to every question. But what is important is that they know where to find out the information and are able to relay it to the customer in an appropriate manner. By appropriate manner we mean explaining the information in your own words rather than simply reading it out from printed information. Every effort should be made to avoid jargon and abbreviations so that the customer understands your explanation; a customer who has never attended an exercise class before is likely to be confused if a member of staff explains it as 'a high-impact, cardio-vascular work-out'. When information is unavoidably complex, it is usually preferable to write down the details for the customer or provide a copy of the information.

activity

THE INFORMATION CLERK AND THE CUSTOMER

Below is an extract from the Epsom Racecourse website advising customers on the dress code for particular race meetings. Take some time to read through the questions and answers. Then in pairs, role play a customer and an information clerk. The customer should ask a question based on any of the information provided. If the information clerk cannot remember the answer they can refer to the information – but make sure that it is then put into your own words.

Dress codes

Whilst we try to keep restrictions to a minimum, we would be very grateful if all customers could be guided by the following dress codes. For the comfort and convenience of your guests and companions, we should be grateful if you would ensure that they are also aware of the dress codes applicable at Epsom Downs Racecourse.

QUEEN'S STAND (Vodafone Derby Day)
Either black or grey Morning Dress with a top hat, or service dress is traditional and obligatory for gentlemen on Derby Day. Ladies are asked to wear formal day dress or a Trouser suit, with a hat.

QUEEN'S STAND (Vodafone Oaks Day)
This remains a very special day in the racing calendar and, whilst Morning Dress is not required, gentlemen are asked to wear a jacket, collar and tie. Ladies do not have to wear a hat but the majority do. Jeans, sports shorts, denim or trainers are not acceptable in the Queen's Stand.

QUEEN'S STAND (Other Days)
Racing outside of the Vodafone Derby Meeting is less formal but the majority of our Queen's Stand visitors like to make coming to Epsom Downs a special day. Therefore, jackets and trousers, with a shirt and tie, are encouraged.

GRANDSTAND BOXHOLDERS
Please would Grandstand boxholders be guided by the Queen's Stand Vodafone Oaks Day dress code, on all racedays.

GRANDSTAND (ALL DAYS)
The Grandstand has a much more relaxed atmosphere but no bare tops please.

Although everyone is welcome at Epsom Downs Racecourse, we do reserve the right in extreme circumstances to either refuse admission to or eject from any enclosure or the Racecourse, any racegoer who, in the reasonable opinion of the Racecourse, behaves or is likely to behave in an unruly manner or in a manner likely to give offence to other racegoers.

Source:www. epsomderby.co.uk

Marketing research

Part of providing good customer service is knowing who the customers are and the type of products and services that they want. To achieve this it is crucial that effective marketing research is one of an organisation's key marketing activities. Marketing research is the process of collecting, analysing and evaluating information and data about customers and markets. Effective marketing research helps organisations to make decisions about the types of products their customers want, the price they are prepared to pay, where they prefer to buy the product and how it should be promoted. In this section we examine:

- The objectives of marketing research
- Primary marketing research
- Secondary marketing research.

Objectives of marketing research

Marketing research can be used to obtain a wide range of information. The objectives of undertaking marketing research commonly involve identifying:

- customer needs
- new and existing markets
- trends and fashions
- changes in markets
- opportunities for market and product development
- competitors
- effectiveness of promotional activities.

Conducting marketing research is a systematic and highly-skilled process. There are two basic types of marketing research:

- Primary (field) research
- Secondary (desk) research.

Marketing research helps organisations such as Great Yarmouth's Pleasure Beach develop new products to meet the needs of customers

144

Unit 3 The Leisure Customer

Primary marketing research

Primary marketing research is also known as field research. It refers to any research that involves contact with past, existing or potential customers. Primary marketing research is what most people think of as marketing research and includes methods such as:

- surveys
- observation
- focus groups.

Before looking at each of these in more detail it is important to understand the difference between qualitative and quantitative research.

Qualitative research:	Quantitative research:
■ looks at consumers' feelings, attitudes, desires and perceptions ■ provides detailed information ■ is often difficult to present statistically or to develop into any general conclusions ■ generally uses open questions that start with 'explain', 'why' or 'describe'.	■ provides more structured information that is statistically measurable ■ enables researchers to draw specific and measurable conclusions from the results. ■ does not explain in-depth reasons ■ generally uses closed questions that start with 'when', 'how many' or 'which'.

Qualitative and quantitative research may differ in their applications. If you (qualitatively) asked 2000 people how the customer service at a visitor attraction could be improved, you could potentially receive 2000 different answers and using all of this information could be difficult. Alternatively, if you asked 2000 customers if they were satisfied with the customer service, it might lead you to find that, of those surveyed, 43 per cent were satisfied with the customer service and 57 per cent were dissatisfied. As useful as these figures might be to give an overall idea of customer satisfaction, quantitative research does not give any detailed information that would explain the results; why were those 57 per cent dissatisfied with the customer service?

In practice, many organisations use a combination of both quantitative and qualitative research. They may ask the original 2000 customers if they were satisfied with the service and then select a smaller group to find out some of the reasons for the results.

Surveys

Surveys are a method of quantitative research that is based on a questionnaire given to a large sample of people. Questionnaires are one of the most widely used research methods in the leisure industry because they are relatively quick and easy to administer and analyse.

The success of a survey depends to a large extent upon the quality of the questionnaire used. A well-designed questionnaire, which includes structured questions, and answers classified into predetermined categories, is quick to administer and the resulting data easy to process.

Compiling a questionnaire is a skilled process that needs careful consideration. One of the most difficult aspects of compiling an effective questionnaire is writing questions that can be easily understood and interpreted in the same way by all respondents. If you want to ensure that your questionnaire is effective you need to carry out a pilot survey. This means testing the questionnaire on a small group of respondents to make certain that all of the questions are easily understood and not misinterpreted. Once you have carried out the pilot you will probably find that some of the questions will need re-wording to make them more effective.

There are three main ways (or contact methods) in which survey information can be gathered:

- by mail
- by telephone
- by personal contact.

Many organisations send questionnaires through the post. The advantage of this is that it is quick to administer, and a large sample can be reached relatively cheaply. The main drawback is that the reply rate can be very poor – as low as three per cent in many cases. Some organisations carry out surveys by asking respondents questions over the telephone. This is more expensive and time-consuming than using the mail but usually has a higher response rate. However, because so many organisations use the phone as a sales tool, respondents are often suspicious, thinking that the purpose is to sell them something.

Another method is face-to-face contact between researcher and respondent. This is clearly more time-consuming and, therefore, expensive, but the response rate is usually higher than to mail and telephone surveys. The contact method used depends largely on the type of research being conducted and the amount of time and money available.

SEA LIFE VISITOR SURVEY

Look at the copy of the first page of the questionnaire that Sea Life Centres give to their visitors, and consider the following:

1 Are the questions quantitative or qualitative?

2 What are the advantages and disadvantages of this?

3 Why do you think that they ask each of the seven questions?

4 What might they do with the responses from each question?

5 What further questions do you think might be on the second page of the questionnaire?

Thank you for visiting Sea Life today. We hope that you have enjoyed your visit. To help us monitor visitor enjoyment and improve what we do, we would be very grateful if you would complete this short survey. Thank you.

Q1 How did you hear about Sea Life before your visit today? Please tick as many boxes as apply.

Website ☐	Recommendation from friend/relative ☐
Holiday guide ☐	Radio ☐
Sea Life leaflet ☐	National newspaper ☐
Road sign ☐	Local newspaper ☐
Saw the Sea Life Tram ☐	Promotional offer ☐
Television news ☐	Posters ☐

Q2 If you've seen the Sea Life leaflet, where did you see it?
Hotel ☐   Holiday park/camp ☐   Tourist Information Centre ☐   B&B/Guesthouse ☐
Self-catering ☐   Pub/Restaurant ☐

Q3 Did you, or anyone in your party, use a promotional voucher/offer when you entered the centre?
Yes ☐   No ☐

Q4 How satisfied overall are you with your visit?
Very satisfied ☐   Quite satisfied ☐   Neither satisfied nor dissatisfied ☐
Quite dissatisfied ☐   Very dissatisfied ☐

Q5 How much time did you spend at Sea Life today?   0–1/2 hour ☐   1/2–1 hour ☐
1–1 1/2 hours ☐   1 1/2–2 hours ☐   2–2 1/2 hours ☐   Over 2 1/2 hours ☐

Q6 Would you recommend a visit to your friends or family?   Yes ☐   No ☐

Q7 Here is a list of things we want to do well at Sea Life. For each one, please rate it by ticking the box which best shows how you feel about it.

	Excellent	Good	Average	Poor	Very Poor	Didn't visit/use
Value for money	☐	☐	☐	☐	☐	☐
Talks/Presentations	☐	☐	☐	☐	☐	☐
Educational value	☐	☐	☐	☐	☐	☐
Environmental/Conservation content	☐	☐	☐	☐	☐	☐
Entertainment value	☐	☐	☐	☐	☐	☐
Range of creatures	☐	☐	☐	☐	☐	☐
Quality of displays	☐	☐	☐	☐	☐	☐
Friendliness	☐	☐	☐	☐	☐	☐
Staff efficiency	☐	☐	☐	☐	☐	☐
Cleanliness	☐	☐	☐	☐	☐	☐
Restaurant/Catering	☐	☐	☐	☐	☐	☐
Gift Shop	☐	☐	☐	☐	☐	☐

PLEASE TURN OVER

Observation

Observation is a research method in which information is obtained by observing customers' behaviour or events. Much research into visitor traffic is conducted by local leisure and tourism departments by counting the number of cars that pass different points at various times. In leisure there are many situations in which observation methods can be used to provide valuable information. Observational research has shown that up to 90 per cent of customers automatically go to the right when entering a souvenir shop. This is valuable information for providers in terms of deciding what goods to display at the first point of customer contact.

Focus groups

Focus group research is when a group of people is encouraged to discuss their opinions and feelings about a particular organisation, product, service or topic that affects an organisation's marketing activities. It has the advantage that the information collected is qualitative and, therefore, very detailed. However, it is extremely expensive, and the information collected is based on a very small selection of respondents. Focus group research is a highly skilled research technique, which is often carried out by qualified psychologists, as the researcher must be able to encourage the respondents to talk freely about the topics that are of interest without leading them to say something that they do not really mean.

Secondary marketing research

Secondary marketing research is also known as desk research and refers to obtaining information from sources that are already published or easily accessible. Desk research is economical and comparatively quick to carry out. It has the advantage that it can be conducted with complete confidentiality – in other words, without competitors finding out! On the other hand, because the information yielded by desk research is not generated for the particular purposes of an organisation, it may not be sufficiently relevant, and more specific (primary) research may be required. There are two main sources of secondary research:

- internal
- external.

Internal sources of information

An internal source of information refers to information that an organisation already has. Most organisations can avoid much of the need for expensive marketing research if they use internal sources of information wisely. For example, a conference centre might look at their customer database to identify which regions the majority of their customers come from and promote heavily in these areas. Some of the most commonly used sources of internal marketing research include:

Sales records	Provide information on the quantity and frequency of products sold over a given period and can often be used to provide a comparison between current and past performance. Information is available from a number of sources, such as customer bills and cash till records.
Usage figures	Provide information about the number of people using a facility rather than sales figures.
Financial information and customer databases	Provide information on customers' accounts, methods of payment and credit arrangements. Many organisations have their own computerised databases that include a range of information on past and present customers. Much of this information is obtained when customers fill in booking forms or registration forms.
Customer complaint and compliment letters	Provide information on aspects of the products and service provided that customers are dissatisfied with or value.

External sources of information

An external source of information refers to information
that has been gathered by a third party, and includes:

Government publications	Both central and local government carry out research and publish the results. The Office for National Statistics (ONS) publishes several very useful volumes of statistics, trends, demographic and census-related data. In all, the government publishes 400 series of statistics, and many publications have specific sections on leisure.
Press reports	National, regional and local newspapers are often a good source of information on current trends, issues and competitor activities.
Trade journals	A trade journal is a publication produced for a particular occupation or industry. Many, such as *Caterer & Hotelkeeper*, *Leisure Management* and *Leisure Opportunities* carry out research and publish the results.
Professional associations	Professional associations are organisations that perform a co-ordinating, informing or leadership role. Within the leisure industry they include the the Institute of Leisure and Amenity Management (ILAM), the Central Council of Physical Recreation (CCPR) and the Institute of Sport and Recreation Management (ISRM). Members of these associations pay a subscription charge in return for a range of services, which frequently includes marketing research information.
Commercial marketing research organisations	Extensive research is carried out by marketing research organisations, such as Mintel and Gallup, which specialise in collecting market data in a particular business sector. The information can then be purchased by organisations.

activity

USING INTERNAL INFORMATION

Arcadia Action is a privately owned company offering week-long activities for 6–14 year olds in the Easter and Summer school holidays. Typical activity weeks include football, tennis, performing arts and art workshops. Arcadia rent premises and facilities from local schools and an FE college. They are considering extending their product range to include a week's computer

course using the new computer suite at a local secondary school. They have maintained an extensive customer database that includes details of frequency of bookings, courses and personal details of customers. They also have sales figures for the last ten years as well as a file of all letters received from customers. In pairs, discuss what information Arcadia might have that would support the development of the computer course.

Selecting a research method

Clearly there are many primary and secondary techniques available to collect marketing research information. Leisure organisations need to identify which techniques are the most suitable for their particular research needs. A number of factors need to be considered when selecting a research method, but the general advantages are shown in the table below.

activity

WHICH METHODS OF RESEARCH?

A national chain of health and fitness clubs is concerned that membership amongst young adults fell by 23 per cent last year. The chain is keen to carry out research to identify the reasons and hence formulate a future marketing strategy. Propose and justify two primary and two secondary methods of research that could be used.

A comparison of the various marketing research techniques

RESEARCH TECHNIQUE	COST	TIME	ACCESSIBILITY	VALIDITY AND RELIABILITY	FITNESS FOR PURPOSE
SURVEY	Cost depends on the extent of survey and sample size. Can be low if questionnaires are produced in-house	Can be very quick to implement, e.g. if telephone surveys and self-completion questionnaires	Postal and telephone surveys can access a wide geographical area. Face-to-face surveys have a more limited accessibility	Good if survey questions are well constructed	Especially good for quantitative research
OBSERVATION	Cost can be very low for quantitative research but rises if qualitative data is required	As with cost, time consuming for qualitative research but relatively quick for quantitative research	Usually fairly limited accessibility to localised area only	Good if well-controlled	Can be used for both qualitative and quantitative research
FOCUS GROUP	Very high in terms of time, small sample size and the need for highly experienced researchers	Very time consuming	Usually fairly limited accessibility to localised area only	Good if well-controlled, but requires highly skilled researchers to be effective	Usually only used for qualitative research
INTERNAL SECONDARY	Minimal since data is usually readily available	Can be very quick if accurate internal records are kept. Very quick if records are computerised	Very accessible	If records are accurate and relevant they will be highly valid and reliable	Especially good for quantitative research. Copies of documents such as complaints letters may provide more qualitative data
EXTERNAL SECONDARY	Much data is freely available, but commercial data can be expensive	Can be very quick. Purchasing commercial data is instant	Wide access to regional, national and international data is available	Dependent on source	Can provide both qualitative and quantitative data

Topic 8 | Promotion

Marketing is an important element of customer service provision. All staff are involved in marketing to some extent, whether it is in the actual planning and implementation of promotions or through knowledge of such promotions and the use of effective selling skills.

In this section we are going to explore the various marketing communications channels that can be used by organisations including:

- advertising
- brochures and leaflets
- direct marketing
- public relations
- sponsorship
- sales promotions
- multi-media applications
- professional presentation skills.

Advertising

Advertising is the paid-for space or time in a publication or on television, which usually aims to persuade consumers to buy a product or service. Advertising is one of the most common marketing communication channels used by leisure organisations, and ranges from national television advertisements costing many thousands of pounds to small classified ads in local newspapers costing just a few pounds.

Practically all leisure organisations undertake some form of advertising, which might be in any or all of the following media:

- newspapers and magazines
- television
- radio
- internet
- point-of-sale material
- posters.

- There are approximately 1330 local and regional newspapers in the UK and 21 national dailies and Sunday papers.

- Over 27 million people read at least one national daily newspaper.

- 30 million read a national Sunday paper.

Newspapers and magazines

National press advertisements are cheaper than many other forms of mass media, such as television advertising, and large national audiences can be reached. Alternatively, press advertisers can target audiences in individual localities or regions by using local and regional paid-for or free newspapers.

Advertising in newspapers is very flexible. Advertisements can be placed or changed at relatively short notice, while the advertising message can be read at leisure, re-read or even cut out and kept for future use. There are a few disadvantages to press advertising, however. The advertisements are static, and cannot show products or services working. With many leisure products this is an important consideration because they are intangible experiences. For example, advertising a product such as a theme park will have greater visual impact on colour television than it would in a black and white newspaper.

Advertisements in magazines have similar advantages and disadvantages to newspapers since they are also a printed medium. Print quality varies, but in most cases it is vastly superior to that of newspapers, with the use of full colour commonplace.

Television

The greatest advantage of television advertising is that it can show products working. Added to this, the use of music, dialogue, personalities, special effects and animation can help to create a stunning visual impact on a mass audience. However, unlike printed advertising, the exposure is very short – usually 10–60 seconds at a time. This means that the amount of information is limited and can be missed altogether if the advertisement fails to attract the attention of the viewer. A further problem for advertisers is the use of remote-control devices that allow viewers to 'zap' between channels when advertisements appear. Television advertising is often backed up by Teletext services that direct viewers to sources of further information.

For many leisure providers, the single greatest disadvantage of television advertising is the expense. Many smaller providers, such as privately owned visitor attractions and council-owned leisure facilities, cannot afford to consider any form of television advertising.

Radio

Some leisure providers use local or national commercial radio stations to promote products to the local population. It is a lot cheaper than television and has the advantage over printed media that music, dialogue and sound effects can be used. However, since radio is not a visual or printed medium, the messages rely totally on the effectiveness of aural communication. This is often a drawback for advertisers because of the tendency of listeners to use radio as 'sound wallpaper'. Nevertheless, radio advertising is often an effective means of promoting specific products and local events, particularly when it can be linked to public relations activities such as live radio coverage of an event.

The magazine advertisement for KFC's new Zinger Salad is made more effective by the strong colours made possible through this medium.

Internet

The rapid increase in the use of the internet has meant that many leisure organisations have realised the benefits of using it as an advertising channel.

The internet combines many of the advantages of both printed and visual advertising media. Customers have the opportunity to browse through a large amount of information at their own speed and print out specific pieces of information that they are interested in. A further advantage is that customers are frequently offered the opportunity to buy products online. Of course, the internet is not without its disadvantages as an advertising media. Many people do not have access to the internet or are simply reluctant to give the personal details required to make an online purchase or reservation.

Point-of-sale material

The term 'point of sale' refers to the place that the customer actually buys a product, such as a ticket or reservation desk, a shop counter or a leisure centre reception desk.

Advertising at the point of sale has the advantage that it targets customers who are clearly interested in the product. Its main disadvantage is that it rarely reaches new markets. It is often used when the marketing objective is to develop existing markets or products. For example, a point-of-sale promotion might be used in a hotel foyer to inform customers about special bargain-break deals or themed dinners. The materials used can include displays of products, posters, leaflets and brochures.

Posters

The use of posters is the oldest form of advertising and is still used extensively by leisure organisations. Posters can be displayed on billboards, bus shelters, on public transport, at sports stadiums or simply on the wall of the provider's own facility. One of the main considerations with poster advertising is that its effectiveness depends largely on its location. For example, a poster advertisement on the London Underground will be seen by a lot of people and they will probably have time to read it properly during their journey; however, it will be a very broad audience. A poster outside a visitor attraction such as a museum will have a limited audience but the targeted market may stop to read it fully.

activity

COMPARING ADVERTISING MEDIA

In pairs, discuss what you consider to be the main advantages and disadvantages of the advertising media listed below. Then suggest three different leisure organisations that might use each medium.

Advertising media: national newspapers, local newspapers, magazines, television, radio, internet, point-of-sale material, posters.

Brochures and leaflets

Brochures and leaflets are one of the most widely used promotional media for leisure organisations. Brochures are used extensively to promote conference facilities, hotels, activity breaks, etc. The obvious advantage of brochures is that a great deal of specific information can be included that potential customers can read at their leisure. Yet, this can sometimes be one of their disadvantages since they may appear too complicated to the customer unless they are laid out effectively.

Leaflets have similar advantages to brochures and provide an effective promotional channel for leisure organisations such as visitor attractions, entertainment venues and special events. Rather than the 'book' format of brochures, a leaflet is usually a single folded A4 page.

The increasing use of computers has also meant that many leisure organisations are now able to produce their own leaflets using simple desktop publishing software.

Direct marketing

Direct marketing is so-called because it directs the promotion to a specific customer – and it is one of the fastest growing methods of marketing communication. One of the main benefits of direct marketing is that it enables organisations to target products at specific markets, for instance when a theatre sends a list of its forthcoming productions to past customers.

There are a number of ways in which direct marketing can be carried out such as:

- direct mail
- telemarketing
- door-to-door distribution.

Direct mail

The process of posting promotional material to a potential or existing customer is known as direct mail or a mailshot.

One of the misconceptions about direct mail is that everyone throws it into the bin without reading it. In fact, research shows that this is not true. However, it is not enough for the customer to simply open a direct mail letter and read it; the promoter also wants the customer to buy the product as a result of reading the mailshot. It is common practice to include a letter in the mailshot explaining the content of the sales literature. The letter may include some form of sales promotion, perhaps offering a discount or prize if an order is placed within a certain period.

Mailshots are also more effective if they appear to have been written to an individual rather than to dozens of customers. Using the word 'you' is effective, as is addressing the recipient by name rather than as Sir or Madam.

But how does an organisation know to whom to send mailshots? Most organisations achieve this by the use of a mailing list. Mailing lists are compiled from information already held on people who have either bought or enquired about a product, or by targeting specific groups of people, using the postcode system. Mailing lists are usually held on a computer database, so it is a very efficient way for many organisations to communicate with existing or potential customers.

Telemarketing

Like direct mail, telemarketing is an increasingly common marketing technique, but it suffers from a number of drawbacks. Many potential customers are simply too busy or are suspicious of unsolicited sales calls and are, therefore, unwilling to engage in a conversation. However telemarketing, in which customers are contacted by telephone with the aim of promoting a particular product, can be successful if properly conducted and targeted.

Alnwick Castle AKA 'Hogwarts'

Door-to-door distribution

Rather than mail materials to customers or contact them by telephone, many organisations deliver direct marketing materials to the customers' homes in person (door-to-door distribution). This can work out a lot cheaper than mail or telephone. It also provides the opportunity for personal face-to-face contact with potential customers, which can encourage customers to try a product or service. For example, a restaurant may send staff out to local houses with discount vouchers, to make contact with residents and ask them if they would be interested in using the restaurant.

Public relations

The Institute of Public Relations (IPR) defines public relations as: 'The planned and sustained effort to establish and maintain goodwill and mutual understanding between an organisation and its public'. In this definition 'public' means the whole range of people who come into contact with the organisation, not just its customers and employees. These may include trade unions, suppliers, press, shareholders or councillors. In 1999 the IPR extended its original definition to 'PR is about reputation, which is the result of all you say, all you do and what others say about you'. In other words, an organisation continually communicates messages to the public, whether it wants to or not.

Public relations includes activities such as:

- Media inclusion
- Community relations
- Corporate communications.

Media inclusion

Media inclusion refers to the inclusion of a leisure product in a screened or broadcast film or programme, or in a printed medium such as a newspaper. An obvious example is a particular resort, visitor attraction or sporting activity being featured in one of the many holiday programmes. This is a growing trend as leisure organisations realise the great PR benefits of film crews using their towns, cities or companies as the backdrop for productions and programmes. The National Trust estimates that media coverage of their properties generates approximately £30 million a year. Similarly, Alnwick Castle in Northumberland has seen a 500 per cent increase in child visitors since part of the castle was used as Hogwarts in the Harry Potter films.

A further example of media inclusion is the use of press releases. A press release is a statement written by an organisation that describes a particular event, occasion or piece of interesting news, which is sent to the media in the hope that editors will publish or air it. In many newspapers – particularly local ones – a large proportion of the editorial is, in fact, made up of stories based on press releases rather than articles written by reporters. The decision as to whether or not to use a press release depends not only on its content but also on the relationship that the organisation has with the paper. As a result, part of PR requires maintaining a good relationship with media staff to ensure that they look favourably on news items submitted. Apart from the fact that it is free, the main advantage of getting editorial coverage based on a press release rather than advertising, is that people are likely to read it properly without thinking that it is trying to sell them something.

MEDIA INCLUSION

In pairs, identify one example of media inclusion (a film or television programme) that has benefited the following leisure organisations or destinations:

1. a hotel
2. a sport
3. the Yorkshire Dales
4. a stately home
5. a visitor attraction.

Community relations

Maintaining a good relationship with the local community (community relations) is an important part of PR. This is often achieved by providing support to various groups or participating in events. For example, the McDonald's chain of restaurants gives the following pledge to remain involved in local communities.

One of McDonald's most important principles has always been to support the communities in which it operates. McDonald's restaurants are, by their nature, sociable places, intrinsically linked to local community life. As such the Company supports community programmes, which operate at grassroots level, usually focused on family – and local environment-related issues. All of the initiatives undertaken by McDonald's reflect the Company's strong social stance and desire to put something back into the community of which it is an integral part. Good corporate citizenship through social and environmental responsibility are important values underpinning the McDonald's approach to business.

Corporate communications

Many organisations establish their corporate image partly through their communications. Corporate communications use consistent and recognisable formats and images such as logos, colours and typefaces on their leaflets, bills, faxes and advertising.

Sponsorship

Sponsorship is when an organisation provides financial support to another organisation, individual or event, in order to gain prestige and status from the association. It is often included in an organisation's public relations activities, since it indirectly enhances customers' perceptions of the organisation and its products and services.

There are many examples of sponsorship in the leisure industry where organisations provide financial support for an event, service or product in return for their name being prominently linked to it.

Sales promotions

A sales promotion is a short-term activity aimed at generating sales or improving public perception. Sales promotions are often undertaken in response to the activities of competitors so that an organisation can keep its market share.

Sales promotions can include any or all of the following activities:

- **Price reductions** (discounting). Discounts are offered to increase sales or usage, often at periods of low demand. For example, many leisure clubs offer cheaper rates at off-peak times.
- **Free gifts and incentives.** These are used to encourage consumers to purchase products or services.
- **Special offers.** This is another form of discounting. Special offers are often run in conjunction with some form of advertising campaign in which consumers have to produce the advertisement (or coupons) to qualify for the offer. For example, Little Chef advertisements frequently feature 'buy-one-get-one-free' (BOGOF) coupons.
- **Competitions.** Many leisure organisations run free competitions to encourage consumers to buy their products and services.
- **Extra products.** This is another form of special offer. Customers are provided with extra products or services at no extra charge. A free bottle of wine with your meal, or free T-shirts when enrolling as a member, are just two examples of extra products being used as incentives to persuade consumers to purchase products.

Multi-media applications

With rapid developments in technology, many leisure organisations use a range of multi-media applications as part of their promotional techniques, including internet websites, CD ROMs, videos and touch screens. One of the main advantages of using these methods is that it makes the information more accessible to the customer. For example, if you visit the website of any of the major theme parks you will be able to take a virtual tour of the attraction, download maps and information about the range of facilities and services, book tickets online and, probably, email enquiries.

Professional presentation skills

Being able to present information effectively and professionally is an important part of both marketing and customer service. For some staff in leisure, for example a guide in a stately home or a fitness instructor, presenting information will be a major part of their job role, but all staff will be required to present information at some time. This will often be in a situation where they are selling products and services to the customer. Developing effective selling skills are vital for anyone working in leisure. They provide numerous benefits for the organisation including:

- Increasing sales and profitability

- Gaining an edge over the competitors

- Ensuring that customers' needs and expectations are met.

However, it is important to understand that providing good customer service should always be more important than simply selling a product to the customer. As a member of staff, your main objective should be to satisfy customers by meeting their needs and expectations. In doing this you will almost inevitably sell the customer a product. But the 'selling' aspect of your relationship with the customer should always be the end result of presenting information professionally and giving good customer service.

---

activity

METHODS OF PROMOTION

Select a leisure organisation that you are familiar with.
- Suggest five different methods of promotion that the organisation could use and justify why you think each would be effective.
- Explain how each method of promotion contributes towards good customer service.
- Describe the ways in which members of staff in the organisation might be directly or indirectly involved in each promotion.

Dealing with customers

The final two topics are the 'doing' part of the unit – in other words we are going to explore the ways in which you, as a member of staff, can provide good customer service.

In this topic we explore how leisure organisations provide customer service to meet the needs of their customers. In particular we look at how organisations and their staff deliver good service through:

- Providing information and advice
- Providing assistance and dealing with problems
- Providing for specific needs
- Taking and relaying messages
- Maintaining health, safety and security
- Handling complaints.

Providing information and advice

Earlier on we looked at the importance of having good product knowledge when providing information and advice to customers. It is also important to have a sound understanding of the range of customers and the different situations that you might experience as a member of staff, and the sort of information and advice that you may be called upon to provide.

---

activity

HELPING YOUR CUSTOMERS

Select one job within the leisure industry that appeals to you as a future career. Write a list of the main types of customers that you think you might need to deal with. Then, for each type, describe five examples of how you may need to give them information or advice.

Providing assistance and dealing with problems

In reality, any customer may have a specific need for extra assistance at any time: a hotel guest who is locked out of their bedroom; a leisure centre customer who has lost the locker key, a wheelchair user who needs assistance getting through swing doors; or a theatregoer who cannot find a reserved seat. In situations such as these, your responsibility is to try to anticipate when customers might need assistance and then provide it. For example, if you see a wheelchair user struggling to get through doors you should not wait for them to ask for help; offer assistance quickly to show that you really care and have anticipated their needs.

Dealing with serious problems such as accidents or illness or are often more difficult to handle. These types of situations can be very stressful for the customer and require tactful and careful handling. The customer may be anxious, upset or even angry, and it is your responsibility to reassure them and show that you are confident and in control of the situation.

Providing for specific needs

Since the introduction of the Disability Discrimination Act 1995 (DDA), all organisations have had a legal responsibility in terms of providing products and services for disabled people.

A part of the DDA gives disabled people important rights of access to everyday services that others take for granted, and is particularly relevant to leisure providers. Under this part of the DDA:

- Treating a disabled person less favourably because they are disabled has been unlawful since 1996.
- Since 1999, service providers have had to consider making reasonable adjustments to the way they deliver their services so that disabled people can use them.
- Since 2004, service providers have had to consider making permanent physical adjustments to their premises.

Many leisure organisations far exceed the requirements of the DDA to ensure that specific needs are met. The Stephen Joseph Theatre in Scarborough provides a range of additional services for visually and hearing-impaired customers as well as wheelchair users, as can be seen below.

Taking and relaying messages

Taking and relaying messages is an important part of customer service for both internal and external customers. There are many examples of when it may be necessary to take messages:

- a customer telephoning to speak to a hotel guest who is not there.
- a sports coach telephoning to say that they have been delayed.
- a customer wanting to speak to the manager regarding a complaint.
- a member of staff phoning to say that they are unwell and will not be in for work.

SJT ACCESS

Wheelchair Users / Mobility Needs

The building is fully accessible for wheelchair users. The SJT has ramp access from the street into the lower foyer where the Box Office has a low-level counter. The building also has a low-level public telephone as well as three fully adapted toilets, each fitted with emergency alarms. Our lift provides level access to both the Round and McCarthy auditoria as well as the Restaurant, Bar and Gallery. We also have a stair-lift which provides access to the Theatre Shop.

There are wheelchair spaces in the Round and the McCarthy which are next to a seat for your escort, and easily accessible from the lift. Please notify the Box Office at the time of booking if you require wheelchair access.

Our training/conference room is also fully accessible and has an induction loop system installed. Contact Jaye Lewis for further information.

Support Dogs

Support dogs are welcome to stay with you during the performance, or we will dog-sit and provide water in the foyer. Your dog will be brought to your seat during the interval and at the end of the performance.

Visually Impaired

Audio-Described Performances are organised for all SJT productions and some visiting shows. The on-stage action is relayed through headsets by a trained audio describer. Touch tours of the set, costumes and props are available before the show. Audio programmes are given free on the evening of the audio description.

Our lift features Braille numbering, and provides level access to all floors. There are some low-light areas within the building – if you require assistance please inform a member of staff. Brochures and programmes are available in large print and Braille, on request. Please inform the Box Office that you are visually impaired so that they can advise you on seating in the auditorium.

Hearing Impaired

Infrared audio and loop systems are available in both the Round and McCarthy Theatres – please book headsets in advance at the Box Office. Hearing aids should be switched to the 'T' position to tune into the loop system. Every SJT production, and many visiting shows, has a sign-interpreted performance by a professional BSL Interpreter. Our regular signer is Steven Conlon, who is based at the Leeds Deaf Centre and has worked as an interpreter for more than 10 years. Please notify the Box Office at the time of booking if you will be watching the signer.

Failing to take accurate messages and ensuring that they are passed on to the right person promptly can have disastrous effects on the customers' perception of the overall level of service offered. Most organisations have standard message pads to allow staff to record all of the necessary details, such as the one shown below.

TELEPHONE MESSAGE

Message for: Mr Sinclair   Date: 26/1/05

Message from: Miss J Collins   Time: 3.40 pm

Message:

Please call me at the office before 6 pm tonight.

Telephone number: 01723 562189 Ext. 126

Message taken by: S Rawlins

---

activity

A DIFFICULT SITUATION

You are working as a receptionist in a residential health and fitness spa in France and have come into the office one morning to find the following message left by a colleague:
'Have just received a call from UK Head Office to say that the mother of one of our guests, Mr Nicholson, has been taken seriously ill and is in hospital. I've checked and we can get the Nicholson family on a return flight to the UK tomorrow evening. Could not contact the family as they were out when I received the message. Please ensure that they get the message promptly.'
You go directly to the family's villa, but only the Nicholson's 14-year-old daughter is there; the rest of the family have gone out for the day and she does not know when they will be back. Explain what you would do in this situation and why you think your method of dealing with the situation is appropriate.

Maintaining health, safety and security

Health and safety issues are one of the key concerns for all leisure organisations and an integral part of good customer service. In fact, failure to comply with health and safety requirements can result in an organisation not being allowed to operate. Most health and safety standards are set by legal requirements. Health and safety regulations have a varying impact on leisure organisations depending on the type of service and facility provided. For example, COSHH (Control of Substances Hazardous to Health) regulations have a greater significance for swimming pools than for art galleries. All organisations must comply with the Health and Safety at Work Act 1974, which covers four main areas:

- the health, safety and welfare of people at work
- the protection of outsiders from risks to health and safety
- the controlled storage and use of dangerous substances
- the controlled emission of noxious or offensive substances.

Apart from complying with legal requirements, many leisure organisations will also make it part of their customer service standards to provide customers with general health and safety advice. Because leisure is an international industry, many providers have to consider the implications of health and safety in foreign countries. In some countries, for example, child seats are not provided in rental cars, whereas in the UK they are standard. Likewise, regulations regarding lifts, balconies and swimming pools in hotels are considerably less strict in some countries than in the UK.

Generally speaking, health and safety considerations take priority over all other customer needs and expectations, even if it means that the customer is not able to receive the products or services that they had hoped for. For example, the fire alarm sounding in the middle of a wedding reception would mean that the wedding party would need to evacuate the building; not the ideal event to include in a celebration, but clearly necessary. However, even if it is not possible to provide the expected service because of health and safety issues, it is vital that the customer is still treated politely and with consideration.

Handling complaints

Dealing with customer complaints is also a part of providing good customer service; if a complaint is handled well a good relationship will be established and the customer may well return in future.

No one likes dealing with customer complaints because it often suggests that someone has not done their job properly. Even when a complaint is about something totally out of your control you may still feel concerned that the customer is disappointed. Sometimes a customer may be angry or directly criticise you; they may even shout at you.

Being able to deal with situations like this is all part of good customer service, although on the first few occasions that you receive complaints you may find them difficult to handle. The following measures provide some useful tips when handling complaints.

■ Listen carefully to the customer.

■ Apologise in general terms for any inconvenience caused.

■ Let the customer know that the matter will be fully investigated and put right.

■ Try to see the problem from the customer's point of view.

■ Keep calm and don't argue with the customer.

■ Find a solution to the problem or refer the issue to a supervisor/manager.

■ Agree the solution with the customer.

■ Take action and make sure that what you promised to do gets done.

■ Make sure that you record details of the complaint and actions taken.

activity

ROLE-PLAY SCENARIOS

Part of the assessment for this unit requires you to demonstrate that you can provide effective customer service. Below are some role-play scenarios that you should act out with a colleague.

1. Mr Jones is an elderly gentleman on a coach trip to an industrial museum. He likes to sit in a front seat because there is more room. When he gets on the coach, the front seats are taken – two by other passengers, and the others by the two couriers who say they cannot move because they have to be next to the microphone, which is situated at the front.
Roles: Mr Jones, two passengers, two couriers

2. Lizzie is three years old and very excited about her first visit to a water park with her parents. She is running around the edge of the pool and collides with a lifeguard, falling over and cutting her knee. Signs are clearly displayed asking customers to refrain from running.
Roles: Lizzie, Lizzie's mother and father, the lifeguard

3. Wayne is attending a Karaoke night at the local rugby club. Wayne has had too much beer and is trying to start a fight with another man who Wayne claims has stolen his girlfriend. The worried girlfriend asks the bar staff to help.
Roles: Wayne, other man, 2 bar staff

4. Maureen is a guide at a stately home. She is showing a group of visitors around when one of the guests faints. A cleaner is working nearby.
Roles: Maureen, fainting visitor, cleaner, rest of group

5. An American couple make the toilets their first visit at a theme park but are disgusted to find them dirty and without soap and towels. They complain to a member of staff, who tells them to go to the customer service desk.
Roles: American couple, customer service clerk

6. A party of visitors arrives at a football match with a member who is in a wheelchair. They have written in advance asking for assistance in gaining access. When the party arrives, the main car park is full and the only available parking spaces are on a lower level reached by thirty steps.
Roles: visitor in wheelchair, car park attendant

7. The fire alarm has sounded at 10:30 p.m. in an hotel. All of the guests have evacuated the building, apart from Mrs Simcox, an elderly lady who is standing at reception in her dressing gown refusing to go outside because it is snowing.
Roles: Mrs Simcox, receptionist

8. Mr and Mrs Rodriguez are from Spain and speak very little English. They have gone into a fast food restaurant to ask for directions to the main shopping area.
Roles: Mr and Mrs Rodriguez, counter assistant

9. Mr and Mrs Cohen are interested in booking a wedding reception for their daughter at a hotel. As devout Jews they have to abide by strict dietary requirements. They would like the hotel to allow an outside chef to oversee the food preparation to ensure that it is kosher. The hotel's chef is not very keen on the idea of an outsider running his kitchen – even if it is only for one day.
Roles: Mr and Mrs Cohen, hotel manager, hotel chef

10. Miss Carmichael has gone to a sports centre to find out about hiring a badminton court. She has a profound hearing impairment but can lip-read.
Roles: Miss Carmichael, sports centre receptionist

Providing acceptable customer service

In the last nine topics we have looked at the ways in which leisure organisations view their customers and continually strive to improve the products and services that they offer to meet the changing needs of their customers. By now you will have recognised that the role of individual staff is crucial in terms of meeting individual customers' needs and therefore allowing an organisation to meet its business objectives. In this final topic we are going to look at the skills that you need to effectively deliver customer service in the leisure industry. In particular we will explore:

- **Interpersonal skills**
- **Communication skills**

Interpersonal skills

The way in which you present yourself to customers, and the interpersonal skills that you use, will have a direct influence on the level of customer satisfaction as well as the image of the organisation you work for. In particular, interpersonal skills contribute to good customer service in terms of:

- dress
- personal hygiene
- personality and attitude.

Dress

Dress and physical appearance are important parts of the overall impression that you give to customers and help to create a favourable first impression. 'Dress' covers everything from clothes and footwear to your hairstyle, make-up and jewellery. Many organisations within the leisure industry provide their staff with a uniform. From a customer service point of view there are many advantages of this.

- It helps create a positive first impression.
- Staff are instantly recognisable as working for a specific organisation.
- It is easy to find a member of staff when a customer needs advice or assistance.

- It can indicate which department a member of staff works in.
- It helps to create a professional corporate image.

It is becoming more common for organisations to provide some sort of uniform or specify what staff should wear. For example, many smaller catering establishments may not provide a uniform but specify that staff should wear white shirts and black trousers/skirts. Organisations also rely on the good judgement of their staff in deciding what is and is not acceptable in terms of appearance. Aspects such as the amount and type of make-up, hairstyles, jewellery and visible tattoos are issues that many staff will need to consider. The most important consideration with dress and appearance is that it should suit the job, the organisation and the customers' expectations. From an organisation's point of view they should also ensure that uniforms are comfortable, easy to maintain and look equally appropriate on staff of all builds.

Personal hygiene

Anyone serving customers should have excellent standards of personal hygiene. No customer will be impressed by a waiter who smells of garlic or a receptionist with dirty finger nails! Equally, dousing yourself with perfume or aftershave when you have not had time for a shower, or chewing gum after a curry or a cigarette, is just as off-putting for customers.

Some jobs in leisure will have stricter requirements for personal hygiene than others due to the nature of the work. For example, someone employed in food preparation will be expected to wash their hands dozens of times a day between separate food-preparation activities to avoid cross-contamination.

Personality and attitude

The impression you give to customers also depends on your personality and how you project it. Your personality will influence the image that the customer forms of the whole organisation. The difference is that only you can actually influence your personality and determine whether the customer is going to see it positively. It is

activity

RIGHT PERSONALITY FOR THE JOB

Using the list on the right, choose three adjectives that you think most closely describe the type of personality that would be needed for the following jobs (you can add your own adjectives if you like):

- Fitness instructor
- Children's activity co-ordinator
- Tutor for an adults' bridge class
- Conference co-ordinator
- Fast food counter assistant.

Mature
Calm
Outgoing
Fun-loving
Serious
Friendly
Reassuring
Efficient
Humorous
Informal

important to realise that there is not one correct type of personality. Different jobs in leisure require different types of personality. The sort of personality required to work as a children's football coach is likely to be very different to that of a maître d' in a five-star hotel.

Your attitude towards the customer is crucial to your ability to deliver excellent customer service. All customers are sensitive to the way you feel about them and will know whether or not you are keen to serve them.

activity

WHERE ARE YOU ON THE ATTITUDE SCALE?

Your attitude towards and understanding of particular customer service situations says a lot about your attitude generally. Below is a quick quiz to see how you score on the 'attitude scale'.

Consider the following statements and decide whether they apply 'always', 'never' or 'sometimes'. If you decide the answer to a question is 'sometimes', explain the situations in which this would apply.

(a) It is all right to call a customer by their first name.

(b) A member of staff should always stand up when dealing with a customer.

(c) It is acceptable to chew gum when talking to a customer.

(d) You should always wait for a customer to start a conversation.

(e) You should maintain eye contact when dealing with a customer in a face-to-face situation.

(f) It is old-fashioned to address a customer as sir or madam.

(g) It is acceptable to get angry with a very difficult customer.

(h) It is wrong to complain about one customer to another customer.

(i) Customers will understand if you are tired or unwell, and make allowances.

(j) All customers are equally important.

(k) Your attitude and behaviour towards the customer will affect the extent to which he or she is satisfied.

(l) The customer is always right.

Answers are given on page 171. Your total number of correct answers will show you where you are on the attitude scale.

8–12 correct answers: an excellent attitude;

4–7 correct answers: not bad but you probably need a bit more practice – try some of the role play exercises;

0–3 correct answers: oh dear, perhaps you should read this unit again – slowly!

161

Topic 10 Providing acceptable customer service

Communication skills

A large part of effective customer service involves dealing with and communicating with customers. Communicating with customers can include:

- Face-to-face communication

- Non-verbal communication

- Telephone communication

- Written communication.

Face-to-face communication

Face-to-face situations have many advantages over other forms of communication, but only if you understand how to use them well. For example, your appearance can help to create a positive impression, particularly if you wear a uniform that immediately identifies you. You can also use facial expressions and gestures to help you to communicate more effectively. Of course, there are also some challenges when dealing with customers face-to-face: you are 'on show' and the customer can see if you lack confidence or the right attitude. You also need to be able to think quickly and make the right response. Unlike written communication, you cannot spend time thinking about the best way of expressing something; the customer will expect you to respond to them immediately.

Oral communication is central to many face-to-face situations.

The ability to speak well does not mean using a posh accent. Of far greater importance is the ability to speak in a way that is comprehensible and acceptable to your customers. 'Comprehensible' means speaking in a way that is understandable and easily followed by the customer. 'Acceptable' means that the way you express yourself should fit the personal image that you are trying to convey. As a quick guide, the following points are worth considering.

- Express your thoughts clearly. Do not mumble or ramble.

- Avoid slang and jargon. In other words, use language that is likely to be familiar to the customer.

- Vary your tone of voice – it makes it more interesting and shows that you are interested.

- Listen to the customer. Good communication skills also involve the ability to listen carefully to customer requests and respond to their needs.

- React with interest by using suitable facial expressions as well as your voice.

Non-verbal communication

Non-verbal communication comprises all forms of communication that do not involve words – spoken or written down. We all tend to focus on what we say or write and overlook the importance of what we communicate non-verbally. However, research indicates that as much as 80 per cent of communication is non-verbal, so it is clearly an important part of customer service.

Body language is one kind of non-verbal communication and refers to the way we use our body to send messages to someone else. Body language includes posture, mannerisms, gestures and facial expressions, all of which communicate messages about what we really think and feel. From a customer service point of view it is useful to be aware of what is known as open and closed body language. Open body language suggest to a customer that you are interested in them, that you are not hostile or aggressive and that you want to listen to them and please them. Closed body language suggests the opposite: that you are uninterested, may be hostile or aggressive and are unwilling to listen to them or satisfy their needs. The table (above, right) gives examples of open and closed body language.

Smiling is the single most important aspect of non-verbal communication. It says that you like and take pride in your job and that you like the customer and want to meet their needs.

Open and closed body language

Open	Closed
Smiling	Frowning
Standing up straight	Slouching
Arms loosely at your side or behind your back	Arms crossed in front of you, or hands on your hips or in your pockets
Head held with chin level to floor	Chin up or down
Eye contact with customer	Avoiding eye contact with customer
Remaining in a comfortable position	Fidgeting, moving from foot to foot, crossing and uncrossing legs
No obvious mannerisms	Fiddling with your hair, hands, clothes
Using gestures that help you to explain what you are saying	Using gestures excessively or for no apparent reason
Showing interest	Showing no feeling at all
Showing concern	Showing lack of concern

Telephone communication

Most organisations use the telephone to provide some part of their customer service. Indeed, some organisations such as call centres, use the telephone as the main method of communication when dealing with customer enquiries. Many of the skills needed are the same that you would use in any customer service situation. For example, you need to be polite, friendly, attentive and efficient. However, additional skills are needed when using a telephone because the customer cannot see you and you cannot see the customer. This means that you cannot use facial expressions or bodily gestures to help the communication process, but must rely totally on your voice and your ability to listen carefully.

Here are some basic rules for using the telephone effectively:

- Speak clearly. Do not eat, drink, chew gum or smoke while on the telephone, as this will distort or muffle the sound of your voice.

- Take notes. Always write down full details of what the customer wants, particularly if the message is for someone else.

- Identify the caller's needs. Remember that the caller is paying for the call and wants to be dealt with quickly and efficiently.

- Listen carefully. Do not interrupt when the caller is talking.

- Explain what is happening. If you transfer the caller to someone else, state what you are doing.

- Smile whilst you are talking – the customer will be able to 'hear' it in your voice!

Written communication

The definition of written communication extends to any information that is written and/or read and includes information that is provided electronically such as on the internet. For most leisure organisations, written communication supports and enhances the other methods of communication that they use.

Typical examples of written communications used by leisure organisations include:

- menus
- tariffs or price lists
- letters
- bills
- brochures and leaflets
- advertisements
- signs
- noticeboards
- programmes
- tickets
- faxes
- websites and emails
- timetables.

The same standard of care needs to be given to written forms of communication as to any other aspect of customer service. The quality of written communication will affect the customer's image both of you and of the organisation.

Here are some final role plays for you to practise your customer service skills. The following scenarios cover a wide range of situations and different customers.

1. Role: Swimming pool lifeguard
Situation: A group of young adult men have been causing disruption in the pool by running along the side of the pool, pushing each other in and generally upsetting other swimmers with their rowdy behaviour. You suspect that they might have been drinking before they came to the pool.

2. Role: Concert booking agency clerk
Situation: An Italian visitor wants to reserve seats for an open-air pop concert in Hyde Park, London. In fact the concert is free and there are no seats. He does not speak much English.

3. Role: Sports centre receptionist
Situation: A customer would like to start taking some form of exercise class or sporting activity. Her preference is for an activity where she will meet other people whilst getting fit. She is hearing-impaired so will need advice on activities that would be suitable.

4. Role: Leisure centre receptionist
Situation: A customer has just returned to his locker and found that his wallet has disappeared. He claims that he is sure that he locked the door as he left. The only other person with a key to the locker is the Duty Manager.

5. Role: Ride operator
Situation: A customer and her two children have been queuing for the Log Flume for 45 minutes. Just as she gets near the front of the queue the maintenance engineer decides that the ride has to be temporarily closed down due to a suspected fault.

PRACTISE YOUR CUSTOMER SERVICE SKILLS

6. Role: Assistant in a children's soft play area
Situation: A customer is concerned that she is not allowed to accompany her young children into the ball pool and soft play area. Her concern is increased by the fact that the area is quite large and therefore it is not possible for parents to actually see their children at all times. The customer is worried about the safety of such an arrangement, particularly since the area is very busy and she is not convinced that the assistants will be able to keep an eye on her children.

7. Role: Conference centre receptionist
Situation: A new customer telephones to speak to a delegate attending a conference at the centre. First make a public address announcement. The delegate does not respond to this so you will need to take a message to pass on to them. (You need a pen and paper for this one!)

8. Role: Cinema attendant
Situation: An elderly customer at the cinema would like to sit at the rear of the auditorium near to the toilets as she has difficulty moving around. The cinema is already very busy and there are no vacant seats in the area that she would like. She did not know that she could have reserved a specific seat in advance.

9. Role: Stately home's souvenir shop sales assistant
Situation: A customer has returned with a video of the stately home that he has recently purhcased. There is nothing wrong with it but the customer is disappointed that the video only features the interior of the house and not the grounds. He claims that this should have been made clear in the description.

10. Role: Fast food assistant
Situation: Lucy is having her sixth birthday party at your fast food restaurant. She and her 10 friends have finished their meal and become bored. They have started running around the restaurant and disturbing other customers. With another half an hour left of the party, the manager has asked you to quickly think of an activity that will keep them occupied (and relatively quiet!).

11. Role: Shop assistant in a heritage museum
Situation: A Swedish visitor would like to buy some souvenir goods but is unfamiliar with English currency. The total cost of his purchases is £46.23 but he has given you three fifty-pound notes. The customer would also like a receipt.

12. Role: Hotel night porter
Situation: A guest rings down in the middle of the night and asks for some indigestion tablets claiming that the fish he had in the restaurant was not cooked properly and has made him ill. It is against company policy to give guests any form of medication. There are no all-night chemists in the area.

13. Role: Jet ski centre manager
Situation: A customer has booked herself and her sister on a day's jet-ski course. On the day of the course the sister is unwell and both customers want a full refund. The booking form states clearly that no refunds will be given if cancellations occur less than 24 hours prior to the course.

14. Role: Video shop sales assistant
A customer would like to become a member of your video rental club. You need the following information: name, address, telephone number, age (to ensure that they are over 18) and proof of identity. They also need to be told about the conditions of renting a video (e.g. the extra cost if videos are returned late, charges made if they damage a video, etc.).

15. Role: Private sports club attendant
A new member has arrived to play a pre-booked game of badminton. Unfortunately she was not aware of the strict rules on appropriate footwear and has not brought suitable trainers.

165

Topic 10 Providing acceptable customer service

INDUSTRY FOCUS

Katherine Duckworth, Sales & Marketing Manager for Alton Towers Hotels

Can you give me a brief overview of what your job entails?

I am responsible, first, for all aspects of sales within the hotels – managing the pricing strategy and revenue management, with ultimate responsibility for all primary hotel revenue, and selling into the leisure and conference market. I am also responsible for both external and internal marketing of the hotels, both 'above the line' such as TV advertising and 'below the line' activity, such as direct mail pieces.

Who are your main target markets and how are their specific needs met?

Research shows that our target market is predominately high-income families and country dwellers – A,B,C1. The services we offer reflect this – our tropical Cariba Creek Waterpark, themed hotels, and nightly entertainment are all aimed at the family.

Alton Towers is renowned for its exceptional level of customer service. How is this achieved?

We use a Customer Service Training Manual. All staff are trained to implement its codes of conduct, and are monitored and appraised by our Customer Service department.

How are levels of service and complaints monitored?

All hotel guests are requested to complete a Customer Satisfaction Survey before checking out (for which they receive a 'kids go free' ticket for the Theme Park). The survey covers the Theme Park, Waterpark, Spa and the hotels themselves, requesting opinions on value for money, customer service, queuing, etc. We also use this tool to gain more information about our guests – their age range, intention to return, and which piece of our marketing activity resulted in them hearing about us. Comments and figures gained from these questionnaires are fed back to senior management for review, and for any corrective action to be taken.

Approximately twice a year, qualitative and quantitative research is carried out within the hotel, by an outside agency. This takes the form of research groups, and provides in-depth information about our guests and their feelings on all aspects of their stay.

Can you give me any examples of how customer service procedures have been changed due to this monitoring?

One aspect that caused dissatisfaction was the fact that guests had to book for breakfast. This procedure was introduced to try and manage the flow of guests through breakfast, and enable them to take advantage of early access to the theme park.

However, after complaints about non-availability of booking times at times of high demand, and guests who hadn't booked being turned away (despite tables being empty) it was decided to trial a free-flow system.

This was introduced at the beginning of the summer holidays, the thinking being that if we could manage this at our busiest time, it would work all year round. It worked exceptionally well (after a few minor hick-ups) and there is now no need to book for breakfast at all – resulting in much higher levels of guest satisfaction.

What is the procedure for training staff in customer service skills?

Every member of staff completes our 2-day 'Creating the Magic' induction training course, covering our company mission, vision and values, customer service, health and safety, and best practice. This provides our staff with the knowledge and skills to help make our guests' stay as magical as they would hope for from Alton Towers Hotels.

Can you give an example of how additional training has resulted from the monitoring of customer service?

Our Call Centre provides a good example. It receives about 1000 calls a day enquiring about the hotels, but the conversion rate from 'enquiring' to 'booking' was quite low. Further investigation revealed that this was because our operators were not offering the right kind of information to enable the callers to book easily. A dedicated sales trainer was appointed who focused the operators on identifying guest needs and supplying the right information to help meet them. Within weeks, the levels of customer service (and the conversion rate) had increased dramatically.

How UNIT 3 is assessed

Unit 3 is assessed by coursework. The evidence should be in four parts, which we suggest you present as four sections within a portfolio. The following guidance outlines how you can achieve the assessment requirements for each of the four parts. The final sections give you advice on the presentation of your evidence and on improving your grades.

1. How the leisure industry views the customer

1.0 Introduction
Give a brief overview of the leisure industry and the reasons why it is important to understand the needs and expectations of its customers. Define what is meant by 'customer service'.

1.1 Leisure customers
Describe the range of customers that use different leisure facilities, products and services.

1.2 Policies and procedures in the leisure industry
Describe what is meant by policies and procedures.

Mission or vision statements
Explain what is meant by mission and vision statements, and describe examples from the leisure industry.

Customer service charters
Explain what is meant by customer service charters, and describe examples from the leisure industry.

Customer feedback procedures
Explain what is meant by customer feedback procedures, and describe examples from the leisure industry.

Complaints procedures
Explain what is meant by complaints procedures, and describe examples from the leisure industry.

Systems for providing goods and services
Explain the types of systems used to provide goods and services, and give examples from the leisure industry.

2. An evaluation of customer service within the leisure industry

2.0 Introduction
In this second part of the assessment you are to report on your findings as a 'mystery customer' in evaluating customer service in a leisure organisation. In the introduction explain how and where you undertook your mystery customer visit, and give a brief overview of the organisation.

2.1 Policies and procedures
Describe the range of policies and procedures used by the organisation and their effectiveness for the customers. This should include evaluation of the appropriateness of the language and layout of such procedures.

2.2 Information provided
Evaluate the effectiveness of information provided to customers.

2.3 Products and services
Evaluate the range of products and services offered and the extent to which they meet customers' needs and expectations.

2.4 Suggestions for improvements
Based on your mystery customer visit, make recommendations as to how the organisation could improve its customer service..

3. Marketing activities used within the leisure industry

3.0 Introduction
Explain what is meant by marketing activities, and why they are important in the leisure industry.

3.1 Product knowledge
Explain what is meant by product knowledge, and give examples of how it applies to staff working within the leisure industry.

3.2 Market research
Explain what is meant by market research, and describe different research methods used by leisure organisations.

3.3 Promotion
Outline the main methods of promotion, and describe examples used by leisure organisations for a range of different products and services.

3.4 Multi-media applications
Explain what is meant by multi-media applications, and describe examples used by leisure organisations for a range of different products and services.

3.5 Professional presentation skills
Explain what is meant by professional presentation skills, and give examples of how they are used by staff in leisure organisations.

4. Providing customer service to a range of customers in different situations

This final part of the assessment requires you to provide evidence of your ability to provide customer service. Your evidence can be from role-plays or from real situations – such as work placement or a part-time job.

4.0 Introduction
Explain why it is important to be able to provide effective customer service, and state where your evidence has come from – role-plays, work placement or part-time job.

4.1 Dealing with customer enquiries
Describe how you have dealt with customer enquiries. Your description should include information on the type of customer, their needs and the specific situation.

4.2 Anticipate and handle issues
Describe how you have anticipated and handled issues relating to customer service. Your description should include information on the type of customer, their needs and the specific situation.

4.3 'Going the extra mile'
Describe ways in which you have 'gone the extra mile' when dealing with customers and therefore exceeded their expectations.

4.4 Evaluation
Evaluate the extent to which you were able to provide acceptable customer service, and make recommendations as to how your performance could be improved in future.

WITNESS STATEMENTS
Your evidence for this section should be supported by signed witness statements that verify that you provided the customer service that you describe. A suggested format for the witness statement is provided on the next page.

Bibliography
List all of the sources of information that you have used to complete the assessment for this unit.

Appendices
Include any relevant supporting information in the appendices, such as examples of marketing materials, policies and procedures, etc.

Improving your grades
Generally, you will get better grades by giving more comprehensive explanations, including better examples and showing a deeper understanding of each topic. Your school or college should be able to advise you in more detail, or you could visit the Edexcel website: edexcel.org.uk for more guidance.

General guidelines on presentation of assignments
Whilst the way in which you present your assessment evidence will not directly affect your grade, it is important that you strive to present it in a professional and well-structured way. The following are a few tips on achieving good presentation.

1. All assignments should be word processed, using a suitable font, such as Ariel. Try to avoid 'casual' fonts, such as Comic Sans.

2. You can use a different font for titles if you wish, but do not use more than two fonts in your work.

3. Be consistent in your font size. Generally, 14 or 16 is suitable for titles, and 12 for the main text.

4. Only use bold for titles – not the whole report.

5. Use italics and 'quotation marks' to show when you have copied text from another source, and indicate the source in brackets after the quote.

6. If you choose to use more than one colour in your work, limit this to two, e.g. blue for titles and black for the main text.

7. Avoid using 'Wordart' for titles!

8. Use 1.5 line spacing throughout your work.

9. Do not cut and paste cartoon-style clipart into your work.

10. If you use photographs in your work, label each image underneath.

11. Insert page numbers into your finished work.

Witness Statement

Student's Name:		Date:	
Description of the situation:			
Description of the customer/s and their specific needs and expectations:			
How customer service was provided by the student:			
Recommendations as to how the customer service provided by the student could have been improved:			
Additional comments:			
Signature of witness:	Position of witness:	Date:	

General guidelines on presentation of assignments

Whilst the way in which you present your assessment evidence will not directly affect your grade, it is important that you strive to present it in a professional and well structured way. The following are a few tips on achieving good presentation.

1. All assignments should be word processed, using a suitable font, such as Ariel. Try to avoid 'casual' fonts, such as Comic Sans.

2. You can use a different font for titles if you wish, but do not use more than two fonts in your work.

3. Be consistent in your font size. Generally, 14 or 16 is suitable for titles, and 12 for the main text.

4. Only use **bold** for titles – not the whole report.

5. Use *italics* and 'quotation marks' to show when you have copied text from another source, and indicate the source in brackets after the quote.

6. If you choose to use more than one colour in your work, limit this to two, e.g. blue for titles and black for the main text.

7. Avoid using 'Wordart' for titles!

8. Use 1.5 line spacing throughout your work.

9. Do not cut and paste cartoon-style clipart into your work.

10. If you use photographs in your work, label each image underneath.

11. Insert page numbers into your finished work.

Web Directory

Government and national associations

Advertising Standards Agency	asa.org.uk
Arts Council	artscouncil.org.uk
Association of Exhibition Organisers	exhibitions.work.co.uk
British Association of Leisure parks	balppa.org
Central Council for Physical Recreation	ccpr.org.uk
Charter Mark	chartermark.gov.uk
Countryside Agency	countryside.gov.uk
Department for Culture, Media and Sport	culture.gov.uk
English Heritage	english-heritage.org.uk
Environment Agency	environment.gov.uk
European Committee on Sport, Youth and Sport	europarl.eu.int
European Leisure & Recreation Association	elra.net
Health & Safety Executive	hse.gov.uk
Hospitality Training Foundation	htf.org.uk
Institute of Leisure and Amenity Management (ILAM)	ilam.co.uk
Institute of Sport and Recreation Management	isrm.co.uk
Investors in People	iipuk.co.uk
National Coaching Foundation	sportscoachuk.org
Quest	quest-uk.org
Ramblers Association	ramblers.org.uk
Recreation Managers Association	rma-ofgb.org
Skills Active	skillsactive.com
Sport England	sportengland.org.uk
Sportsaid	sportsaid.org.uk
VisitBritain	visitbritain.com
Youth Hostels Association	yha.org.uk
Institution of Occupational Safety and Health	iosh.co.uk

Governing bodies

British Olympic Association	olympics.org.uk
Fitness Industry Association	fia.org.uk
Football Association	thefa.com
Rugby Football Union	rfu.com
Sport, Recreation and Allied Organisations (SPRITO)	sprito.org.uk

Voluntary groups

Historic Houses Association	haa.org.uk
National Trust	nationaltrust.org.uk

Private sector organisations

Alton Towers	alton-towers.co.uk
Business in Sport and Leisure	bisl.org
Center Parcs	centerparcs.com
David Lloyd	davidlloydleisure.co.uk
Fitness First	fitnessfirst.com
Flowsports (recruitment agency)	flowsports.co.uk
Gala Bingo	gala-bingo.co.uk
Madame Tussaud's	tussauds.com
Manchester United	manutd.com
Odeon Cinemas	odeon.co.uk
Sports Industries Federation	sportslife.com
UCI Cinemas	uci-cinemas.co.uk
Virgin (recruitment agency)	virginactive.co.uk

Other useful sources

Leisure Opportunities	leisureopportunities.co.uk
Mintel (research)	mintel.co.uk
Oympics Office and Association	olympics.org.uk
Research and Market	researchandmarkets.com
Springboard (careers)	springboarduk.org.uk
World Leisure News	worldleisurejobs.com

Acknowledgements

The authors and publishers would like to thank the following for their help:
Peter Wilson; Katherine Duckworth of Alton Towers Hotels; Michael Beadle
of Xscape; Martin Steers of ISRM.

The publishers would like to thank the following for permission to reproduce
pictures on these pages (t) = top, (b) = bottom, (l) = left, (r) = right:
Cover: Getty Images; page 12 (t) Empics; (b) Rex Features; p.13 Empics; p.14
(t) Rex Features; (b) Empics; p.15 Photofusion; p.16 Rex Features; p.19 (t) Rex
Features; (b) S & R Greenhill; p.20 Alan Edwards; p.22 Empics; p.21 (l)
Graham Woodall; (r) Alamy; p.23 (l) Courtesy of David Lloyd Leisure; (r)
Empics; p.24 Roger Scruton; p.25 (l) David Lloyd Leisure; (r) Rex Features;
p.26 Rex Features; p.28 (t) S & R Greenhill; (b) Alamy; p.29 Alamy; p.30
Photofusion; p.31 (t) Rex Features; (b) Collections/Mansell; p.32
Collections/Robert Deane; p.33 Roger Scruton; p.34 Corbis; p.36 (t) Alan
Edwards; (b) Empics; p.37 Alamy; p.38 (t) S & R Greenhill; (b) Popperfoto;
p.39 Corbis; p.40 Rex Features; p.41 John Walmsley; p.42 Paul
Talling/Derelict London; p.43 Roger Scruton; p.44 (l) Photofusion; (b) Empics;
p.45 Empics; p.46 (t) Corbis; (b) Alamy; p.47 (t) Rex Features; (b)
Collections/Graeme Peacock; p.48 Actionplus; p.49 (t) Rex Features; (b)
Corbis; p.50 Rex Features; p.51 S & R Greenhill; p.52 Corbis; p.53 Empics;
p.58 Topfoto; p.59 Rex Features; p.60 (t) Photofusion; (b) Rex Features; p.61
Empics; p.62 Still Pictures; p.63 Photofusion; p.66 Actionplus; p.67 Rex
Features; p.68 Science Photo Library; p.69 Empics; p.70 David Lloyd Leisure;
p.77 Alan Edwards p.78 (t) Alan Edwards; (b) Corbis; p.84 Alan Edwards;
p.85 Alan Edwards; p.86 Courtesy of Badgers Café, Llandudno; p.87
Collections/Ben Boswell; p.88 Rex Features; p.90 PA/Empics; p.93 Courtesy
of Clubmark; p.94 Alamy; p.96 Corbis; p.97 Corbis; p.98 Alamy; p.103
Abbey; p.104 Rex Features; p.105 Empics; p.110 Alamy; p.113
Collections/Andy Hibbert; p.118 (t) David Lloyd Leisure; (b) Alamy; p.119
Alamy; p.120 (l) Corbis; (r) Rex Features; p.122 (t) S & R Greenhill; (b) Alamy;
p.123 Roger Scruton; p.124 Chessington World of Adventures; p.125 Rex
Features; p.126 Photofusion; p.127 Courtesy of Vue Cinemas; p.128 (t)
David Lloyd Leisure; (b) Photofusion; p.132 (t) Alamy; (b) S & R Greenhill;
p.133 Courtesy of Warwick Castle; p.134 Alamy; p.135 Roger Scruton;
p.136 Alamy; p.139 Alamy; p.140 Roger Scruton; p.141 Photofusion; p.142
(tl) Alan Edwards; (tr) Alamy; (b) Rex Features; p.143 Empics; p.144 S & R
Greenhill; p.148 Alan Edwards; p 150 Actionplus; p.151 Roger Scruton;
p.153 Alamy; p.154 Roger Scruton; p.156 Photofusion; p.160 S & R
Greenhill; p.161 Empics; p.162 Alamy.

Answers to WHERE ARE YOU ON THE ATTITUDE SCALE? (page 161)

(a) sometimes, (b) sometimes – consider a customer in a wheelchair,
(c) never, (d) never, (e) always, (f) never, (g) never, (h) always, (i) never,
(j) always, (k) always, (l) sometimes – but you should always act as if the
customer is right!

William Collins' dream of knowledge for all began with the publication of his first book in 1819. A self-educated mill worker, he not only enriched millions of lives, but also founded a flourishing publishing house. Today, staying true to this spirit, Collins books are packed with inspiration, innovation and practical expertise. They place you at the centre of a world of possibility and give you exactly what you need to explore it.

Collins. Do more.

Published by Collins

An imprint of HarperCollins*Publishers*

77 – 85 Fulham Palace Road
Hammersmith
London
W6 8JB

Browse the complete Collins catalogue at
www.collinseducation.com

© HarperCollins*Publishers* Limited 2005

10 9 8 7 6 5 4 3 2 1

ISBN 0 00 719808 6

Lindsey Taylor and Ray Barker assert their moral rights to be identified as the authors of this work

British Library Cataloguing in Publication Data
A Catalogue record for this publication is available from the British Library

Commissioned and project managed by Graham Bradbury
Cover Design by Blue Pig
Cover picture courtesy of Getty Images
Series design by Patricia Briggs
Book design by Sally Boothroyd
Series managed by Kay Wright
Picture research by Thelma Gilbert
Production by Sarah Robinson

Printed and bound by Printing Express Limited, Hong Kong

Index

Index

Index